Piaget, Psychology and Education

edited by *Ved P. Varma and Phillip Williams*

Piaget, Psychology and Education

Papers in Honour of Jean Piaget

F. E. Peacock Publishers, Inc.   Itasca, Il., 60143

ISBN 0-87581-220-1

Published first in Great Britain for
Hodder and Stoughton Educational,
a division of Hodder and Stoughton Ltd, London,
by T. & A. Constable Ltd, Edinburgh

Printed and published in the United States of America 1976
by F. E. Peacock Publishers, Inc.
401 W. Irving Park Road
Itasca, Illinois 60143

Preface

This book is published as a tribute to Jean Piaget on the occasion of his eightieth birthday. There is no need to extol the contribution which Piaget has made to human learning, for there can be few if any individuals with interests in psychology and education who have not met the influence of the Piagetian school.

It is clearly not possible to do full justice to Piaget within the covers of one volume. He is an extremely prolific writer whose own works number some 1500 titles (a complete listing covering the period 1907 to 1974 is provided in the *Catalog of the Jean Piaget Archives*, published in the USA by G. K. Hall & Co., and available in the UK from George Prior Associated Publishers Ltd). Not only has Piaget himself written widely on central issues in developmental and educational psychology—in addition there are fields of study and application which have been given new illumination and fresh stimulus by the techniques which he has used and the theoretical framework which he has erected. So for the purpose of this book contributors have been asked to cover a selection of different topics, not all of which have been of major concern to Piaget himself. Inevitably this means that topics which some readers feel—rightly—are of great relevance to Piagetians have had to be omitted in order to accommodate some more tangential but nevertheless important themes.

The first part of the book deals with some broad questions in a mainly theoretical way. The second part focuses on a set of rather more specific topics, which are nevertheless all treated from a mainly theoretical standpoint. The third part covers some questions which have more direct relevance to education.

Contributors have been asked not necessarily to stress the Piagetian approach, but rather to present a set of reasonably high-level reviews of the current position in their special fields.

The Editors

Contents

Preface   *v*

The contributors   *ix*

Jean Piaget: a biographical sketch
    Eric A. Lunzer   *xi*

PART ONE

1. An appreciation of Piaget's work
    Eric A. Lunzer   *3*

2. The course of cognitive growth
    J. G. Wallace   *15*

3. Environment and intelligence
    P. E. Vernon   *31*

4. Emotions and intelligence
    E. James Anthony   *43*

PART TWO

5. The measurement of development
    Colin Elliott   *57*

6. Perception and cognition: where do we stand in the mid-seventies?
    George Butterworth   *74*

7. On the social origins of symbolic functioning
    John and Elizabeth Newson   *84*

8. Moral development: the cognitive-developmental approach
    D. Graham   *97*

9. Memory: theory and application
    Ian M. L. Hunter   *109*

PART THREE

10. Programmes for cognitive growth
   K. Wedell   *123*

11. Understanding scientific concepts
   K. Lovell   *132*

12. Mathematical thinking in children
   K. F. Collis   *144*

13. Schooling and moral development
   J. B. Biggs   *155*

14. The thinking and education of the adolescent
   E. A. Peel   *172*

15. Language programmes for disadvantaged children   *182*

   Part I: Recent research on the language of disadvantaged children   *183*

   Part II: A survey of language programmes for disadvantaged children   *188*
   Maurice Chazan and Theo Cox

References   *201*

Index   *227*

The contributors

E. James Anthony
Blanche F. Ittleson Professor of Child Psychiatry and Director, Eliot Division of Child Psychiatry, Washington University School of Medicine, St Louis, USA

J. B. Biggs
Professor of Education, University of Newcastle, Australia

George Butterworth
Lecturer in Psychology, University of Southampton, England

Maurice Chazan
Reader in Education, Department of Education, University College of Swansea, Wales

K. F. Collis
Associate Professor of Education, Department of Education, University of Newcastle, Australia

Theo Cox
Lecturer in Education, Department of Education, University College of Swansea, Wales

Colin Elliott
Director, British Intelligence Scale Project, Department of Education, University of Manchester, England

D. Graham
Senior Lecturer in Psychology, University of Durham, England

Ian M. L. Hunter
Professor of Psychology, University of Keele, England

K. Lovell
Professor of Educational Psychology, University of Leeds, England

Eric A. Lunzer
Professor of Educational Psychology, University of Nottingham, England

Elizabeth Newson
Senior Lecturer in Child Development and Joint Director, Child Development Research Unit, University of Nottingham, England

John Newson
Professor of Child Development and Joint Director, Child Development Research Unit, University of Nottingham, England

E. A. Peel
Professor of Education and Head of the Division of Educational Psychology, School of Education, University of Birmingham, England

Ved P. Varma
Consultant Psychologist; formerly Educational Psychologist, London Borough of Brent

P. E. Vernon
Professor of Educational Psychology, University of Calgary, Alberta, Canada

J. G. Wallace
Professor of Education, Department of Education, University of Southampton, England

K. Wedell
Senior Lecturer, School of Education, University of Birmingham, England

Phillip Williams
Professor of Educational Studies, The Open University, England

Jean Piaget: a biographical sketch

Jean Piaget is perhaps the only living psychologist whose name is a household word. He has been internationally famous for at least forty-five years. And he is a mere eighty years old.

He was born in Neuchâtel in 1896 and has lived in Switzerland all his life. There was a brief period in his very early twenties when he worked at a number of centres in Germany and later in Paris. For the rest, apart from lecture tours, conferences and visits abroad to receive honorary degrees, Piaget has remained in Geneva and scholars from all over the world have come to see him and to study under his guidance. They have come not only because of his reputation as a psychologist, but because of the breadth of his interests and the all-embracing scope of his ideas. He is a biologist, a logician and an epistemologist. In addition, he is the foremost figure in education and was for many years director of the Bureau International d'Education under UNESCO.

In each of these fields, Piaget has been a prolific and profoundly original writer. His first publication appeared when he was in his mid teens. His primary interest was then in biology. The reports which he published, based on his observations of the adaptive variations of freshwater molluscs, gained him his first offer of a post—as assistant curator in the museum at Geneva. Piaget had to turn the offer down, as he was still at school. He continued his studies in biology at the University of Neuchâtel, gaining his first degree in 1915 and his doctorate in 1918, when he was still only twenty-two.

Piaget's work as a biologist was more than a youthful pursuit to be set aside in favour of psychology. For it was out of his researches on ecology and adaptation that he evolved his central theme: that adaptation is based on the achievement of a successful equilibrium in the interactions of the organism and the environment. In more primitive species, these adaptions are physiological and behavioural. But in man they extend to knowledge in the form of internalised action. The study of psychology, and more particularly of the origins of cognition, was therefore a natural extension of Piaget's work as a biologist. Nor has he allowed his early interests to lapse. Throughout his life he has maintained an active interest in botany; and despite his involvement in psychology and education, not to speak of his work in logic and epistemology, he has also kept abreast of the most important developments in theoretical biology. His recent works include a most thought-provoking study of certain features that are common to genetics and cognitive psychology: Biology and Knowledge *(1967, translated 1971).*

Piaget's first initiation into psychology included a period of study under Bleuler. Doubtless he found psycho-analysis insufficiently rigorous, but from it he gained a keen perceptiveness which he later brought to bear in his observations of children. Herein too lies the origin of Piaget's famous 'méthode clinique' by which he was able to discover so much about the mechanism of thinking in children and the rationale underlying replies which others might have dismissed as errors of no account. Piaget's introduction to experimental psychology at about the same time was to bear fruit not only in his experimental studies of cognition, but perhaps most prominently in his careful studies of perception: The Mechanisms of Perception *(1961, translated 1969).*

From 1919 to 1921, Piaget held a post in Binet's laboratory under Henri Simon in Paris, where he worked on the standardisation of Burt's tests of reasoning. This initiation had two effects. First, he was able to go beyond the categorisation of children's answers as 'right' or 'wrong'. Further questioning enabled him to establish how and why a reply took the form that it did. This is the line of investigation that was to be Piaget's principal preoccupation throughout his career. Second, and as a corollary to this, Piaget became disenchanted with psychometrics—and has remained so to this day, believing that other methods, and notably the clinical method, permit the investigator to go beyond statistical recording of surface data to the analysis of process itself.

It was in 1921 that Piaget was given his first appointment in Geneva. This was at the Institut Rousseau, then under the direction of Claparède. Later this was to become an inter-faculty institute of the university—and Piaget himself was its director from 1933 to 1971. He was now free to continue his own lines of investigation and these resulted in the rapid publication of a whole series of works, beginning with The Language and Thought of the Child *(1923, translated 1926) which immediately gained him an international reputation. They were original, far-reaching, penetrating and provocative. In the course of these works, Piaget was able to demonstrate to an unbelieving world the extent to which children's thinking differs from that of the adult, particularly in its lack of objectivity, in its ability to dissociate action and observation and in its all-pervading egocentrism—best defined as an inability to conceive of the existence of an alternative point of view. In addition to the works on* Judgment and Reasoning, The Child's Conception of the World *and* The Child's Conception of Physical Causality, *these include his celebrated volume on* The Moral Judgment of the Child *(1932), which draws as much on sociological theory as it does on psychological analysis. These works have been criticised for their almost exclusive reliance on verbal questioning. Yet their principal conclusions remain valid, and many of the more detailed findings have been since replicated by the careful studies of Laurendeau and Pinard (La pensée causale, 1962). It is interesting to note that at this time Piaget was far more inclined to stress the role of social interaction, as well as that of language, than he has done in his more recent writings. Did he over-react?*

Following the publication of these early classics, Piaget began to turn his attention to the origins of intelligence, joining the ranks of his illustrious predecessors, Preyer, Sully and Valentine, who relied on detailed observations of their own children as source material for the interpretation of child development as a whole. Because of his training as a biologist as well as his deep insights into psychology and epistemology, Piaget's observations were both more probing and more detailed than those of his predecessors. His finely documented analysis of the successive stages from reflex to the beginnings of representation remains the most comprehensive in the field, an obvious and essential reference point for the construction of diagnostic developmental scales such as those of Woodward and Uzgiris and Hunt. These researches appeared in article form in the early thirties. The three books on The Origins of Intelligence, The Child's Construction of Reality *and* Play, Dreams and Imitation *came out in the late thirties, but were not translated until twenty years later.*

These studies enabled Piaget to advance his understanding of the relation between action and thought and to establish the critical role of object conservation. He could now resume his studies of development from five to ten from an entirely new standpoint, using practical situations instead of verbal interview. Moreover, he was fortunate in being able to call on the collaboration of outstanding researchers trained in his methods, including Alina Szeminska and Barbel Inhelder.

This was the era which produced what are now his best-known studies, those bearing on the development of conservation, of classification, of seriation and of transitivity. Piaget and Szeminska's work on number appeared in 1941 at the same time as Piaget and Inhelder's work on physical quantities. Within the same series, works on time and movement came out in 1946, on space and geometry in 1948 and on chance in 1951. Most influential of all was the summary entitled The Psychology of Intelligence *(1947, translated 1950). The translations of these and related works have given rise to a gigantic body of literature in English-speaking countries: both fundamental and applied, as well as providing a constant point of reference for curricular reform in the sixties.*

During the same period, no one knows how, Piaget found time to write a three-volume treatise on genetic epistemology, an essay on philosophy in the grand manner, as well as a highly individual and imaginative study of logic. Perhaps the crowning achievement was the publication of The Growth of Logical Thinking *(1955, translated 1958). This supremely original work has not gone uncriticised (the reviews of Parsons and Bruner in the* British Journal of Psychology *for 1959 are themselves classics in the field). Nonetheless, it remains the most impressive body of evidence on the subject of thinking in later childhood and adolescence, and it is still the key psychological reference for the redesigning of curricula in science and mathematics at the secondary level.*

Throughout this period, despite his preoccupations with experimental psychology and philosophy, Piaget at the same time occupied a leading position in the educational field as Director of the Bureau International d'Education. His astonishing grasp of the problems of education on a world scale emerges most clearly in the two essays Science of Education and the Psychology of the Child *(published in one volume by Longman, 1971), one of which was written in 1935 and the other thirty years later.*

From 1957 onwards, Piaget was able to supplement the work of the Institute at Geneva, by bringing together a stream of scholars under the auspices of the Centre international d'épistémologie génétique. This enterprise was financed first by the Rockefeller Foundation and later by the Ford Foundation. From all over the world, psychologists, logicians, epistemologists and mathematicians were eager to associate with Piaget in the elaboration and evaluation of his ideas. Some came for periods ranging from six to twelve months; others attended only for the annual discussions or 'Symposia'. The results of this continuing endeavour are contained in a series of monographs 'Études d'épistémologie génétique' which now runs into more than thirty volumes. The series contains some of Piaget's own most important statements. (Fortunately, extracts from several of these appear in translation in Furth's Piaget and Knowledge, *1969.) The number and above all the calibre of the scholars who have worked with Piaget is impressive. Nearly all will allow that they gained at least as much as they contributed. They include such internationally well-known figures as François Bresson, Mimi Sinclair, Daniel Berlyne, Benjamin Matalon, Jerome Bruner, Seymour Papert, Leo Apostel, Jean-Blaise Grize, Jan Smedslund and Joachim Wohlwill—and the list is far from exhaustive. As for the many distinguished scholars in the field who have gone to Geneva for shorter visits, it would probably be easier to list those who have not!*

For fifteen years, from 1957 to 1971, Piaget continued to fill the two-fold role as director of the Institute and leader of the new Centre. His published works since 1958 include The Early Growth of Logic *(1959, translated 1964), essentially a complement to* The Growth of Logical Thinking, *as well as two important new departures: the works on Mental Imagery and Memory, these being studies of the interaction between intellectual organisation and cognitive processes which are in a sense more peripheral.*

In 1971 Piaget retired as Director of the Institute, having reached the age of seventy-five. But his work as head of the Centre continues unabated. At the time of writing he is engaged in exploring what psychological steps are necessary for an individual learner to come to terms with the concept of 'Category' in mathematics. The scope and power of his thinking are as impressive as ever, and so too is his sheer productiveness as a writer on an ever-widening range: titles of recent publications include Sagesse et illusion de la philosophie *(1965),* Études Sociologiques *(1967), and* Structuralism *(1968, translated 1971).*

In psychology and education, the impact of his work is so considerable that one would not attempt to sum it up in a paragraph. I have tried to do so in a separate chapter and that too is far from adequate. Meanwhile, Piaget is only eighty and intellectually as strong as ever. It is more than probable that the publications yet to come will be as influential as their predecessors. This volume is one which celebrates Piaget's eightieth birthday. We salute him and look forward to his hundredth!

E. A. Lunzer

Part One

Eric A. Lunzer

1. An appreciation of Piaget's work

Piaget is among the outstanding psychologists of all time. In the field of developmental and cognitive psychology he is unique. His publications are so numerous that the very reading of them would represent a lifetime's work for an ordinary man. Yet his ideas are also so seminal that in the ever-growing field of child psychology hardly a paper is published without some reference to one or more, often to several, of his works. Many report studies conducted within a Piagetian framework. They set out from assumptions and findings contained in the work of Piaget himself and go on to report extensions of this work. Often the result of such studies has been to confirm, but at the same time to extend and to clarify, the findings of Piaget himself. One thinks at once of the numerous replications and extensions carried out in the sixties by Lovell and his associates in Britain, by Elkind, Wohlwill, Goldschmid and many others in America, by Smedslund in Norway and by others all over the world (see Modgil 1974).

But not all are of this kind. In the later sixties and seventies especially, just as earlier in the thirties and forties, one reads many excellent studies which set out to question some of Piaget's assumptions. Experiments are reported which suggest that this or that finding is liable to an interpretation quite different from that of Piaget, and the findings that they describe accord better with these alternative interpretations. One recalls the work of Kohnstamm, of Gelman, of Bryant and of others. Above all, one thinks of the lively controversies between Bruner and Piaget and of even earlier criticism by the Russian psychologist Galperin, and Vygotsky before him.

But this is not to diminish the work of Piaget nor to denigrate it. It is the fate of every great scientist to find not only that his views are challenged, but that sooner or later new findings emerge which require modification of his theory or even its overthrow. The hallmark of his achievement is not that his theory stands forever unchallenged, but rather that it opens up new fields of enquiry, while at the same time providing a comprehensive and comprehensible interpretation of phenomena which were till then seen as unrelated. Such a man asks new questions and the questions that he asks lead to discoveries that are valid. In these respects the place of Piaget is assured.

Briefly, the question that he asked is this: is the extension of knowledge a gradual accumulation of new bits of information or is it the result of successive coordinations such that the acquisition of any new piece of knowledge is simply not possible without some frame of reference within which it will be meaningful? The discoveries that he has made range over the child's acquisition in every area of knowledge from mathematics to science and moral judgment; they cover each of the major dimensions in terms of which we structure our experience—time, space, number and causality—and they extend over the whole span of development from babyhood to adulthood. The interpretation of these discoveries is indeed open to question. Their validity is not. Equally, the fundamental importance of the question that he asks is incontestable. For it is the question itself which led to these discoveries and which continues to stimulate new and fruitful research, often on the part of workers whose theoretical perspectives may be very different, save in this one essential respect: that they accept the importance of the question itself, and they share the view that it is open to empirical enquiry.

Yet while it is easy to recognise and demonstrate the magnitude of Piaget's achievement, it is a great deal more difficult to capture what it is that makes him unique, different not only from great scientists in other fields but different too from his own colleagues in psychology. What is required here is not a judgment in the dimension of valency, of better or worse, but rather a statement of the kind of contribution Piaget has made and still continues to make. What are his peculiar strengths? And why is it that so many scholars who recognise his eminence none-the-less find it difficult to come to terms with what Piaget has to say?

Any attempt to answer these questions—and what follows is no more than one man's attempt—must take account of Piaget's epistemological interests as well as his scientific work. No less important is some recognition of the state of psychological thinking at the time that Piaget commenced on his great enterprise by contrast with the current state of the science. Third, I would suggest, is the need to acknowledge and respect the fact that scientists may differ from one another in their use of theory. No scientist of any stature can dispense with theory, and each will make his personal contribution to the development of scientific theory. But while some prefer to keep theoretical inferences very close to their observations at any given moment, others are more prone to make imaginative leaps, often beyond what might be warranted on the basis of existing evidence. Sometimes, but not always, these leaps turn out to be justified, and further progress in research will then produce the evidence that was lacking at the start. There is no doubt at all that Piaget falls into the second class. Finally, there is the need to separate out Piaget's scientific contribution from questions of application. This is not to deny the importance of application or even the urgency of making the best use of scientific evidence in the formulation and implementation of educational policy. It is to note that making inferences from theory about what would constitute good practice is a perilous enterprise, although a necessary one. The inferences that one makes will nearly always entail additional assumptions about matters of facts that are not yet proven, as well as particular philosophical or ethical orientations which are indeed important and inescapable, but have little to do with scientific evidence. So it is that one's inferences can sometimes be wrong. Or their rightness may be a matter of opinion and not one of fact. And this without prejudice to the coherence or the experimental validity of the theory upon which they are based.

While Piaget's contribution to general psychology is not in doubt, it is well to recognise that Piaget himself has always preferred to follow his own line of thinking. On those occasions when he has accepted the interests and findings of others as points of departure for new work, it is because he felt that they lent themselves to the further development of his own ideas. Indeed, Piaget regards himself as the founder of a distinctive branch of psychology: genetic epistemology. There are many who would agree that the questions Piaget asks form a distinctive branch of the science, and one which requires its own methods of research and its own modes of evaluation. Many others, including many of his admirers and followers, would not go so far, preferring to see him as an outstanding contributor to the field of developmental psychology, one who has brought his own distinctive insights to bear on the subject, but whose work must stand evaluation in the same way as that of any other scientist in the field. Nevertheless, Piaget's own conception of his aims provides an important key to the understanding of his work.

Epistemology is a branch of philosophy. It is concerned with the nature of knowledge and its origin. Among the questions that it poses there are some which are of particular concern. Is all the knowledge that we possess ultimately rooted in perception? If it is, then, since perception is notoriously fallible, can there be certainty on any point, and if so, upon what basis? Since both logic and mathematics present themselves as likely representatives of a kind of knowledge which is not open to empirical falsification, does this mean that reason is a peculiar faculty of human beings which is somehow immune from all other kinds of knowledge and also independent of experience? If they are so, then what is their relation to the rest of nature, of which human beings and human brains are clearly a part? And finally, if logic and mathematics are innate and inviolate, what is it that permits new discoveries in mathematics, and above all how is it that new systems of mathematical transformations are first invented in their own right and later seen to model the interrelations of physical phenomena which were either unknown or not considered when the mathematicians did their work?

It is Piaget's central belief that at least some of these questions are not entirely matters for philosophical speculation and *a priori* reasoning. To know what knowledge man can possess and what reason we possess and how these are formed is at least in part a matter for empirical investigation. We who are now men and women and who pose these conundra about human reason and knowledge in the abstract were once children. Much of our knowledge was acquired in the course of our early experience. But how is it with our respect for logic and coherence in mathematics? Is reason indeed innate? Here Piaget set out to do something which few philosophers have done before him and none so relentlessly. He went and looked at children, and he gave them problems some of which were practical and others verbal. He recorded both their behaviour and their verbal comments, always looking to infer the kind of reasoning which these implied. And the answers that he found were as startling and disturbing to philosophers and psychologists alike in the twenties as today they are old hat. Children of four, five and six have only the most rudimentary comprehension of magnitude and number, and their ability to categorise and order, or even to recognise contradiction in their judgment, is remarkably wanting. It is far short of what would be needed to substantiate the claim that reasoning in the then accepted sense can be regarded as innate.

Just as Piaget's concern with an empirical approach to epistemology underlies his interest in the development of logical thinking in children, so it determines the principal directions of his work as a whole. Philosophers have long been aware that the ways in which we assimilate and categorise our experience are determined not only by our sensory modalities, but above all by the ways in which we experience the major categories or dimensions that structure our conception of the world: space, time and causality. It is therefore no accident that Piaget has concentrated so much of his effort in trying to establish the genesis of these concepts from infancy to adolescence and from reflex or random interaction with the object to the construction and validation of scientific models. Within these, too, it is no accident that Piaget has chosen to investigate the origins of conservation—of length, distance, area, volume, weight, duration, and so on. For these are the key measures in terms of which one must ultimately order our observations if these are to result in the construction of testable scientific models.

However, the argument must be taken one step further. For a fuller understanding of Piaget's approach, we need to take account of his philosophical views as well as his philosophical interests. Piaget defines his position as a form of structuralism. Structuralism may be thought of in two ways. On the one hand it is the view that in the final analysis all knowledge about things can be reduced to knowledge about interactions between things, together with knowledge about our own interactions with the things that we know. This is simply to say that knowledge results from a mixture of experiment, which gives rise to general laws governing the behaviour of matter and energy at various levels of organisation, and observation, which is itself a function of the interaction between our own sensory end-organs and the forms of energy to which they are most sensitive. One thinks at once of Kant's demonstration of the unknowability of the 'thing in itself', and also of Wittgenstein's dictum that 'the world is the totality of facts and not of things'.

But Piaget's structuralism goes further. Considering that scientific knowledge takes the form of laws and even everyday knowledge relies on the recognition of regularities in the behaviour of nature, Piaget is led to the view that the various sets of laws, and even the regularities themselves, combine to form systems or structures, and these have a great deal in common with mathematical structures. To describe a structure one needs a minimal set of axioms which define its elements, the operations that are permissible, and the transformations which these produce. The notion of 'set' in mathematics and the fundamental axioms of logic are perhaps the most familiar examples. Structural descriptions of this sort are essentially circular, since operations are defined in terms of elements and transformation, and so on. Nevertheless, continued application of the elementary axioms and laws produces an ever-growing if not infinite body of theorems about the behaviour of the system. As noted earlier, mathematical and logical structures are self-sufficient in that they are not themselves subject to physical laws, although they may serve as models for these laws. Piaget has tried very consistently to describe knowledge as a growing structure in just this sense.

This is why Piaget argues that the growth of knowledge (French: 'intelligence') presupposes a series of structures—auto-regulations, concrete operations, formal operations—and that the succession of these must depend on the internal mechanisms of intelligence, the principle of equilibration, and not on perception, language or even neurophysiological development. Once again, one is reminded of a great idealist philosopher: Leibniz, except that for Leibniz it is the elements or monads that do not interact, while for Piaget it is the structures. Nor is it quite correct to say that Piaget denies any interaction. Indeed, he maintains that interaction is essential for the growth of knowledge, since knowledge feeds on experience. Nevertheless he insists that the most fundamental changes in intelligence are governed by internal laws, while experience simply provides the content which spurs the subject to effect novel and more comprehensive, more economical and less contradictory equilibrations.

At this point I can imagine that some readers will be tempted to stop. For the kind of view I have just described runs counter to Anglo-Saxon tradition both in science and in philosophy. The propositions just set out are far too ambitious in their scope and also far too abstract in their formulation to be palatable to most readers. For my own part, I have no wish to defend them on philosophical grounds, even if I had the necessary ability. But I would claim that one needs to take account of Piaget's position as a structuralist in order to appreciate the directions and emphases of his work. From the views just described stem his insistence on the role of cognitive conflict in the development of understanding; his attempt to find a unifying principle in the evolution of intellective behaviours in a wide variety of situations, especially at what he takes to be the critical ages of five to eight and eleven to sixteen years; and his enquiries into the role of intellectual development on the character of perceptual behaviour, of imagery, of memory and of language.

If Piaget had been a bold and ingenious speculative theoretician and no more, his ideas would perhaps have held little interest for those whose main preoccupations lie elsewhere—and that includes the vast majority of scientists and educators alike. But it happens that Piaget is not just a philosopher. He is also a brilliant pioneer in translating his ideas into something like a scientifically testable form. This is not to say that they have been scientifically proven. Indeed, it can reasonably be argued that, taken as they stand, few of his ideas are testable. For instance, it would be difficult to test the principle that the influence of cognition on language acquisition exceeds that of language on cognitive development. But whereas the use of language to clarify a principle of cognitive organisation suggests itself readily to researchers, the notion that the transformational complexity of a rule may be such that its acquisition requires some minimal level of cognitive organisation is far less obvious. Less obvious too is the prediction of just what kinds of interpretation might result from failure to understand a transformational rule, or from failure to establish what rules of usage determine the selection of an appropriate transformation. And these are questions that are indeed testable.

Piaget's philosophical orientation is indeed more in the European tradition than in the British or American. One might even say that the appearance of rigour within some of its compartments all too often masks certain exuberance in the construction of the edifice as a whole. For instance, one may question whether axiomatisation is as appropriate to the description of cognitive behaviour as it is to that of logic or of language. Even if it is, one may ask whether the kinds of insights that one obtains by looking at the overall pattern of replies to a diagnostic interview can ever produce the hard data that are needed as back-up for an acceptable axiomatisation. Yet even here the scepticism should be tempered with admiration and gratitude. Piaget's ideology may well be over-ambitious; it has none-the-less helped him to discover new lines of research, whose validity is independent of their origin. To take three examples. Piaget's studies of imagery and its dependence on knowledge offers a line of enquiry quite different from that of Paivio and Bower. His studies of memory and reconstruction extend and complement the work of Underwood and of Norman. Sinclair's Piagetian approach to language comprehension and production extends the analyses originating from the work of Chomsky, Fodor and Roger Brown.

Perhaps, too, it was Piaget's philosophical independence that enabled him to anticipate the revolution in psychological thinking that separates current emphases from those which dominated the work of psychologists in his youth. At that time psychology was largely influenced by the controversy between a mechanical style of behaviourism and a question-begging form of mentalism (Gestalt psychology). This was largely because the only physical analogues then available for the study of mental processes were mechanical, so much so that the telephone switchboard and the common slide-rule were never very far from one's thoughts. Today that controversy is all but forgotten. Nearly everyone recognises that the business of cognitive psychology is to disentangle the sequence of transformations which enable the subject to utilise sensory information in such a way as to produce behaviour which is finely regulated and well-adapted to the exigencies of the environment. All are agreed that perception itself involves a series of transformations on sensory cues. No one ignores the role of expectancy and of categorisation in the determination of which cues are used and which are discarded. Nor is there disagreement about the need to postulate some form of conceptual or verbal coding of perceptual data. Even beyond this there are few who would question the validity of experimentation designed to elucidate the kinds of transformations on data that are involved in making inferences, or the role of inference in problem-solving. It is within the newly-won territory that one finds ample material for disagreement and the discovery of researchable problems—for instance, to elucidate the interrelation between stimulus equivalence and response equivalence; or to unravel the mechanisms which permit the recovery of relevant material from the long-term memory store and hence to discover just how this material is filed in the brain; or the problem of knowing just what sorts of transformations are in fact executed when one is asked to decide whether a particular verbal formula is consistent with a given state of affairs or with another verbal formula or with a series of such formulae.

What has happened in between? No doubt historians will differ in their replies. Some may point to advances in physiology, notably in elucidating the role of the reticular formation as a sort of information filter and in clarifying the nature of visual response to patterned visual stimuli. Others will mention advances in experimental psychology, as in the work of Harlow, Broadbent, or Sperling. Others might go farther afield, and refer to developments in linguistics, biology and ethology. For my own part, I believe that the main impetus for a fundamental change in psychology came from the rapid development of cybernetics and computer technology. Unlike telephone switchboards, computers do not simply relay information: they process it. Unlike switchboards, they do not treat all information in a standard and simple manner: they are the repositories of earlier information, suitably transformed, and it is this which determines how they will deal with the new. And of course there is nothing mysterious about how they operate, because human beings construct the machines and human beings develop the programs which determine their operation. Since it is necessary and reasonable to study and develop the art of programming for machines, so it is no longer unreasonable to conduct enquiries that deal with the programming of human behaviour. There is no longer any justification for restricting oneself to the description of external stimuli and observable fragments of behaviour.

Be that as it may, the phenomena investigated by Piaget in the twenties and thirties and forties were well in advance of his time. His concern with the central role of knowledge in the determination of perception and response anticipated the present concern with information processing. This is surely one of the reasons why his work had a more favourable reception abroad after the Second World War than it did in the thirties. For Piaget's organising scheme is something like a self-modifying program and his logical structures can be thought of as specifying the kinds of transformations on input that occur at any stage of development. At least to this extent, the *Zeitgeist* appears to have caught up with Piaget. At the same time, Piaget himself had modified his research procedures. While he continued to rely on the diagnostic interview as his principal technique, he had introduced two radical alterations. The questions that were put to young children no longer centred on things that were abstract or beyond their ken, like the origin of the wind or the kind of reality that attaches to dreams. Instead they bore on the movements and dimensions of concrete objects, many of which were entirely familiar. Also, because these objects were present in the situation, the child could manipulate them himself, and often (but not always) the response that was called for was not verbal at all, but practical, as in the seriation of rods, or the arrangement of objects in classes, or the reproduction of the horizontal axis when one tilts a container which is half-full of water.

As a matter of fact, the range of experimental situations that have been investigated by Piaget is so wide that it is quite difficult for anyone interested in developmental psychology to devise an experiment which is potentially fruitful without finding that Piaget and his associates have already explored some set-up which is identical or very similar. Invariably when this is so, it will be found that Piaget has drawn attention to the principal ways in which the child's approach to the problem differs from that of the adult. Here one is bound to point to another of Piaget's supreme talents, and one which has not been mentioned so far. It is his remarkable flair for empathy, his ability to put himself into the shoes of the child, to think as the child would think—and then to turn round on that thought and analyse its characteristics and its mechanisms. Strange as it may seem, empathy is by no means a universally characteristic of psychologists, and is certainly not always evident in those whose main contribution has been in some fundamental area of research. Indeed, there was a time when an ability or a willingness to empathise was looked at askance, as if it were a culpable betrayal of one's scientific integrity. No doubt the brilliant and far-ranging but essentially unscientific intuitions of Freud were still felt as threatening in the early part of this century, as though the very existence of such ideas could not but impede the progress of objective research. We are now perhaps a little more tolerant, prepared to allow that it matters little whether a man's first intuition of an idea came about by empathy or by reference to a mathematical model or a physical analogue, so long as the idea is testable by means of controlled experiment.

It has previously been remarked that at least some of Piaget's broad ideas are not easily tested, but this is by no means true of his findings, for these are indeed testable and that is their strength. It is why they continue to serve as a quarry for more searching experimental analysis. In so far as Piaget has revealed the principal ways in which child behaviour differs from that of the adult, the accuracy of his observations nearly always stands the test. But this is not at all to say that every aspect of Piagetian theory is thereby verified and must be taken as sacrosanct. It does not even follow that Piaget's clinical method is the only valid procedure for studying the development of thought. It is excellent for a first approximation: to discover whether a phenomenon is present and to arrive at a preliminary descrip-tion of it. But it is also too fluid and flexible, insufficiently standardised and replicable, and it allows too much scope for interpretation to serve as the principal technique of enquiry once a phenomenon has been shown to be genuine. For the task is then to establish precisely the conditions under which the phenomenon appears and what are the influences that cause it to vary—and here the experimental method is clearly superior.

So long as one recognises the extraordinary productiveness of the clinical method in the hands of Piaget, it is no disrespect to point to its limitations. Equally, to treat the whole of 'Piagetian theory' as if it were a repository of eternal wisdoms is more of an insult than a tribute. It is to regard Piaget as a cult figure instead of a scientist.

Precisely because of his great inventiveness, the works of Piaget contain not a few speculative notions which can hardly stand scrutiny. For instance, there is the idea that children's first intuitions of space are topological: are we to understand that little children confuse coffee cups with doughnuts and wedding rings? All that can be said is that there are occasions when they use continuity/discontinuity as a cue. For the rest, the problems are first to identify what cues are innate and which are the product of learned equivalence, and second to establish the relations between visual or kinesthetic cues on the one hand and spatial conceptualisation on the other.* I believe that Piaget's treatment of formal reasoning falls into a similar category, and especially his attempt to explain the experimental control of variables in the adolescent by postulating their 'possession' of the INRC group.† By the same token it may be suggested that the notion of 'horizontal décalage' (see Wallace, p. 17—Ed.) is little more than a catch-all for anomalies in experimental data which cannot be accounted for by Piaget's stage theory, while 'vertical décalage' differentiates between behaviours that differ so greatly both in level of conceptual abstraction and in amount of previous learning involved that a single label in unhelpful.

Opinions differ about whether success or failure in each of the many problems allocated to the concrete and formal stages can be explained by reference to a single mechanism. The co-occurrence of a large number of gains about the period of five to seven years has been widely recognised (White 1965). I have argued elsewhere that all or most of these seem to depend on the child's awareness of the criteria of his own actions (e.g. in classifying, enumerating, measuring) in relation to opposing criteria that he might have used and did not (Lunzer 1970). This is one of the things Piaget means by 'prise de conscience'. In regard to the developments of 'formal reasoning', I have suggested that at least one feature common to all or most of the relevant problems consists in the ability to accept lack of closure (ALC) (see Collis, p. 148—Ed.). ALC occurs when the initial information available or obtained by the subject does not permit him to make unambiguous inferences about any of the variables with which he is concerned, but instead permits a reduction of alternatives, so that the final determination can only be made at a later stage, when more information has been obtained (Lunzer 1976a). Nevertheless, this feature in itself is quite insufficient to account for the great variety of conceptual advances associated with progress at the secondary level and beyond. These must depend not only on the availability of a fairly considerable body of more or less organised previous knowledge (Gagné 1966), but also on a variety of procedures for synthesising apparently disparate elements, including several kinds of abstraction (Lunzer 1976b). Nevertheless, the acquisition of complex intellectual behaviour still poses many unsolved problems, so that it is difficult to make precise statements about the interaction between specific learning, general learning and intellectual readiness. Just how should one describe the task of solving simultaneous equations or making up a relevant set of such equations on the basis of information given in the problem? This is just one example taken from a vast area where there is an obvious need for more objective research.

Yet the fact remains that, even if one is a little sceptical about the generality of

* It is here that Piaget's own researches offer several novel departures in technique as well as a wealth of experimental evidence. See especially, Piaget and Inhelder (1956) and Piaget and Inhelder (1971).

† A group of transformations, consisting of four operations: identity, inverse, reciprocal and correlative. See Inhelder and Piaget (1958, pp. 307ff).

Piaget's four major stages,* one cannot but be grateful that the intuition of these stages has produced so great a wealth of evidence on the various ways in which child and adult need to elaborate and modify their information-processing strategies to enable them to come to terms with the requirements of a technological and cultural society. For there is a sense in which these stages can be regarded as broad and interesting epistemological descriptions of different patterns of adaptation: the sensorimotor stage is characteristic of adaptation at the sub-primate level; intuitive or context-specific representation might be held to describe the mode of adaptation of some real or notional primitive societies; concrete reasoning represents a beginning of codification perhaps associated with the beginnings of literacy and the exercise of suzerainty over a wider area than the confines of a tribe; while formal reasoning is a prerequisite for the evolution of mathematics, of science and of technology and perhaps, too, for the evolution of literature out of myth, of music out of dance and of art out of craft. But there is also a sense in which the intuition of these stages has enabled Piaget to devise a large number of precise experimental set-ups within which it can confidently be predicted that the whole approach of the child will be different as a function of some mixture of maturation and experience associated with growing older and growing up in society.

It is entirely legitimate and even essential to probe further: to study the extent to which performance can be modified by training or by variation in the language used to orient the child to what is required of him. Nor should one be surprised if, as a result of introducing these finer distinctions, one finds that the unity of the stages begins to recede in importance. But it does not follow that one can easily substitute some other equally broad hypothesis as a counter-theory to Piaget. For instance, the evidence does not support the theory that defect of short-term memory can by itself account for failure of operational solutions in children under seven (McLaughlin 1963), for the correlations between behaviour in different Piagetian tasks are very much higher than those between these and short-term memory (Lunzer 1976c). Short-term memory will therefore account for only a very small percentage of the common variance. Similarly one cannot account for these developments by reference to the effects of variations in the language used by the experimenter.† For the fact remains that older or abler children do not 'alter where they alteration find'—nor do they 'bend with the remover to remove' (for they resist counter-suggestion!). Likewise the effectiveness of training procedures (itself still a matter of controversy) cannot be taken to argue the irrelevance of the original phenomenon. For once again one must bear in mind that the same behaviours tend to appear 'spontaneously', that is, without specific training. It has even been argued that all children are capable of transitive logical inferences from

* Piaget speaks of four stages in his 1965 paper 'Education and Teaching since 1935' (see Piaget 1971). More often he omits the second, 'representation' (cf. Inhelder and Piaget 1958, Piaget 1970)—presumably on the grounds that it does not constitute an equilibrium. The omission may be appealing to a (Piagetian) logician, but can make no sense for developmental psychology. It amounts to saying that representation and language are important for cognition only in so far as they give rise to consistent logical argument.

† The effect of such variations is nevertheless brilliantly illustrated in recent papers by Margaret Donaldson and Peter Lloyd (1976) and James McGarrigle and Margaret Donaldson (1976).

birth—on the basis of a single experiment which, however brilliant, is capable of quite another interpretation.*

In sum, just as the work of Piaget contains some ideas which may be considered as fanciful and some which have only a limited usefulness for a fairly specific phase in the development of the science as it covers the psychology of cognition, there are others which will continue to be powerful and productive for some time to come. Mention has already been made of the importance of the concept of coordination in drawing attention to the kinds of inferential links that are essential at any given level of conceptualisation. Another important theoretical contribution is the distinction that Piaget draws between execution and reflexion: the ability to do something presupposes a programme for doing it, but it does not entail the ability to reflect on that programme and describe what one is doing. The latter is essential for certain kinds of generalisation and for the solution of new problems. Piaget's notion of 'prise de conscience' recalls Bartlett's idea of 'turning round on the schema'. No less potent, surely, is Piaget's identification of the role of cognitive conflict in bringing about major change. This is not to deny the potential value of 'meaningful reception learning' as described by Ausubel, but rather to bring out what I take to be a general problem of some importance: under what conditions is it appropriate to guide the child's learning in such a way that right behaviours are stressed and rewarded and interfering wrong behaviours are simply ignored (and certainly not deliberately provoked by the teacher to point out a difficult contrast), and when is it desirable to elicit an inappropriate strategy to enable the learner to realise its inadequacy? It seems to be the case that there are situations where the latter course is indeed desirable (Inhelder, Sinclair and Bovet 1974). Failure to appreciate the significance of this problem may well account in part for one of the defects of so many curricula: children are taught the answers to questions which they have not put, and cannot even understand.

I would suggest that one of the principal objectives in the study of cognitive development may now be to bring about a rapprochement between the Genevan approach and that of the new behaviourists (Bloom, Carroll, Gagné, and others). On the one hand, it may be fruitful to view the spontaneous development of operational behaviour as the outcome of transfer from related but not identical tasks. On the other hand, it seems essential to supplement the kind of hierarchical conceptualisation envisaged by Gagné, a hierarchy based on relevant previous knowledge, by studying the complementary role of the Piagetian hierarchy, which deals not so much with the knowledge relevant to success in a particular task, as with the way in which these elements need to be fused together to enable the subject to cope with more complex relations such as reciprocity, functional dependence, multiple interaction and so on.

In conclusion, the true measure of Piaget's greatness lies in the many new fields of research that he has opened up. The only sincere tribute that can be paid

---

* See the articles by P. E. Bryant and T. Trabasso (1971) and by Benedicte de Boysson-Bardiès and Keven O'Regan (1973). Bryant's demonstration of the universality of comparative perceptual evaluation is exceedingly well-taken, but its relevance for inference is unclear (Lawrenson and Bryant 1972).

by his admirers if they are scientists is to explore these avenues without fear. To do so effectively one must use every technique that is available and one must explore every reasonable interpretation of the data that these may yield. Some will have their origin in Piaget's own writings. Others will not. But it will surely be many years before all of his insights can be incorporated into some comprehensive theory which supersedes his own. One may safely guess that when this does happen, that new theory will integrate more of Piaget's work than it rejects.

J. G. Wallace

2. The course of cognitive growth

The absence of a generally accepted theory of cognitive development continues to restrict progress towards the solution of a range of fundamental educational problems. A few of the more obvious issues are the adaptation of educational experience to the individual child (Glaser and Resnick 1972), the diagnosis and treatment of mental handicap (Mittler 1973) and the provision of a comprehensive theoretical underpinning for the construction of mental tests (Hearnshaw 1972; Wiseman 1972). The failure of psychologists to produce the desired theory becomes understandable, if not excusable, when the magnitude of the task is appreciated.

Kessen (1962), in discussing a variety of possible orientations towards the study of development, outlines the three qualities which define a complete theory of cognitive growth. Firstly, it must be compatible with a cross-sectional approach in terms of the sequence of states through which the child passes in the course of development. Secondly, a theory which only provides a normative account of the sequence of states is incomplete since provision must be made for the inclusion of stable differences in state characteristics between children. Finally, it must comprise general rules governing the transition from state to state in development. The remainder of this chapter will be devoted to an assessment of the current position in cognitive developmental research in relation to the state, individual differences and transition issues.

State and stage in development

Piaget's theory of intellectual development continues to dominate work on cognitive development from a state orientation. Consequently, a convenient method of characterising the current position of research on this theme is to relate it to the fundamental features of his theory:

1.   Stages occur in an invariant developmental sequence. Ages of attainment may be assigned to stages for a particular population, but these vary considerably between populations due to maturation, the previous experience of individuals, motivation and cultural milieu.

2.   The admission of variations in ages of attainment is the only concession to

individual differences in development. Every child must traverse the same stages in a constant order which is assumed to be a fixed feature of the organism–environment interaction, and to be both organismic and experiential.

3.   Once constructed, the logical structures underlying stages are generally applicable. The exact performance consequences of this attribute are unclear. Piaget (1941) asserts that 'at a given level and for a given concept the (eight) different possible groupings appear to be constituted at about the same time'. In performance terms this means that, for a concept such as weight, children should acquire principles such as conservation and transitivity at or about the same time. Somewhat later, Piaget (1956) once again explicates generality of application in terms of the groupings underlying the stage of concrete operations, but this time maintains that when a particular grouping is constructed successful performance appears synchronously on the diverse range of tasks to which it is relevant. As Wohlwill (1973) points out, on this basis construction of the multiplication of relations grouping, for example, would simultaneously give rise to an understanding of double seriation, representation of points in a coordinate system and the principle of compensatory relations between weight and distance in the lever.

4.   Piaget's stage theory is couched in structural rather than process terms. An account is offered of the logical structures which underlie performance, but not of the process that determines the step-by-step temporal unfolding of mental processes and resulting behaviour when a child is confronted with a problem such as a conservation task (Pascual-Leone 1975). Two main reasons for this relative emphasis on structure rather than process have been outlined by Cellérier (1972). The first is Piaget's preoccupation with epistemology. Structures are excellent building-blocks in 'the reconstruction of the Kantian *a priori* categories of knowledge as developmental necessities'. The second factor is the adoption in his main work on groupings of a type of mathematical formalisation which is 'at least twice removed, in its degree of abstraction, from the actual actions and situations with which the child or the adult deals' (p. 117).

During the last fifteen years a considerable number of research studies have been conducted with a view to establishing definitely the truth or otherwise of the Piagetian stage theory with its rigidly predictable developmental sequences and its disregard for individual differences. Despite progressive refinements of method aimed at removing from the experimental data all variation due to extraneous factors, the most striking feature of the results of these studies is the degree of inter- and intra-individual variability obtained. The only direct support for the view that all the groupings appear at about the same time for a given concept and for the simultaneous attainment of successful performance on all tasks which draw upon the same grouping is provided by the results of experiments conducted in Pinard's laboratory at Montreal (Lemerise and Pinard 1971; Dagenais 1973). The efficacy of such studies as a means of confirming or disconfirming the Piagetian stage hypothesis has been questioned by Brainerd (1974). Support for the synchronous development hypothesis can, also, be derived from Osherson's (1974) data, but this is only of indirect relevance to the Piagetian stage theory since his experiments were concerned with 'logical thinking in the strict sense' and required the subjects to make distinctions between logically valid and fallacious arguments. In general, the experimental evidence indicates that principles, such as conservation, are successfully applied at different times to different concepts and to different test situations representing the same concept. Comparisons of performance on quantity, weight and volume conservation tasks exemplify the former, while conservation of quantity assessed first with balls of Plasticine and then with an elastic band affords an example of the latter.

Not only is evidence of synchronous relationships lacking, but the search for regular asynchronous relationships has proved to be fruitless. The results of Smedslund's (1964) well-known study, for example, revealed that not one of the fourfold tables covering the relations between pairs of items tapping aspects of concrete reasoning contained an empty cell indicating an exact developmental relationship. There was, thus, no support for the existence of a regular order of acquisition within the set of items. Even when the focus is narrowed to a single item, exact developmental relations are elusive. Smedslund's (1966a, b, c) studies of a single concrete operational task involving sequences of addition and sub-traction operations on two initially equal, hidden collections demonstrated that the same logical task structure, with identical perceptual and conceptual contents, still gives rise to radical differences between children in the relative difficulty of items.

What has been the reaction on the theoretical plane to the widespread inconsistency in developmental relationships detected by the empirical studies? Piaget accepts the evidence that principles are successfully applied at different times to different concepts and to different test situations representing the same concept. His concession to the former is the concept of 'horizontal décalage'. This refers to a repetition which takes place within a single developmental stage and involves a single general level of functioning. A cognitive structure (the conserva-tion principle) can first be successfully applied to task X (quantity) but not to task Y (weight); later, as a result of repetition of the same developmental process, the same organisation of operations can be extended to Y as well as X. In the case of tasks involving the application of the same operations to different objects (conser-vation of a quantity of water and conservation of a quantity of plasticine), Piaget states that they may give rise to 'slight décalages' explainable 'by the difference in the perceptual or intuitive conditions' (1941, p. 266). 'Horizontal décalage' is purely a descriptive concept, a label for this aspect of the experimental data rather than an explanation of the developmental processes which give rise to it. The general emphasis of Piaget's theory remains on the uniformity of the develop-mental paths traversed by individual children and on the generality of application of the logical structures which determine the sequence of development.

It has been left to others to consider the full import of the empirical data for the basis of Piaget's stage theory. Pinard and Laurendeau (1969) maintain that, since the intervention of 'horizontal décalages' linked to differences in content seriously blur the developmental picture, investigation of generality of application of logical structures should be concerned with the intra-concept level of generalisation and directed to answering the question whether for the same conceptual content, and material content if possible, the different groupings underlying the concepts are achieved in synchrony. This viewpoint is in line with the earlier of the two explications of generality of application by Piaget (1941) quoted above.

Pinard and Laurendeau stress the extreme methodological difficulties involved in an experimental attack on this question and stress that asynchronous developmental relationships obtained without resolution of these difficulties should not be considered as evidence which invalidates Piaget's view. If, on the other hand, asynchronism among the constituent groupings of a given concept was found in a study which resolved the methodological difficulties, Pinard and Laurendeau assert that this would seriously undermine Piaget's conception of stage since it would deny one of its most essential characteristics. Wohlwill (1966) takes a more liberal view of the relationship between Piaget's 'stage' and empirical results. He maintains that if evidence of a regular order of succession or developmental sequence in the appearance of the constituent groupings of a single concept is established, this supports rather than weakens Piaget's position. This liberal view of the 'stage' concept has given rise to a number of proposals which take Piaget's stage theory as their point of departure but introduce significant modifications to bring it into line with the results of empirical studies.

A four-phase model of development is suggested by Flavell and Wohlwill (1969). The first three phases are said to correspond respectively to the Piagetian stages of preoperational thought, IIA, IIB and IIIA, but their approach involves a new way of coping with the apparently inconsistent performance data obtained in studies of the stages issue. Instead of attributing the inconsistency to extraneous factors and attempting to remove it by progressive refinements of experimental method, they incorporate the situational and individual variables from which it springs into their theory. They distinguish between two determinants of the child's performance in a cognitive task. These are derived from the competence-performance distinction in psycholinguistics and comprise, on the one hand, the rules, structures, or 'mental operations' embodied in the task and, on the other, the actual mechanisms required for processing the input and the output.

On this basis three parameters are defined which jointly determine a child's performance. The first of these, P_a, is the probability that a given operation has become fully established and is functional in a particular child. P_b, the second parameter, is an attribute of the task. It represents the likelihood for any given task that the necessary operation, if functional in the child, will in fact be called into play and its end product translated into the desired output. The influence of task-related variables varies with the age of the child. This variation is represented by the third parameter, k, which expresses the weight that P_b corresponding to a particular task carries for a given child, depending on his ability to abstract the information required to utilise a particular operation and to code and process information generally. The form of the interaction of the three parameters is expressed in the equation $P(+) = P_a \times P_b^{(1-k)}$. This indicates the probability of a given child, characterised by particular values of P_a and k, solving a task with a particular value of P_b. This equation forms the basis for the description of the formation of new cognitive structures in terms of a four-phase process.

Since proposing this model of development, Flavell and Wohlwill's views on the states issue have diverged. Flavell (1971, 1972) has increased the emphasis on individual and situational variables and moved farther away from the Piagetian conception of identifiable developmental states subsuming a broad range of performance which is attributable to the same underlying structures. He discusses development in terms of the child's repertoire of cognitive 'items'. These are cognitive skills, rules or strategies which typically go through a protracted process of development before reaching their final level of 'functional maturity' defined in terms of the range of appropriate situations in which the item is evoked and successfully applied. The applicability of an item such as transitive inference, for example, continues to extend long after the generally accepted end point of the Piagetian stage of concrete operations at ten to eleven years. From this standpoint the study of cognitive development involves unravelling the network of inter-relationships of cognitive items, and Flavell (1972) has presented a detailed discussion of a variety of possible relationships.

Wohlwill (1973), in contrast, argues that Flavell has gone too far in devaluing the stage concept and underestimating the degree of order and regularity in development and of constraints on the forms which the interrelationship of developing elements of a structure may take. To handle this regularity Wohlwill proposes that the nature of the developmental relationship between cognitive items or skills can be appreciated if the attainment of a stage is conceptualised as a node in a network. The paths converging on the node represent the course of development of individual cognitive items. The rates at which these paths are traversed varies from child to child, but the node must be reached on all of the paths before development along any of the paths which diverge beyond it is possible. There must be complete stabilisation of all of the items involved in the stage before the disequilibration process marking movement towards the following stage can begin. The scope of applicability of such stages is confined to specific subsets of concrete operations which, as indicated above, may be defined in terms of specific concepts or of particular groupings.

Wohlwill's proposal has much in common with von Bertalanffy's (1960) suggestion that the psychological development of the child may be of an equifinal nature in which equifinal phases are reached from different starting points and in different ways, and maintained until a change in internal or external conditions brings about a new development in the system and sets it on the way by diverse routes towards another equifinal phase. There are, also, indications that the individual paths converging on the stage nodes in Wohlwill's scheme may themselves provide further examples of equifinality. Wallace (1972), in an experimental study of the development of conservation of discrete quantity, found that children added this cognitive skill to their repertoire by a variety of routes.

It is clear from the above selective review that the reaction on the theoretical plane to the inconsistent developmental relationships detected by empirical studies is the adoption of more complex models of development characterised by greater

B

flexibility and affording much more scope for individual differences. This represents a departure from three of the four basic features of Piaget's theory listed at the outset—the invarying sequence of stages, restriction of individual differences to variations in ages of attainment, and the general applicability of the logical structures underlying stages.

There are, also, indications that the fourth feature, the relative emphasis on structure rather than process, is inconsistent with current trends. Interestingly enough, some of these indications are to be found in the more recent work of the Genevan group. Cellérier (1972) attributes to Piaget an increased concern with process and outlines the consequences of this alteration of emphasis for his general theory of development: 'This type of analysis gives rise to a picture of cognitive development as a parallel evolution of cognitive categories, each composed of a neat "filiation" of progressively stronger structures. It has been recently complicated by the discovery that many different schemes and concepts may be applied by the child to the same problem, also that this seems to be a general rule, and that the different cognitive categories seem to evolve at slightly different rates. The net result is that lateral interactions . . . appear at the decomposition and recombination level. These interactions (Piaget describes them as reciprocal assimilations between schemes, resulting in new coordinations) take place between elements that are heterogeneous in two ways: they originate from different categories and their degrees of completion are not necessarily the same. Thus, Piaget's picture of development now incorporates vertical relations (intra-category filiations), horizontal ones (inter-category lateral interactions) and oblique ones (interactions between elements of different "operatory levels").' This marked shift in theoretical viewpoint is closely linked with series of learning experiments conducted by Inhelder (1972) and aimed at observing 'not the coordination process, but a close series of snapshots of its effects: how the schemes are decomposed, what are the successive recombinations that are generated and tried out, what are the guiding constraints their generation is subjected to' (Cellérier 1972). Further confirmation of an increasing emphasis on process is provided in Piaget's (1974) report on the development of children's awareness of how they succeed in carrying out a variety of sensorimotor tasks.

The tendency to emphasise process rather than structure in the study of developmental states is not confined to Genevan revisionism. Illumination of the step-by-step temporal unfolding of mental processes and resulting behaviour is the prime objective of the attempts to apply the methodology of information processing analysis devised by Newell and Simon (1972) to cognitive development. The main features of the approach and its educational implications have recently been discussed by Broadbent (1975). The basic paradigm initially involves posing the question 'What routines for processing information would a child need in order to perform this task?' The ultimate objective is the construction of a computer program which is a completely explicit, demonstrably sufficient theory of the processes involved in task performance.

Using this approach, Baylor and Gascon (1974) and Young (1973) have produced programs which are theories of the developmental states providing the process basis of the performance of individual children on Piagetian seriation tasks. A different strategy has been adopted by Klahr and Wallace (1970, 1972, 1973, 1975), who focus on normative rather than individual performance and seek to construct programs which are state theories covering an increasingly broad range of tasks. At the time of writing, a program has been produced which represents a theory of the processes underlying performance in quantification, class inclusion, conservation and transitivity tasks.

An alternative approach to the study of developmental states in process terms has recently emerged from work on human memory. The main objective of the work is the investigation of the representation of knowledge in memory and, following Quillian (1968), the basic method involves the construction of semantic networks which constitute models of the representation of specific items of knowledge. These networks are characterised as directed graph structures and in their fully explicit form are expressed as computer programs. Although the bulk of this work is concerned with semantic memory in adults, there are indications of an increasing interest in the developmental dimension. Norman *et al.* (1975) outline successive states of the network structures which may underlie a child's acquisition of language. On a more specific level, Gentner (1975) has analysed the network structures underlying the verbs 'give, take, buy, sell, spend-money, trade', derived an order of acquisition for them and predicted an order of developmental acquisition of the verbs on this basis which was confirmed by subsequently obtained experimental data.

The adoption of a process approach to the analysis of developmental states is not confined to the area of language. Greeno (1975) in an attempt to demonstrate that 'principles now understood and incorporated in cognitive theories can be applied in the formulation of instructional objectives' has produced descriptions of the states underlying successful performance on a range of tasks involving quantitative concepts. The tasks comprise fractional numbers as taught to nine-year-olds, Euclidean geometry for thirteen-year-olds and auditory psychophysics as presented to eighteen-year-old undergraduates. The state descriptions may have considerable significance for future research strategy, since Greeno has employed both Newell and Simon's methodology and semantic networks in their construction.

Individual differences in development

In his celebrated Presidential Address to the American Psychological Association, Cronbach (1957) highlighted the distinction between the two disciplines of scientific psychology: between psychometrics, the study of individual differences, and experimental psychology, the search for the basic laws governing all human and animal functioning. The existence of this gap between the two approaches can be illustrated in many ways, but for the present purpose the most significant distinctions are the relative unconcern of the psychometrists with the construction of formal theories to underpin their work and the relative disinterest of the experimentalists in individual differences.

Developmental psychology is no exception to the situation in the discipline as a whole and distinct psychometric and experimental strands can be distinguished in developmental research. Wohlwill (1973), however, points out that the study of developmental change does not readily fit either the psychometric or the experimental model, since the study of age changes in behaviour differs from differential investigation of other interpersonal characteristics and there are critical distinctions between a controlled experimental approach to developmental and nondevelopmental problems. Developmental issues have their own peculiar methodological and design requirements which cannot be provided by either approach alone. In the context of the present discussion it is evident that if a valid theory of cognitive development which incorporates stable differences between children in state characteristics is to be constructed, a conjunction of experimental and psychometric expertise will be required.

There are trends in both psychometric and experimental research which give grounds for guarded optimism that acceptance of the joint importance of formal theory and individual differences is becoming more widespread. Psychometrists have traditionally emphasised the content of performance rather than the processes underlying it. This is exemplified in the practice of naming group factors derived by factor-analytic techniques, such as the familiar v, k and n, after the nature of the tests for which they have high loadings. Concern with performance content and successful prediction explain the absence of a unifying theory of cognition underpinning test construction which has been castigated by Hearnshaw (1972). An increasing interest in the processes underlying performance can, however, be traced through Eysenck's (1967) paper on intelligence assessment, Guilford's (1967) inclusion of basic psychological processes in the framework for his scheme of ability factors, and Bunderson's (1965; Dunham and Bunderson 1969) studies of the changing relationship between cognitive processes at different points in the performance of concept attainment problems. More recently it can be detected in the current state of aptitude-treatment interaction (ATI) studies. There is an impressive degree of unanimity about the reasons for the generally negative results of attempts to obtain disordinal interactions between measures of individual differences in ability and educational treatments. Bracht (1970), Glaser and Resnick (1972), Cronbach (1975) and Cronbach and Snow (1975) agree that the aptitude constructs used are not a productive way of measuring individual differences which interact with different educational methods because these measures stem from a psychometric, selection-orientated tradition that does not relate to the processes underlying performance. Both educational treatments and aptitudes should be characterised in terms of specific processes; in the words of Glaser and Resnick (1972) 'successful attempts to adapt instruction to individual differences will depend upon a line of research on process variables in instruction and performance that is only now beginning to emerge' (p. 253). The proliferation of such process-based research will undoubtedly produce an increasing interest among psychometrists in cognitive theory and, as an inevitable result, cognitive development theory.

A complementary tendency towards a greater concern with individual differences can be detected in the theoretical discussions and empirical research of some experimentalists (Underwood 1975). An indication of this trend, as Glaser and Resnick (1972) point out, is the application of the process constructs of contemporary theories of learning to the conceptualisation of individual difference variables advocated by Melton (1967). A clearcut empirical example of this approach is the work of Rohwer (1971) on individual differences in the process of mental elaboration in paired associate learning. Less clearcut, but none-the-less closely related, examples are provided by the large number of experimental studies of the influence on the learning process of differences in cognitive style or personality characteristics. Although concerned with individual differences in learning processes, these studies, as Kagan and Kogan (1970) have indicated, do not have 'the beneficial guidance of strong theory and, on occasion . . . become empirically barbaric'.

The increasing concern of experimentalists with individual differences is not confined to empirical research based on contemporary learning theories. The discussion of the states issue in the previous section provides evidence of a similar tendency in experimental research on cognitive development being conducted from a variety of theoretical viewpoints. Further examples of this trend will be cited in the next section, which is devoted to a consideration of transition rules in development.

Transition rules in development

The research emphasis on process *within* states is paralleled by an increasing interest in the processes involved in transition *between* states. The current position can be characterised in terms of the framework suggested by Piaget (1957, 1960) and Smedslund (1961). They distinguish four main points of view on the nature of the transition rule in cognitive development. These provide support for the claims of maturation, equilibration, learning and nativism.

It is generally accepted that maturation is a necessary but not sufficient condition for development and that it sets limits to the rate of development. Neurophysiological research is beginning to illuminate the specific nature of these maturational constraints. Hutt (1973) has summarised some of the evidence for a close relationship between behaviour and learning in early development and differential maturation of brain structures. There is, for example, an interesting correspondence between White and Held's (1966) finding that the mean age for the onset of visually guided reaching by infants is three and a half months and the data obtained by Wall which suggests that information about a manipulated object has a specific route to the brain via the dorsal roots, which complete myelination at three and a half months. A similar correspondence exists between landmarks in the development of visual discrimination which appear at three and five months and the completion of the myelination of features of the visual system.

An interesting example of the assignment of an important role to maturation in the construction of a neo-Piagetian theory of cognitive development is provided by Pascual-Leone (1975). It is not possible to provide an adequate account of the theory in a few sentences, far less evaluate it, but an attempt will be made to outline the features which are of particular significance for the transition rule issue.

Pascual-Leone adopts the Piagetian conception of a scheme as his basic unit of analysis in tackling cognitive development. A scheme is defined as an ordered pair of active components. The first one is a 'releasing component' or set of conditions which are activated by external or internal input, while the second is an 'effective component' which provides the basis for the execution of internal or external actions. Any given input activates a set of schemes which is termed the 'field of activation'. Not all of these schemes are applied and actually contribute to producing the child's actions. Only those which are dominant in 'activation weight' determine the response, while the weaker schemes are inhibited.

The activation weight of schemes is decided by the operations of independent neurophysiological processes called 'scheme boosters'. The developmental importance of maturation is represented in a scheme booster, the M operator. M is a central working memory in which task-relevant schemes can be placed in order to boost their activation weight. The number of different schemes which M can boost simultaneously increases with age. Pascual-Leone presents an account of the growth of the capacity of M in terms of chronological age and of Piaget's substages. Each transition from substage to substage corresponds to a unit increase in M.

M is only one of six scheme boosters included in the current version of the theory. Although the other five cannot be considered here, there are two general features of Pascual-Leone's account of cognitive development which will be mentioned, since they provide a convenient way of defining the framework for the remainder of the discussion of transition. Both features are included in a list of requirements which any developmental theory should satisfy. The first is expressed in the prescription that a theory should be 'capable of explicitly representing the step-by-step temporal process of behavioural unfolding'. This can only be achieved by an increasing emphasis on the processes involved in the transition between developmental states. The second requirement is that any account of the transition process should recognise that learning on the basis of experience cannot explain the appearance of behaviour which is 'truly novel' in the sense that, although learned schemes are components of it, no learned scheme is responsible for fitting the components together. This distinction between learning on the basis of experience and the processes involved in reorganising the results of such learning provides an interesting perspective from which to consider theories of transition. In particular it characterises the standpoint adopted by Piaget on the transition issue.

Piaget (1959) makes a distinction between the acquisition of content and structure in intellectual development. The former is brought about by learning on the basis of experience while the latter, which comprises the active formation and reorganisation by the child of the logical structures necessary to cope with the content derived from experience, is identified with the process of equilibration. As development proceeds, learning and equilibration together lead to the acquisition of content and logical structure concurrently. They are, thus, to be regarded as complementary rather than competing transition rules.

As Wohlwill (1966) has pointed out, for all its formal elaboration and complexity, Piaget's theory remains basically a structural analysis of children's performance on cognitive tasks at different levels of development. His treatment of the transition problem, the nature of the processes by which these changes take place, is much less complete. The accounts of equilibration in terms of the complementary processes of assimilation and accommodation resemble Piaget's accounts of the developmental stages in being abstract and divorced from the actual, step-by-step performance of the reorganisation process in relation to specific content. The single exception is a description of the emergence of conservation of continuous quantity (Piaget 1957, 1960). This deals only with the classic experimental situation using clay, however, and is not directly concerned with the processes determining performance since it is based on a sequence of four strategies defined in terms of variations in the probabilities of response to two dimensions of the situation.

The increased concern with process in Piaget's current view of developmental states is, according to Cellérier (1972), paralleled in a recent revision of the equilibration model. This resembles Pascual-Leone's (1975) account of the emergence of truly novel behaviour in being based on the idea that a child's functioning in a problem environment is determined by a process that produces new rules and concepts by decomposing and recombining those which he already possesses. The new combinations are evaluated on the basis of their effects on the external problem environment and the outcome gives rise to a new recombination sequence. A cyclic chaining of external observations and internal combinations is thus established. By generating the extension of certain rules, new properties of the environment can be discovered and these new properties serve to invent new rules that can then be used to discover new properties. The cycle stops when nothing new is generated, under a given definition of the problem environment. Although this revised version of equilibration is a better starting point for process analysis than earlier accounts, it is still a considerable distance from providing a step-by-step account of the operation of the reorganisation process.

The most prominent variants of learning theory in contemporary research on development are to be found in Skinnerian experimental analysis of behaviour and social learning theory as exemplified in the work of Bandura (1969, 1971). The objectives of the experimental analysis of behaviour are entirely concerned with the control of learning through the manipulation of experience or, in Piaget's terms, the acquisition of content. The basic paradigm involves the modification of the behaviour of individual children by the addition or subtraction of target behaviours. These modifications are produced by sequences of experience founded on classical and operant conditioning principles and designed specifically to achieve the behavioural objectives. The wide range of children's behaviour to which this approach has been applied is illustrated in the surveys produced by Risley and Baer (1973).

The nature of the objectives of the experimental analysis of behaviour are not conducive to concern with novel learning as defined by Pascual-Leone. If the acquisition of the desired content proceeds satisfactorily, there is no need to study the reorganisation process initiated by the results of this learning. Consequently, on the theoretical plane, stimulus and response generalisation are the only processes appealed to which are relevant to novel learning. Accounts of their operation are as far removed from the step-by-step performance of the reorganisation process in relation to specific content as Piaget's descriptions of assimilation and accommodation. This situation is consistent with the distinction originally drawn by Carnap (1958) and highlighted by Pascual-Leone (1975) between a behaviouristic method with its emphasis on behavioural control, the production of selected responses, and the method of structure analysis which aims at producing a theory that is sufficiently comprehensive to generate predictions of the response which a subject would make to any specified circumstances in the environment. If Kessen's criteria are to be met, a cognitive developmental theory of the latter rather than the former type is required.

Social learning theory is founded on a broader theoretical basis than the experimental analysis of behaviour and exhibits greater concern with the function of the reorganisation process in transition. Both of these features are well illustrated in a comparison of the accounts of observational learning offered from the two theoretical viewpoints.

New patterns of behaviour are created by organising constituent responses into certain patterns and sequences. As Bandura (1971) points out, the two theories of modelling, learning on the basis of observing the behaviour of a model, differ on the location of this response integration, on whether it occurs at an externally observable, peripheral level or a covert, central level. Explanations of observational learning based on operant conditioning (Baer and Sherman 1964; Gewirtz and Stingle 1968) assume that it proceeds by rewarding the overt actions performed by a subject which resemble the behaviour of a model and ignoring those which do not. Response components singled out in this way are sequentially chained by the influence of reinforcement to form more complex units of behaviour. Since, in this view, observational learning requires overt responding and immediate reinforcement, behaviour is organised into new patterns in the course of performance.

Social learning theory, on the other hand, distinguishes between learning and performance of matching behaviour: 'Observational learning can occur through observation of modelled behaviour and accompanying cognitive activities without extrinsic reinforcement. By observing a model of the desired behaviour, an individual forms an idea of how response components must be combined and temporally sequenced to produce new behavioural configurations' (Bandura 1971). The 'cognitive activities' and 'idea' formation referred to by Bandura involve the application of a process of cognitive organisation to internal representations of the observed behaviour stored in the form of imaginal and verbal memory codes. It is the results of this internal reorganisation which provide the basis for the performance of the observed behaviour by the individual at a future time under the control of externally applied, self-administered or vicariously experienced reinforcement. Both acquisition of content and the consequent reorganisation process are accorded important functions in Bandura's account of observational learning. No attempt is made, however, to describe the operation of the process of cognitive organisation in abstract terms or in relation to specific content.

Discussion of nativism does not centre on its claims to be the transition rule in development, but rather on the extent to which it must be drawn upon to complement the processes of maturation, equilibration and learning. The proposition that 'an empty box cannot fill itself' is accepted even by the most extreme protagonists of learning theory, who find it necessary to assume that a basic behavioural repertoire of reflexes and conditionability of the organism are innate. The emphasis on nativism in attempts to produce cognitive developmental theories has fluctuated over the years, reaching a peak some forty years ago. This was followed by a trough which extended until the last decade, which saw a steady increase in the importance accorded to nativist explanations. The current emphasis on innate processes stems from research on language acquisition and is to be attributed to the influence on developmental psycholinguistics of the work of Chomsky and his followers in linguistics.

The influence of Chomsky's (1967) viewpoint on the empirical level is to be seen, in particular, in the emphasis on syntax exemplified in the detailed studies of syntactic development carried out in the 1960s. On the theoretical level it underlies the widespread assertion of the existence of a separate, specifically linguistic competence or innate language acquisition device (McNeill 1970), although, as Morton (1971) points out, it is not entirely clear that Chomsky himself asserts that the innate basis is language-specific.

Since 1970, developmental psycholinguistics has been increasingly influenced by views derived from linguistics which are at variance with Chomsky's theory. A shift in emphasis in linguistics from syntax to semantics (McCawley 1968; Fillmore 1968) has been reflected in developmental psycholinguistics in an increasing concern with the process of acquisition of the cognitive structure which provides a basis for the acquisition of syntax. Empirical evidence that children's syntactic development is closely related to prior mastery of certain conceptual relations has been provided by Bloom (1970), Bowerman (1973) and Slobin (1973), while a theoretical case for the primacy of certain semantic aspects has been made by Macnamara (1972), Schank (1973a, b) and, from a Piagetian viewpoint, by Sinclair (1973).

This increasing emphasis on semantics is contributing towards a shift in opinions on the innate basis of language acquisition. An indication of the nature of the change is provided by McNeill (1970), who finds it necessary to propose the existence of both 'strong linguistic universals' and 'weak linguistic universals'. The former are categories and rules which are found in all languages and are based on language specific innate endowment, while the latter are linguistic structures which reflect universals in cognition or perception that are not language-specific. The shift is seen in a more clearcut form, however, in the view that there is no innate language acquisition device or specifically linguistic competence, but rather a range of innate cognitive universals which give rise to universal features of language. An indication of the range of specific variants of this general theoretical position is provided by Morton (1971).

The concept of 'cognitive universals' provides a link between studies of language acquisition and the other main strand of current research which bears upon the relationship between nativism and transition. This stems from a cross-fertilisation of the ideas of Piaget and Chomsky, since the fundamental question tackled is the extent to which logical principles such as conservation and transitivity are innate. The initial experimental studies were conducted at Massachusetts Institute of Technology by psychologists involved in research on language acquisition. Mehler and Bever (1967), on the basis of data derived from 2:4- to 4:7-year-old children, asserted that non-conservation behaviour does not indicate the absence of this principle from children's innate endowment, but only the existence of a temporary developmental phase during which dependence on inappropriate perceptual strategies undermines an existing conservation performance capability. This conclusion stimulated an immediate flurry of experimental activity (Beilin 1968; Rothenberg and Courtney 1968; Achenbach 1969; Calhoun 1971; Gelman 1972) and opened up an area of research of fundamental importance.

The most comprehensive case for the innate nature of logical principles has been made by Bryant (1974). Consistent with the research strategy which Bryant regards as optimal, the theory of the nature of the relationship between perception and understanding which he has produced represents a retrospective attempt to accommodate a range of experimental results covering the diverse topics of transposition, transitivity, orientation, position, size, number invariance and cross-modal transfer. The nub of the theory is the view that logical principles such as transitivity must be assumed to be innate since they are necessary to make up for the relative rather than absolute method of perceptual coding employed by young children in making comparative judgments.

Justice cannot be done to Bryant's detailed arguments in the confines of a paragraph, but two brief points will be made. On the empirical level it is clear, as Russell (1974) points out, that validation of the theory will require experimental studies of children under the age of four despite the notorious methodological difficulties involved. Such studies are currently under way. Few results are available as yet, but first indications are not entirely favourable to Bryant's view. Bornstein (1975), while confirming the absence of an absolute code for orientation, for example, reports that four-month-old babies' ability to discriminate colours is consistent with possession of an internal absolute frame of reference rather than dependence on a constant external framework.

Bryant's view also suggests an interesting theoretical question. How would the relative–absolute coding distinction fare if tested by the production of step-by-step process models of relative and absolute performance on comparison tasks? In the case of the task in which a child has to judge whether two books presented successively on a table top are in the same orientation, for example, it is possible that process analysis would reveal that neither mode of performance employs transitive inference. In both cases judgment may be based on a direct comparison of representations of situations one of which is retained in memory while the other is derived from the present situation. The difference between the two modes might lie in the form of the representations of the situation. In the relative mode orientation is represented in relation to a frame of reference, the table top, which is specific to the situation. In the absolute mode the representations which are compared are expressed in terms of a generally applicable frame of reference, based on the horizontal and vertical axes, which has been constructed as a result of experience of a range of spatial frames of reference in specific situations. This alternative interpretation is derived from a theoretical position which attributes both the construction of a generally applicable orientational frame of reference and of logical principles such as transitivity to the operation of the same innate processes for the detection of regularities in interaction with the environment.

Piaget's (1968) views on innate endowment are consistent with such a theoretical position. He argues that an innate neurological and organic *functioning* is required to permit the formation of the structures involved, for example, in conservation and quantification in general. No *structural* hereditary programma-tion is presumed. Conservation is not regarded as being 'wired in', but emerges as a result of the operation of a 'functional kernel' via 'a series of self-regulations and equilibrations in which even the errors play a functional success-promoting role'. Piaget thus draws a distinction between the process of equilibration which is presumed to be innate and structures such as the groupings of operations under-lying successful performance on class inclusion, conservation and other operational tasks. The latter are constructed in the course of development as a result of inter-action with the environment and the functioning of the equilibration process.

An attempt to produce an outline of a theory of cognitive development incorporating a view of innate endowment similar to that of Piaget has recently been made by Klahr and Wallace (1975). The approach adopted conforms to the information-processing paradigm described in the discussion of developmental states. The basic unit of analysis employed is the production or condition-action link as defined by Newell and Simon (1972). As in the case of Bryant's work, space limitations prevent any attempt here at outlining the theory as a whole, but the features concerned with innate endowment will be briefly indicated. The existence of three types of innate processes is assumed. In the order in which they are accessed in memory, these comprise a basic repertoire of sensory encoding productions (Blakemore 1973; Bower 1974), strategic productions that confer problem-solving capabilities such as means-ends analysis, and a group of systemic productions which are the source of the system's developmental, self-modification capacity. Systemic productions detect regularities in the system's interaction with the environment and add new processes to its repertoire as a result. They also increase the information handling capabilities of the system by detecting and eliminating redundant processing. On the basis of these innate processes the present version of the theory provides an account of the development of such logical principles as conservation, class inclusion and transitivity.

Conclusion

This review of research on cognitive development has, of necessity, been highly selective and presented in broad strokes which omit much of the qualitative richness and diversity of both the empirical and theoretical work. In summary, however, it appears to be beyond contention that the appearance of a generally accepted theory of cognitive development conforming with Kessen's criteria is not imminent. Trends can be discerned which provide grounds for optimism in the medium to long term. In particular, the increasing emphasis on process in studies relevant to the state and transition issues and the widening of the theoretical basis of work on individual differences may yet produce a theory of cognitive development adequate to provide solutions to the educational problems listed at the outset.

P. E. Vernon

3. Environment and intelligence

In the 1920s and 30s, when Piaget's work was first becoming known to British and American psychologists, he was sometimes criticised as being an arch-maturationist. Mental development seemed to consist in the appearance at particular ages of a fixed sequence of structures or schemata, from the sensorimotor to the formal stages, regardless of any facilitating or retarding effects of the environment. This of course was a misinterpretation, though it could still be said that Piaget has paid relatively little attention to analysing those aspects of environment which contribute most, and is not much interested in individual differences in rate of growth, whether genetically or environmentally determined. In fact, long before Hebb and J. McV. Hunt, indeed back to his first biological work on molluscs, he was an 'interactionist', who recognised that, while behaviour patterns or schemes are determined neurologically from within, they develop only through adaptation, that is by assimilating, and accommodating to, environment. Intellectual development is the counterpart of biological development, and Piaget makes quite clear its dependence on neurological maturation, physical stimulation, social interaction, and finally the tendency to reach organisation and equilibrium. Thus he short-circuits fruitless discussions regarding the effects of heredity and environment by insisting that both are essential at every stage.

Moreover, intelligence is not some kind of faculty or innate power that causes mental development. It is present in the simplest adaptations of the lowly organism; but behaviour becomes progressively more intelligent the more complex the pathways between stimulus and response, that is, the more behaviour depends on mental structures and abstract thinking. Thus, as Hunt (1961) and the present writer (1955a) have pointed out, there is a remarkable convergence between Hebb's and Piaget's views on intelligence, despite the fact that Hebb was a behaviourist concerned with the brain processes that could account for the building up of perceptual and conceptual skills, whereas Piaget was more an epistemologist concerned with the underlying logic of the infant's adaptations and the older child's thinking.

This chapter will, then, deal mainly with environmental and genetic determinants of intelligence as conceived by Hebb, since it is more amenable to quantitative assessment than Piaget's conception. Test scores or Mental Ages represent a cruder cross-section of overall level of mental development than the attainment of various types of concrete or formal operations, but they are alternative descriptions of essentially the same phenomena. Thus Inhelder (1968) shows that severely retarded children, who would obtain low psychometric IQs, are held up at the sensorimotor and preoperational stages. Several studies have reported moderate to low correlations between, say, conservation performance and intelligence tests; but these have involved somewhat restricted samples or tasks. When the present writer applied a short battery of Piagetian tasks, along with conventional ability tests, to representative groups of children, the 'g' or 'V' factor loadings of the former were around 0·80 (Vernon 1969).

However, some evidence on environmental factors is available from Piagetian-based research. Conservation and other tasks have been given in numerous underdeveloped or relatively primitive societies around the world (cf. Berry and Dasen 1972; Brislin, Lonner and Thorndike 1973; Modgil 1974). Commonly the same sequence of development is found as among European children, though the rate of development may be slower, depending partly on the degree of isolation of the culture from Western ideas, or the prevalence of superstitious thinking, partly on the absence or poverty of schooling (cf. also Bruner's *Studies in Cognitive Growth*). In some cultures even adults mostly fail to conserve. However, the findings are often irregular and difficult to interpret, presumably because in naturalistic settings it is impossible to specify the crucial aspects of environment, or to control representativeness of sampling. In some instances, also, the usual sequence of concepts is disturbed, possibly because performance is affected by the cultural familiarity of the particular materials or questioning employed. We will not attempt, therefore, to survey this interesting and popular type of research further, except to mention one study which appeared to demonstrate clear genetic determination rather than environmental effects. De Lemos (1969) claimed that full-blooded Australian aboriginal children were poorer in conservation than children with part-European ancestry, although reared in the same environment. Dasen (1972), however, was unable to confirm it on a further sample, hence this lead seems to have petered out.

Piaget himself appears reluctant to make any recommendations to teachers or parents on how to accelerate—or to avoid inhibiting—mental growth; and the results of training experiments seem too complex to justify easy generalisations. Numerous inferences have been put forward by educational psychologists (e.g. Aebli 1951; Hunt 1961; Duckworth 1964), but these are usually without much experimental support. Children do not build up more advanced concepts just by being told; they have to discover them through their own activity, preferably in collaboration with peers. Nevertheless, the insightful parent or teacher can do much to provide materials and opportunities at the appropriate times, and stimulate children to explore and experience. Parents should be ready to answer children's 'Why' questions, or put them in the way of finding out. (Presumably the impatient, overburdened, or authoritarian lower-class parent, who operates through Bernstein's 'public' code, tends to retard development.) Even though the effectiveness of school teaching would appear to be downgraded, the teacher has important functions in motivating and interesting children. The acquisition of a new structure or stage depends on matching the environmental stimulation or new experience to already available structures; that is, new experiences should be in advance, but not too much in advance, of the present stage. In addition, the greater the variety of stimulation and practice, the better stabilised a structure becomes, and the more transferable to other similar situations; this is the essence of the accommodation process. Reliance on verbal instruction is particularly to be deprecated, since children can readily acquire, and regurgitate, verbal or number concepts and rote skills without understanding them or realising their transferability to other problems. The building up of effective structures and logical thinking is primarily perceptual and practical, and verbal representation of ideas is secondary. However, such representation facilitates rapid thinking, and thought and language become increasingly interdependent among older children and adults.

Psychometric approaches

The very difficulties of experimental research on such matters suggests that conventional psychometric approaches to the effects of environment can usefully complement Piagetian psychology, particularly by throwing light on the sources of individual differences in intellectual growth. These psychometric approaches can study both general and specialised abilities, i.e. all-round level of complexity of concepts and reasoning, or development along special lines—spatial, number, etc.

There is no need to recapitulate the nature–nurture controversies of the 1920s and 30s: we will merely mention in passing Terman's, Spearman's and Burt's assumption that the IQ as measured by reliable tests is so largely fixed by heredity that it gives good predictions of any kind of intellectual achievement throughout life; the increasing doubts sown by the results from different ethnic groups (e.g. on Army Alpha); by the long-term variability of IQs, and the effects of foster home upbringing (including the famous Iowa studies). The impasse appeared to be resolved when Hebb, in 1949, pointed out that the confusion was largely semantic, since people habitually use the term 'intelligence' in two quite different senses. Hence he proposed to distinguish the basic genetic potential of the individual— Intelligence A—from the developed intelligence which we can observe in his behaviour and thinking—Intelligence B. The latter is the product of the interaction between Intelligence A and the stimulating (or inhibiting) properties of the environment in which the individual has been reared. This is much the same as the biologist's distinction between genotype and phenotype. Our tests, of course, are based on taking samples of Intelligence B, the all-round level of development of cognitive processes; they are quite incapable of directly measuring Intelligence A. And in so far as the range of processes that we can sample is quite limited, different tests, e.g. verbal and performance tests, yield scores which may not correlate very highly. Hence the present writer (1955b) suggested that we need a third construct, Intelligence C, to distinguish test results. Psychologists and others, when talking about intelligence, often fail to make it clear whether they are referring to present level of intellectual functioning, or to scores on a particular test, or to genetic potential.

But while Hebb's formulation has received general acceptance, it does not in fact tell us how far genetic differences and maturation of the brain with age determine present level of functioning, nor how effective are different kinds of environmental stimulation in modifying this level. Hence the recurrence of controversies in the 1960s and 70s, made all the more bitter by growing humanitarian concern over the effects of economic, social and educational deprivation on children in the poorer strata of white society, or in ethnic minorities such as blacks and Indians in the USA, immigrants in Britain, and young people in underdeveloped countries generally.

Now it is far more difficult to assess the effects of environment than appears at first sight. We tend to forget that much of the experience that stimulates mental growth is common to everyone within a cultural group. Almost all children see the same kinds of objects, hear similar speech, and receive a fairly standardised schooling during the main period in which they are building up conceptual skills, though at the same time, of course, there are great differences between the home environments of different children. The question that really interests us is how far do any differences, or changes that we can control or manipulate, such as planned welfare measures, improvements in education, or training in thinking tasks, affect—not specific behaviours—but the all-round level represented by Intelligence C. Such effects are far more limited and harder to demonstrate than the total effects of environment implied by Piaget or Hebb. We commonly assume such effects without bothering to search for evidence. For example, it seems entirely plausible that children whose mothers talk to them a lot and explain things, are therefore going to improve in Intelligence B. But it is another matter to prove it, or to rule out alternate hypotheses, such as that mothers who so treat their children are of above average intelligence and pass on their genes to their offspring; or that mothers of this kind have provided environments with many additional advantages, and these advantages rather than the talking are responsible. Thus when Wolf (see Bloom 1964) obtains a multiple correlation of 0·76 between thirteen home variables and child IQ, and Fraser (1959) in a similar study of four hundred Scottish twelve-year-olds obtains r_m 0·69, these really prove very little about environmental effects. Rather they show that parental education and encouragement are *either* better indicators of parental genes, *or* are more potent stimulators, than parental income or SES (socioeconomic status). Similarly, social class or ethnic group differences in child IQ in themselves prove nothing about environment, however suggestive they may be. One of the most frequently committed fallacies in studying ethnic differences is to partial out, or hold constant, SES on the assumption that this will control for major environmental differences. Some of the evidence cited below indicates, beyond any reasonable doubt, that genetic factors are involved to some extent in ability differences between social classes. Hence matching for SES eliminates considerable genetic as well as environmental variance. Urbach (1974) points out that *ad hoc* theories, which attempt to account for group differences in terms of deprivation of the disadvantaged groups, are apt to be indefinitely extensible. Since they can explain anything, they explain nothing.

Nevertheless, there is a considerable amount of well-controlled research which does support environmental effects, and some of the more striking examples will be listed.

Evidence of environmental influences

1.   Hebb and his colleagues reared rats and dogs, some of them in the highly restricted environment of a cage, others as pets with a free range of a rich environment. The latter showed greater learning and problem-solving capacities as adults. Similarly Levine (1960) found that the handling, and even painful stimulation, of baby rats increased their later responsiveness. Such results cannot of course be transferred directly to human growth. But, coupled with the ample demonstration of the severe short-term effects of sensory deprivation on human intellectual functioning, they are strongly suggestive.

2.   More compelling are the reports by Spitz (1945-6), Goldfarb (1955) and Dennis and Narjarian (1957) of the effects of extreme poverty of physical, and especially social, environment on infants in institutions. Retardation, and even regression, in motor, perceptual and intellectual development were observed. This work lacked any controls, and it is possible that some of the children might have grown up to be low-grade defectives in any environment.

3.   Skeels's (1966) long-term follow-up study did take care of this point. He tested twenty-four seriously retarded children in a very unstimulating orphanage around the age of one and a half years. Then thirteen of them were transferred to an institution where they received more care and attention, albeit from mentally defective girls. Most of the thirteen were later adopted into good foster homes. After twenty-five years both groups were traced, and those who had not been transferred were all still institutionalised, or in low-grade jobs, whereas the transferred ones appeared to be normal adults who were self-supporting in a wide range of jobs. Skeels claims an average rise in IQ for the transferred group of about thirty points, though in view of the unreliability of the initial tests given in infancy, the behavioural observations are more convincing.

4.   Another striking report by Koluchova (1972), though based on only two cases, concerned a pair of twins who were reared till the age of seven in incredibly deprived circumstances, with virtually no human contacts. When first rescued they were severely subnormal with IQs in the forties; but after only four years of more normal upbringing they were testing at ninety-four and ninety-five points.

5.   Recently an important study by Heber (see Clarke and Clarke 1974) in Milwaukee has received a good deal of publicity, though full details are not available, and certain weaknesses have been criticised. Forty children of mentally retarded mothers, whose mean IQ under normal conditions of upbringing in the slums would probably have been about 80, were divided into twenty experimentals and twenty controls. The experimentals attended a centre from the age of three months and were provided with a specially stimulating environment for seven hours a day, five days a week, designed to develop their cognitive and language skills. Simultaneously their mothers were given an educational programme including home-making and child-rearing. On the Gesell scale up to

fourteen months the two groups were equivalent, but on various infant intelligence scales given between two and four and a half years it is claimed that the mean IQs were 122·6 and 95·2 respectively, a difference of 27·4 points. By six and seven years the mean IQs of the experimentals had dropped to 112 and 110, though they were still far above the controls, who had dropped too. This has been referred to as a 'total immersion' programme, and Heber agrees that the high level of stimulation will have to be continued if the IQ difference is to persist into later childhood. We must await the outcome before concluding that genetic lack has been fully overcome by environmental stimulation, also noting that it would obviously be impracticable to arrange similar programmes for all deprived or below-average children.

6.   Foster-child studies are particularly difficult to control because of the likelihood of selective placement. However, the work of Freeman et al. (1928), Burks (1928) and Leahy (1935) suggested that a good, as contrasted with a poor, foster home can bring about a gain in IQ of up to twenty points.

7.   Other frequently cited investigations have indicated lowering of average IQ in British gipsy and canal-boat children who receive no schooling, also in American children living in remote rural communities in the Appalachian mountains.

8.   Klineberg (1935) and Lee (1951) found that black children whose families emigrated from the southern states to New York and Philadelphia gained in IQ according to length of residence in the northern cities, where economic and educational conditions were improved. But it was noteworthy that the maximum rise averaged some six to eight IQ points; that is, they did not make up the full fifteen to twenty points which usually differentiate white and black means. But equally, of course, amelioration in the northern cities was far from ideal.

9.   Further evidence of the importance of schooling, this time at the secondary level, comes from Husén's (1951) study in Sweden. This showed that young adults who had received full secondary or higher schooling were some twelve IQ points in advance of others of the same IQ in childhood but who had dropped out early. Lorge's (1945) findings in the USA were similar, and Vernon (1957) found that the quality of schooling between eleven and fourteen made a difference of seven IQ points between boys who attended good English grammar schools and others attending poorer secondary modern schools. Almost certainly the former also received more encouragement and cultural stimulation at home; that is, the difference was not wholly attributable to schooling as such, but it was none-the-less environmental.

10.   One other very clearcut demonstration of environmental effects occurred in Newman, Freeman and Holzinger's (1937) study of identical twins reared apart. They found IQ differences between some pairs ranging up to twenty-four points, and the bigger differences were associated with bigger differences in the cultural level of the homes and the education received. Unfortunately the numbers were small, and this finding has not been replicated.

11.   The most extensive attempt to raise effective intelligence by means of schooling was that of the Head Start programmes in the USA, which set out to

overcome the handicaps of young children from deprived environments by giving them some kind of kindergarten training, usually for a few months before they entered first grade. The programmes were very diverse in conception, methods and coverage; but in those instances where proper follow-up was conducted, including comparison with control groups, the general result was that there was either no difference between 'treated' and 'untreated', or that a small initial gain disappeared after another year in school. Only occasional programmes that focused on linguistic drills or other clearly defined study skills showed some effectiveness, but these did not attempt to raise intelligence in general. It is quite possible also that there was some improvement in social adjustment or attitudes to schooling, though no satisfactory evidence seems to be forthcoming. Psychologists have tried to excuse the failure of Head Start by saying that the intervention was 'too little and too late'; but the fact remains that many of them did expect well-designed programmes to work.

12.   The term 'environment' also includes biochemical and physical conditions before, and around the time of, birth; and a good deal of evidence suggests that inadequate diet during pregnancy and the first year of life, also maternal stress, or birth difficulties, affect the formation of brain tissue, and therefore the intelligence of the offspring. Results obtained in Western cultures are somewhat contradictory (cf. Jensen 1973a; Gottfried 1973), but the severe effects of protein deficiencies, which are common in underdeveloped countries (e.g. marasmus), are well attested.

13.   Quite a different phenomenon is the effect of practice or coaching on intelligence test performance. In the heyday of the '11-plus', in the 1950s, many studies indicated that children who were thoroughly familiarised with taking group tests obtained IQs averaging some ten points higher than did the completely unsophisticated. However, this does not, of course, represent any improvement in Intelligence B; the effects of training or practice were specific to the particular test format and types of items. Nevertheless such effects have important implications, both for individual diagnostic testing and for survey studies, since the tester may or may not be aware of how much previous experience of the test, or other similar tests, his subjects have had.

14.   There are other conditions at the time of testing which are liable to invalidate Intelligence C as a good measure of Intelligence B, though one would hesitate to classify them as 'environmental'—for example, the interpersonal relations between tester and testees. While it is no doubt true that highly disturbed children may score lower than they should if good rapport is not established, the experienced clinical psychologist can generally allow for this. In group testing it is commonly stated that black children feel anxious under a white tester, and would score better with someone of their own race. The published evidence tends to be highly contradictory; Shuey (1966) and Sattler (1970) conclude that the case is not proven.

15.   Finally, an investigation which is often wrongly cited as showing environmental effects is that of Rosenthal and Jacobson (1968) on teachers' expectations. The authors claimed to show that when teachers were informed that certain children in their classes (who were actually picked at random) are likely to make unusual gains in ability, their IQs did improve significantly over those of children

not so nominated. In fact this research contained numerous weaknesses, and subsequent replications have entirely failed to confirm the results. Hence the publicity it has received, and the frequency with which it is quoted even by psychologists, are quite unwarranted. Self-fulfilling prophecies doubtless do occur, particularly in school achievement; but there is no adequate demonstration of their influence in the development of general intelligence.

Discussion

While the cumulative impact of the above evidence is impressive, some general comments are in order. Firstly, the effects of environmental changes are mostly rather limited. Even with the removal of a child to a much superior environment over several years (as in fostering), the maximum gain appears to be about twenty IQ points. However, in more extreme cases of deprivation, or of 'total immersion', mean changes may reach thirty to forty points or more. More often such conditions as several years of good schooling seem to produce seven- to twelve-point rises; and short-term educational interventions are quite ineffective. Certainly there is no justification for statements such as Hunt's that, by applying what psychologists like Piaget have taught us about cognitive development, we could raise the mean intelligence level of the population by thirty points. We do not have any recipe for bringing up children to be more intelligent beyond the very general conclusion that the educational level of the home and parental aspirations for achievement tend to favour superior intelligence.

Secondly, although it seems that several environmental conditions—healthy pregnancy, perceptual and linguistic stimulation in the early years, conceptual stimulation later, appropriate schooling—all contribute to intellectual growth, it does not follow that by improving all of these, their effects would be cumulative. Normally they tend to occur together, or to be highly correlated. Hence the combination of, say, five conditions might be scarcely any more effective than two of them, just as in a multiple correlation, two good predictors cover so much of the variance in the criterion that the addition of three more predictors fails to raise the coefficient appreciably.

Thirdly, Jensen's (1969) suggestion that environment acts mainly as a 'threshold variable' deserves further study. Like the effects of diet on physical growth, environment may make a lot of difference to mental growth at the bottom of the scale; but above a moderate or reasonable level, it adds very little more. Clearly the biggest changes claimed (by Skeels, Koluchova and Heber) have been among the most severely deprived. Yet at the same time the findings of Lorge, Husén and Vernon show that favourable environment does affect the above-average as well as below-average adolescents.

Fourthly, while high IQ children often appear to have benefited from good environments, it is also probable that the child with high genetic potentiality tends to create a better environment for himself. Parents and teachers who recognise his quickness in picking up things react by providing more stimulation than they would to an average child, and if they fail to do so he is likely to seek out experiences on his own, through reading, hobbies, etc. Conversely, the lower the genetic potential, the less provocation he is likely to get from adults, and the more he is likely to prefer routine, unstimulating experiences. It is interesting that social psychologists are currently coming to reject the notion that socialisation of the child results simply from 'shaping' by his social environment, and are allowing that his own structure determines the kind of experiences he receives (see Schaffer 1974). The same could be said of language development; yet cognitive psychologists continue to think of children as wholly manipulable.

Evidence of genetic determination

Again, we will pick out what seem to be some of the strongest points:

1.   Physical attributes such as height are largely genetic (though height itself is also affected by diet and healthy living), thus there is no reason to think that neurological characteristics, which underlie Intelligence A, are any different. Moreover, by selective breeding we can produce rats which are superior in maze learning; thus the same should be expected for human abilities.

2.   The resemblances in intelligence between offspring and their parents, or between siblings, might well be attributed to home upbringing, but the *differences* can hardly be accounted for environmentally. Parents of average ability can have very bright children, and siblings often vary widely in IQs. Genetic theory would predict such variations.

3.   Though adopted children tend to gain in good foster homes, Skodak and Skeels (1949), Lawrence (1931) and others have shown that child IQ correlates more highly with true-parent than with foster-parent ability.

4.   Inbreeding is known to be genetically harmful. In a well-controlled study in Japan, Schull and Neel (1965) found that the offspring of first-cousin marriages average seven points lower in IQ than the offspring of unrelated parents. No environmental explanation seems conceivable, whereas Jensen (1973b) points out that this fits in neatly with genetic theory.

5.   Ethnic group or racial differences in the USA cannot be explained purely in terms of cultural advantage. Both Mexican Americans and American Indians are, on average, much more culturally disadvantaged than negroes, but yet score higher than negroes on non-verbal intelligence tests (Jensen 1973a).

6.   The siblings of high IQ negroes score lower than siblings of white children of equal intelligence. Each group, in other words, tends to regress towards its own population mean, as would be expected on genetic theory.

7.   The most frequently cited evidence, that from identical twins, is also the most ambiguous and difficult to interpret. The IQs of such twins certainly intercorrelate far more highly than do those of non-identicals or siblings; but we cannot assess how much more similar are their environments and upbringing. When separated at, or soon after, birth and brought up in different homes, the

correlation is lowered, but still averages 0·82 over four different investigations; this should be contrasted with the correlation of only about 0·25 found for un-related children reared in the same home. It is from these figures that Burt (1966) and Jensen (1969) calculate the heritability of general intelligence to be about 80 per cent, leaving 20 per cent attributable to environmental differences. Their particular techniques of analysis have been questioned, and in addition identical twins are a rather peculiar sample from which to make inferences regarding heritability in general. Though Burt denies it, there is evidence that when one or both such twins are adopted they tend to be placed in culturally similar homes; also, they have experienced the same uterine environment and have usually received the same maternal handling until separated. Thus part of the persisting resemblance might still be attributable to environment. In that case the 4 to 1 ratio might be exaggerated, though it probably reaches at least 2 to 1, i.e. two-thirds genetic to one-third environmental variance.

However, as Jensen himself points out, there is no fixed, universal ratio. The available figures apply to white British or American samples, who were all reared in a fairly homogeneous cultural environment. Were it possible to do similar studies with twins reared in different environments ranging from Western middle class to Australian aboriginal, the environmental variance would certainly be far larger, and genetic variance might well drop to 50 per cent or below. More generally stated, one cannot legitimately infer from within-group variance to between-group, though if the former is high it is probable that the latter will be substantial also. Thus even if the 80:20 per cent ratio was established beyond doubt, one would still need extreme caution in extrapolating to differences between groups such as American blacks and whites who constitute somewhat different cultures, yet who also share many common cultural elements. When the environments that shape the development of intelligence in contrasted groups are quite dissimilar, no valid conclusion regarding genetic differences can be drawn, since there is no common basis of comparison.

Conclusions

Suppose we accept a ratio of about 2 to 1 within Western white society; this by no means implies the fatalistic notion of an intelligence fixed at birth. It allows for considerable changes attributable to favourable or unfavourable environments, even exceeding thirty points in the case of severe deprivation; and it is consonant with the quite wide variability of the IQ that has been demonstrated in the course of growth, say from five to fifteen years. In the present writer's view, then, the violent quarrels between hereditarians and environmentalists are unnecessary, and harmful to the prosecution of scientific research. The evidence that both sides have produced is by no means incompatible when reasonably interpreted. Jensen (1973a) claims indeed that all the IQ changes reported by Skodak and Skeels, and Newman, Freeman and Holzinger, lie within the limits anticipated by his 80:20 per cent ratio. This is perhaps somewhat overoptimistic, but the suggested 67:33 per cent ratio should surely cover all the observed variations and changes attributable to a normal range of Western environments.

Another point that needs to be stressed is that scholastic and vocational achievements always show lower heritability figures in twin research than does Intelligence C. It follows that such influences as personality makeup, motivation, parental attitudes, provision of opportunities, and variations in amount and kind of schooling, are correspondingly more important in determining real-life success. At the same time it is stupid to ignore genetic limitations, particularly in all-round intellectual growth. For example, dull children cannot be turned into bright ones just by improving their education, by supplying hints to parents, or by social legislation. This does *not* mean that improved health, education or social conditions are worthless. The general population probably is more intelligent (i.e. better in Intelligence B) than it was a hundred years ago, particularly in countries which were then very backward, for example Russia. The point is, though, that the genetically able benefit as much or more from any such improvements as do the less able. Hence these measures do nothing to wipe out hereditary differences. Indeed, rather the opposite: Herrnstein (1971) has drawn attention to the paradox that, if it were possible by social and educational measures to eliminate all environmental differences, so that every child had an equal chance to develop his potentialities fully, then it would follow that all remaining individual differences would be hereditary in origin. A further misconception that needs to be countered is that acceptance of high heritability implies denying that cognitive skills and concepts are learned from the society in which children are reared. What we are saying is that individual differences in the rate and amount of learning depend more on genetic factors than on environmental variations.

Many critics of Jensen reject his arguments on the grounds that they treat heredity and environment as quite distinct factors, whose effects are additive (apart from a small interaction term which Jensen estimates at about 1 per cent), instead of admitting that they interact with one another from conception onwards. In fact, Jensen admits such interaction in the development of any phenotype, but holds that it is still meaningful psychometrically to calculate the relative contributions to the phenotype of genetic and environmental differences. While accepting this contention, the writer still sees dangers in abstracting heredity and environment as separate, unitary, agents. The prominence of the '*g*' factor in cognitive tests, and of economic and educational class differences in white society, may blind us to the complexities of psychological growth. Other approaches than the psychometric may be more profitable, such as studies of animal genetics and learning, or Piaget's work.

If we agreed that both environmentalists and hereditarians have made their points, and that their data are not irreconcilable, could we not shelve the problem of relative importance, to which we know there is no single, straightforward answer? Unfortunately humans, including social scientists, are far too prone to polarise and stereotype their concepts and attitudes. The controversy is not so much one of psychological theories and methodologies as of political and social philosophies. In the present climate of opinion in the Western world, we naturally dislike the notion that any one group of people is innately 'inferior' in ability to other groups, especially since the definition of 'superior' ability is set by the dominant group. Moreover we fail to realise that, because certain groups differ somewhat in their gene pools, i.e. in their potentialities for development along different lines, this tells us nothing about the mental characteristics of any individual member of either group. If we could overcome such irrational thinking, we might be more successful in modifying social and educational environments to suit individuals with differing patterns of abilities, instead of imposing a single system which inevitably condemns large numbers of children to fail.

Note   Some sections of this chapter are taken from a book by the writer on *The Psychology and Education of Gifted Children*, which is to be published shortly.

E. *James Anthony*

4. Emotions and intelligence

More than any other psychologist in the present century, Piaget has been pre-occupied with the relationship between emotions and intelligence to the comparative neglect of emotions for themselves. His treatment of affect occupies only an insignificant portion of his general opus and is difficult to disentangle from the omnipresence of cognition. The many brilliant insights that illuminate his investigation of the intellectual process are absent. One could, in fact, read all thirty volumes describing his psychology and be left with the conviction that the emotional life of the child has been entirely overlooked. In an earlier article the present author went so far as to caricature Piaget's approach by describing it as a 'psychology without emotion' (Anthony 1957). In this presentation almost twenty years later, some effort will be made to modify this global and somewhat erroneous epithet.

The inseparable tie

Piaget has persistently maintained from his earliest writings that affect and intelligence were two distinct but complementary and inseparable aspects of behaviour, performing different but essential functions in adapting the individual to his environment, and undergoing a parallel development with corresponding stages. Neither affect nor intelligence could be regarded as prior, predominant or causal with respect to each other. The two components had developed a *modus vivendi* in the operations of everyday life. What remained mysterious and intriguing to Piaget was the reciprocal nature of the relationship. To understand this he would have needed to know more about affect than he did, but time was running out. He had already spent half a century in pursuit of reason and to set up a new 'clinical interrogation' into the workings of the emotions would have demanded at least another fifty years.

It is therefore not surprising that he preferred to take the easy way out and state that many of his findings about intelligence could be applied with equal validity to affect, allowing for appropriate modifications. The one system furnished a paradigm for the other. Since, however, the affective system did not contain logical structures it could not aspire to complete equilibrium. Nevertheless, the parallelism was close: 'I think that in the affective field one would also find the equivalent of what logic is in the cognitive field; it would be structurations of social concepts in the form of scales of moral values . . .' (in Tanner and Inhelder 1960, p. 99).

Such a statement has more heuristic than empirical value, and Piaget is well aware that he has few data to support it. He therefore goes on to add: 'However, this does not concern me and I will limit myself to what I have experience of, that is to the facts of logical structures' (op. cit., p. 99). A little further on he says, perhaps with his tongue in his cheek, that he has 'not the slightest desire to generalise from the case of logic to all the rest of mental life' (op. cit., p. 106). Yet, this is what he does on the basis that affect and cognition are but two sides of the same coin. This enables him speciously to present a comprehensive system with only half of it actually under construction. The emotional half is almost non-existent. In truth, affect is the ghost in Piaget's psychology.

Piaget's theory of affect

The affective system about to be described is scattered through Piaget's work in a way that often makes it inaccessible to his readers. It should be understood that since this affect theory is largely latent in Piaget's general theory, inferences have been made as to what formulations he might have made had he pursued the matter more consistently and comprehensively.

To start with, there is no doubt that Piaget, like Schachtel (1959) and Binet, takes a positive view of affects as they are manifested from the start of life in the infant's almost joyful exploration of his immediate environment. The Piaget baby, in Greenacre's words, appears to be conducting a love affair with the world as he almost ceaselessly experiments on it. Step by step he constructs reality, creates environment and conceptualises objects, the whole process being saturated with excitement, curiosity, surprise and delight. This portrait of active commerce with the world is the hallmark of Piaget's outlook and it is essentially a composite of cognition and affectivity. The model is an epigenetic one in every respect, presupposing a constant interaction between maturational and environmental forces and a constant interaction between the individual and his external world. The differentiation of self from non-self and the changing structure of each is mutually derived from this continuing dialectic. The motivation behind this activity is not material reward, but the sheer pleasure of doing and getting done. To use Buhler's expression, it is *Funktionslust*.

In describing Piaget's affect system in general terms, it might be summarised as follows:

1.   It is an interactional system in which affects reach out to the environment and accompany 'practical' and reflective intellectual activity. If to think is to be operational, to feel is also to be operational. Feelings energise the total process.
2.   Like the cognitive system, it is served by the invariant functions of assimilation and accommodation striving toward equilibrium. The incoming environmental data are taken in and modified by the individual's current structure.

3.   This current structure has been gradually generated by affective experiences from the beginning of life and undergoes alteration with the changing demands of development.

4.   At a certain stage, consciousness emerges and allows for the development of autonomy, socialised behaviour and self-awareness. With the resolution of egocentrism the child begins to differentiate between his own feelings and perspectives and those of others.

Affective development

Piaget (1932, 1953-54, 1973) has consistently insisted that intelligence and affectivity undergo interrelated and parallel developments. From birth onward the infant is subjected to alternating states of pleasure and unpleasure which he slowly comes to link to sources in the environment. As his concept of objects is refined, his feelings toward them become graded into positive or negative affective responses that are associated with positive or negative affective states within him. Because there are more important sources of satisfaction and distress than inanimate objects, human beings are especially liable to have strong positive or negative values attached to them. Piaget believes, and the work of Décarie (1966) confirms it, that there is a close correlation between the cognitive development of the schema of the permanent object and the evolution of object relations in the psychoanalytic sense. Piaget himself had suggested (on the basis of a single subject) that the first object to be endowed with permanence was a human object. During this early period of sensorimotor intelligence, feelings are very much intra-individual and presocial. The range is limited to elementary emotions and sentiments, perceptual affects, pain and pleasure, and secondary reactions related to effort, tiredness, joy, success and failure.

With the development of language and other symbolic capacities, feelings gradually become socialised and inter-individual. The child develops intuitive affects of sympathy and antipathy, becomes able to understand how others feel about something and to separate this from his own feelings. He also begins to construct a self-concept based on the evaluations of others and on their attitudes towards him. The first moral feelings appear connected to beliefs, absolute prohibitions and prescriptions which clearly stem from parents. Conduct is punished strictly in terms of transgression without reference to intention or mitigating circumstances.

A distinct change takes place during the period of concrete operations. More equilibrium becomes possible at this time and Piaget is recorded as wondering to what extent psychoanalytic latency is a function of the equilibration process (Tanner and Inhelder 1960). The child can now form groupings of values and grade them according to their relative priorities and mutual affinities so that his evaluations and his motives become consistent with one another. He can now postpone affectivity in accordance with future needs and, because of this temporal 'decentering', he can bring more of his behaviour under the control of his 'will'. His morality also undergoes changes as he comes under the increasing influence of the peer group. While the rules of the game were of no importance in practical and symbolic play, they now come into the forefront as important but flexible conventions that are drawn up and decided upon by the players. Morality is altogether less primitive, less exacting and more in keeping with the principle of mutual respect between equals.

With the onset of the formal stage, feelings become increasingly 'decentered' and evaluations and motivations are based on sentiments attached to collective ideas and ideals. The adolescent learns to think and feel in terms of his social group and to judge according to its standards. His intellectual capacity, in terms of operational activity, is now on a par with the adult so that his angry and resentful and rebellious feelings can now be sustained by criticisms based on sound propositional thinking.

It is of interest that as Piaget has developed stages in the resolution of egocentrism, present-day analysts have begun to detect stages in the diminution of narcissism. The interrelationship between these two developments—narcissism and 'narcissism without Narcissus' or egocentrism—is susceptible to genetic analysis since the one can be assessed clinically and the other experimentally.

Affective structures

Piaget is never tired of bringing intelligence and emotions together in a unified picture: 'affective life, like intellectual life, is a continual adaptation, and the two (that is, affect and intelligence) are not only parallel but interdependent, since feelings express the interest and the value given to actions of which intelligence provides the structure' (Piaget 1973).

Since affective life, like cognitive life, is part of the total adaptation of the individual to his environment it involves:

1. The same functions of reciprocal, recognitory, reproductive and generalising assimilations.
2. Assimilations that comprise earlier assimilations from earlier situations and present situations to earlier ones.
3. As with cognitive assimilations, a continual accommodation of these schemas to the current situation.
4. The construction of affective schemas similar to cognitive schemas and representing relatively stable modes of feeling and reacting.
5. As with the cognitive process, a process of equilibration that continues between affective assimilation and accommodation.
6. In so far as equilibrium is achieved to some extent between affective assimilation and affective accommodation, a conscious regulation of feelings, values and sentiments under the direction of the will. If there is a primacy of assimilation over accommodation, unconscious symbolic activity begins to occur.

The preoperational affects with their simple regulatory mechanism and their focus on 'basic feelings' such as interest, pleasure, joy, success and disappointment are very comparable to preoperational intelligence (sensorimotor and intuitive) with similar schema systems, while the operational affects associated with values, moral sentiments, ideals, etc., correspond to the operational cognitions, also with similar systems of schemas.

The significant people during the early stages are at first incorporated into general schemas relating to both person-objects and thing-objects, but soon the person schemas are enriched with new feeling stemming from the transfer of feelings previously connected with the child's own body. They thus get an added investment. These first personal schemas are later generalised and applied to other people. As Piaget puts it, 'He may assimilate all other individuals to his father's schema or the type of feelings he has for his mother will tend to make him love in a certain way, sometimes all through his life, because here again he partially assimilates his successive loves to his first love which shapes his innermost feelings and behaviour' (Piaget 1951, p. 207).

There are two special features relating to the early personal schemas: firstly, they hold closely to the principles of assimilation with regard to being reproduced, recognised or generalised, and secondly, the cognitive and affective are always equally manifest in them. It is only later that intelligence and emotions show predominances; thus, when one speaks of 'affective schemas', one is always speaking of cognitive-affective schemas although one or the other may be salient: 'We do not love without seeking to understand, and we do not even hate without a subtle use of judgment' (Piaget 1951).

The affective schemas are also accompanied by accommodation, the role of which is increasingly differentiated. Again in *Play, Dreams and Imitation in Childhood*, Piaget offers an illustration of mother and father 'fixations' (in the language of psychoanalysis) exposed to the mechanism of accommodation: 'A normal individual may find in his emotional life all kinds of traces of infantile behaviours connected with his relation to his mother. He will, however, add to them, and anyone who marries with a mother fixation runs the risk of considerable complications in his married life. Similarly the man who continues throughout his life to be dominated by an idealised image of his father, or who, on the other hand, pursues the dream of a freedom he never acquired in his youth, must of necessity have diminished powers. Equilibrium consists in preserving the living aspects of the past by continual accommodation to the manifold and irreducible present' (Piaget 1951, p. 208).

In comparison with intellectual schemas, affective schemas seem generally to remain more unconscious, possibly because they are exposed to less accommodation, but it is also true that the assimilation of affects takes place with less awareness than cognitive assimilations. The only way in which one becomes aware of affective assimilations is through symbolic activity which is closely linked to the affective schemas.

Piaget has repetitiously and almost obsessively insisted on two distinct functions, intelligence and affect, that are at the same time two aspects of the same general function, and it clearly has more than a metatheoretical significance for him. His analytic friends might compare this to the classical association of the tender and sexual components of loving and there is more than a hint of this in some of Piaget's associations.*

The language of affects

According to Piaget, the language of affects had the following characteristics:

1.   It was independent of verbal signs.
2.   It contained two sets of symbols, metaphors (conscious) and cryptophors (unconscious).
3.   It was used almost exclusively in dreams, daydreams and play.
4.   It was idiosyncratic, autistic and rooted in the unconscious.

The child spoke this kind of affective language when he was under internal pressure. It chiefly appeared in play where compensatory activity was involved partly in satisfying the ego and partly in fulfilling a definite affective purpose.

Affectivity and symbolism were closely connected. Secondary assimilations occurred with affective symbols and the more intense the affectivity, the more frequent were the assimilations. The 'cryptophors' were different from the usual play symbols in that they were more directly related to the child's ego and involved relatively permanent affective schemas.

Dreams represent another form of affective language and appeared to be a continuation of symbolic play both in its primary and secondary varieties. It is surprising what a close resemblance there is between dreams and symbolic play at the corresponding developmental level. Although Piaget understands children's dreams in much the same way as Freud does, he speaks of them as the assimilation of reality to the ego. In contrast to the waking, operational world, affects are predominant in dreams and the cognitive process is vague and uncertain.

Affective content

The content associated with affect is most vivid in preoperational or non-operational activities such as symbolic play, dreams and fantasies. It is at this stage that Piaget's clinical interrogation is most clinical and where he shows himself to be very much at home with feelings and emotions.

He divided symbolic play into three groups: those relating to the child's own body (eating and excreting); those relating to love and hate relationships within

* In this same context, Piaget (1951, p. 210) presents a dream which is clearly one of his own (Freud had a similar habit when confronted with a difficult theoretical issue). The dream runs as follows: A student of natural science (which is what Piaget was in the early part of his life) dreamt of *two* birds and wondered whether they were two quite distinct species or merely *two* varieties of the *same* species. Someone in the dream disagreed with this second conclusion and this dream figure was associated with a college friend who had once maintained that the only difference between physical (sexual) and ideal (tender) love was one of degree, the dreamer maintaining the opposite view!

the family; and those bearing on birth anxieties. These were very similar to the content found in the dreams and fantasies of adults undergoing psychoanalysis (according to Piaget). Secondary or unconscious symbolism always revealed its presence by certain affective signals such as undue excitement and embarrassment.

The following vignettes, furnished by Piaget (1951), inform us once again of his striking sensitivity to the cognitive-affective processes of very small children.

1.　'*On masculine protest*' Girl (5:8) 'Why do boys need a long thing for that? They could do it through their navel.' Girl (3:3)—looking at two male statues: 'It's a good thing they've got two things for water to come out; if they hadn't they'd quarrel.'

2.　'*On birth fantasies*' Girl (3:3) Said of her doll that 'when he was born he stayed for a long time inside me; he had sharp pointed teeth and afterwards they became smooth'. (3:9) When someone was arguing with her, she said: 'No, don't do that. You know I have a little baby inside me and it hurts him. You know, when my little baby is born, he'll kick you and knock you down.' (3:10) She explained to her doll who apparently wanted to be inside her again: 'No, you're too big now, you can't.' (3:10) She said to her father: 'I want to go back inside you, and then when I come out I'll be a little baby again. I'll be called Y (the masculine form of her name) because I'll be a boy.' (5:9) She played at being in bed for a confinement declaring that a certain doll was hers 'because it came out of my inside'.

3.　'*On ambivalence toward parent figures*' Girl (5:3) Enlisted one of her imaginary companions to cut off her father's head as a means of avenging her at a time when she was on bad terms with him. 'But she had some very strong glue and partly stuck it on again. But it's not very firm now.' (In passing, Piaget points out that ambivalence towards fathers is less disturbing than towards mothers. The father is often a nuisance, but his removal is not too disturbing a matter.)

4.　'*On guilt*' A child★ would often look for animals to add to his natural history collection. On days when he had anything to reproach himself with, he had the feeling that his bag was a bad one and that it was so because of his misdeeds.

Piaget's sensitivity to affective material is striking. For example, he states (1951) that the case of the little girl above who wants to cut off her father's head and then stick it on again, but not too firmly, denotes 'how skilfully a balance be achieved in symbolism between aggressiveness and its opposite, and how frequently in play the attitude to the father varies according to whether the parents are together or the father is alone'. All those with whom the child lives generate affective schemas which are a summary or blending of the various feeling roused by them. It is these schemas which determine the main secondary (unconscious) symbols and help to explain later attractions or antipathies.

In the case of the little naturalist, Piaget considers the question as to whether the sense of guilt originates from masturbation or from a universal feeling of 'immanent justice'. He says (1932): 'It cannot be denied that we can observe in masturbators a systematic fear of the retribution residing in things—not only the

★ Clearly one of Piaget's memories.

fear of the result their habits may have upon their health, the fear of making themselves stupid, etc., but also a tendency to interpret all the chance misfortunes of life as punishments intended by fate.' He feels that the question whether guilt is inherent, which arises in relation to punitive child-rearing, cannot be answered unless one could bring up a child in very special circumstances.

The affective and intellectual unconscious

Piaget (1973) has tried very strongly to make a case for the existence of an intellectual unconscious which he has insisted is 'remarkably comparable' to the affective unconscious postulated by Freud. However, he did not visualise it as a separate region of the mind, a limbo of forgotten ideas and affects waiting for a stimulus to emerge, but rather as part of a continuous movement along a conscious-unconscious spectrum. He had always been impressed by Binet's comment that 'thought is an unconscious activity of the mind', meaning that although the ego was conscious of the contents of its thought, it knew nothing of the structural and functional reasons that forced it to think in a particular way and it knew nothing of the innermost mechanisms that directed this thought. He regarded the discovery of the affective unconscious as 'one of the great discoveries of Freudian psychoanalysis' and felt very much that unconsciousness was needed in the field of cognition. He noted the following similarities between the intellectual and affective unconscious:

1.   Cognitive repression has a similar inhibiting role to that of affect repression. In the cognitive sphere, this means that an earlier schema cannot be integrated into the system of conscious concepts and is therefore eliminated by one of two processes—conscious suppression or unconscious repression. (Unfortunately the illustrations that he offers for unconscious repression of an intellectual idea would not be convincing to any psychoanalyst.)
2.   The 'return of the unconscious' from the intellectual unconscious consists of a reconstruction through conceptualisation where the cognitive unconscious (and this would be true of the affective unconscious according to Piaget) is furnished with sensorimotor or operational schemas organised into structures that carry the potential of future intellectual activity. Likewise, affective schemas express what the subject can feel, not what he is currently unconsciously feeling.
3.   The conceptual reconstruction characteristic of 'becoming conscious' may encounter conflict on the way and manifest itself in partial or distorted form. This would be tantamount to an 'intellectual complex'. Catharsis in the affective sphere is similar to cognitive conceptualisation.
4.   Conceptualisation, catharsis and remembering do not represent the emergence of dynamically conflicting ideas and feelings, but consist of a reconstruction of past schemas (intellectual and emotional) in terms of the present. According to Piaget (1973), memory works 'like a historian who reconstructs the past, in part deductively, on the basis of documents which are always to some extent incom-

plete'. He offers this analogy in opposition to Freud's picture of the archaeologist 'digging up the past'. The past is only there schematically. This was where he saw the big difference between Freud and himself. Both believed that all feelings and thought have a history and that 'no external influence represents an entirely new beginning but is always assimilated to all that has gone before, and may modify the subsequent course of the history by giving it an impulse in a partly new direction'. But the understanding of how this assimilation took place and in what form the organisation of the old and new factors existed was radically different. For Freud, such past experiences as infantile conflicts continued to operate in the unconscious so that subsequent emotional life always consisted in the identification of the new situation with past ones.* Piaget disagreed on principle with such a formulation. Cognitive memories were not retained in the unconscious but rather as schemas of actions or operations that were constantly adapted to the present and oriented toward equilibration as a continuous structural process. He thought, without much evidence, that the same was true of affective schemas and in this he agreed with newer trends in psychoanalysis.

A common language for emotion and intelligence?

Piaget has been preoccupied with questions of convergence and divergence between emotional and intellectual forms of equilibration. Tanner and Inhelder (1960) record him as having wondered to what extent it was possible to express affective conflict in the language of equilibrium. He took some classical emotional conflicts, as expressed in the language of psychoanalysis, and attempted to transpose them mathematically:

1.   'The Oedipus stage represents a certain form of affective equilibrium, characterised by a maximisation of the "gains" expected from the mother and by a minimisation of the "losses" expected from the father. Then in this connection it would be of interest to examine whether the equilibrium point corresponds merely to a Bayes strategy the criterion of which would be a simple maximum of "gains minus loss", or whether it corresponds to a "minimax" strategy, with a search for the minimum or maximum loss which the subject supposes a hostile environment is trying to inflict on him. It is evident that a problem such as this cannot be treated in general since it depends for its solution on the overall environmental conditions for each child. Besides these problems of "cross-sectional" equilibrium at any given moment raised by each of the essential phases of affective development, there remains also the essential problem of the equilibrium between the previous affective schemata of the subject and the exigencies of the present position' (op. cit., p. 8).

* In 1915, Freud had made a formulation comparable to Piaget's: 'A comparison of the unconscious affect with the unconscious idea reveals the significant difference that the unconscious idea continues, after repression, as an actual formation in the system Ucs, whilst to the unconscious affect then corresponds in the same system *only a potential disposition* which is prevented from developing further.'

C

2.   With respect to the interactions between the genesis of the object concept and object relations, one can observe at almost the same ages and in both fields (intellectual and emotional) 'a parallel transition from an initial state of centration on the subject's own activities . . . to a final state of decentration wherein the subject becomes conscious of his subjectivity, and "places himself" with respect to a world of external objects and persons' (op. cit., p. 16). If one accepts the thesis of equilibrium, then the loss and gain strategy can be used to explain both the cognitive development of the object concept and the affective development of the object relation. The two, Piaget was sure, cannot be very different: 'It is not entirely unreasonable to believe that the fact of maintaining "objectal" relations with the persons about him is, for the infant, a much more costly strategy, although much more remunerative in affective values of all kinds, than to be content with merely giving play to his sucking reflexes or even his sphincters' (op. cit., p. 16). 'An explanation in terms of profit and loss of the phases of affective development does not signify that the subject (the infant) has himself made a calculation of his interests in each situation lived through. This calculation is made solely in the sense that the fact of experiencing positive or negative values (an affect consisting essentially in attaching value to a given action) amounts precisely to enriching or empowering oneself, from the viewpoint of functional exchanges with surrounding persons.'

It would seem reasonable to suppose that a common, 'uncontaminated' language based on information or games theory would allow one to discuss intellectual and emotional reactions in the same terms and within the same framework so that the two might become closely associated in theory as well as in practice. It is not enough to say that intelligence and emotions are two sides of the same coin: one has to say a great deal more about the coin in question.

The collection of affective data

One of the reasons why Piaget has neglected emotional development is that he had no data and no proven method of collecting any. But clinicians who have made use of his 'method of clinical interrogation' combined with 'concrete manipulation' of experimental material have felt that the technique was easily adaptable to the collection of affects and was in fact not far removed from play therapy. The difference lay in the purpose of the interviewer.

Two examples (Anthony, in press) are offered of interviews in which a clinically oriented investigator was conducting the examination and biased it in the affective direction.

1.   The first illustration is taken from the protocol of a typical Piaget-type experiment conducted with a little girl who was asked to predict whether an array of objects would sink or float in the water. 'She misses two out of the first three predictions and begins to look at first embarrassed, then anxious, and finally very ashamed of herself. When the next question is put to her she recovers, comes smiling up to the examiner, and places an appealing hand on his shoulder. She

shakes her head and says, "You don't want to be wrong again, do you? You want to be right, don't you? Why don't you just do it and see what happens?" On the cognitive side she behaves very much in keeping with Piaget's expectations, but there are also some surprises that seem more related to her affective than cognitive behaviour. Her past history reveals constant intellectual deflation by her teacher-mother who is markedly ambivalent towards her daughter and is frequently punitive. The father, in contrast, overpraises and also overstimulates the girl, who is unable to say with which parent reality lies.'

2.   In another experiment on the making of shadows, K, a five-year-old girl, is extremely interested in the phenomenon but afraid of the candle. 'It will burn me—will it burn me up—will I be dead?' But she is absorbed by the problem and torn between her emotional dread and her intellectual curiosity. B, a boy aged five, appears to be more absorbed with the phenomenon of sex differences, and each time K leans forward to examine the shadows, he pulls up her skirt and examines her underwear. He is asked where the shadows come from and his answer is 'from inside K's panties!'

It seemed almost impossible for a clinically trained examiner to carry out a straightforward Piagetian test without soliciting intellectual-emotional response from the subject. What is surprising is that so many of the protocols from Geneva appear to contain hardly any of this affective material. It seems likely this particular type of data is excluded on the grounds of being 'romancing' or 'teasing' responses. The children were probably sent back to the classroom as 'untestable'. On the other hand, Genevese children may be much more conforming.

Conclusion

There is an affective system within Piaget's psychology which has its own development, its own structures, its own language, but not, unfortunately, its own supporting framework of empirically obtained data. The system is not rewarding in itself, being somewhat desiccated and impersonal, but in conjunction with Piaget's rich cognitive system, it offers a rich field for research.

Affective development, according to him, would begin as a group of reactions which are at first isolated and uncoordinated between themselves, but which later become more and more coordinated until they finally constitute a whole. The stages would depend, according to Piaget (1973), 'on the progressions in this development from isolated elements into a coordinated whole. In these processes of affective coordination, then, we can find stages which might correspond to, or would at least compare more closely with, the stages of cognitive development.' Because of his Gestalt background, Piaget believes that emotions, like perceptions and thoughts, cannot be understood without reference to the wholes in which they are organised, but he disagrees with Gestalt psychology in believing that the wholes can be analysed into component relations and that these relations between parts and whole are very necessary for the understanding for the different psychological phenomena.

The psychoanalytic influence is also very obvious, both in comparing Piaget's system with Freud's, in attempting to transpose Freudian constructs into Piagetian constructs, and in finding a common language for both. There is no doubt that his affect theory owes its greatest debt to Freud.

Jersild (in Carmichael 1946, 1954) had done his best to point to the crucial importance of researching the interaction between intelligence and the emotions, but neither he nor a successor to him found a place in the 1970 edition of *Carmichael's Manual of Child Psychology* (Mussen 1970). Kurt Lewin, who had been one of the first psychologists to examine the emotional aspects of human living within a laboratory, was also excluded. It is therefore some compensation for his point of view to quote from one of his last statements about the psychologist's task in today's world: 'The psychologist finds himself in the midst of a rich and vast land full of strange happenings: there are men killing themselves; a child playing, a child forming his lips trying to say his first word; a person who, having fallen in love and being caught in an unhappy situation, is not willing or not able to find a way out; there is the mystical state called hypnosis, where the will of one person seems to govern another person; there is the reaching out for higher and more difficult goals; loyalty to a group; dreaming; planning; exploring the world; and so on without end. It is an immense continent full of fascination and power and full of stretches of land where no one has ever set foot. Psychology is out to conquer this continent, to find out where its treasures are hidden, to investigate its danger spots, to mass its vast forces, and to utilize its energies. How can one reach this goal?' (Lewin 1940).

One way is to examine both intelligence and emotion and the relationship between them.

Part Two

Colin Elliott

5. The measurement of development

Introduction

It is perhaps fitting that in a book which is intended as a tribute to the work and influence of Jean Piaget some attempt should be made to suggest ways in which observations of children's cognitive development can be transformed into measurement. Piaget's *méthode clinique*, while being fruitful in producing insights into the ways children think, does not readily lend itself to measurement. The technique is essentially observational, and has been used primarily to identify invariances in the stages of cognitive development through which children pass. As Tuddenham (1970) has pointed out, Piaget has always been principally interested in identifying invariant stages through which all individuals pass in the acquisition of knowledge, rather than in individual differences in rate of development. Such stages are ordered hierarchically, so that to reach a given stage, all earlier stages must have been passed through. However, to postulate general laws of development, to which all individuals conform, is not to deny the presence of individual differences in development which may be shown in the rate at which children pass from one stage to another, such as in the transition from concrete to formal operational thought. Individual differences may also be shown within a stage, for it is evident that because an individual can operate at a certain stage with one class of problems, he may not be able to do so with other problems. For example, if a child can conserve length and number, there is no certainty at all that he can conserve area or volume, which are generally reckoned to be harder tasks. Piaget (e.g. 1971) himself emphasises the existence of horizontal décalage, or time lags within a stage of development,* where a child is able to solve problems in some content areas, but not in others. Such individual differences in development both within and between stages are, of course, grist to the mill of the differential psychologist.

A distinction has already been drawn between observation and measurement. It cannot be emphasised too strongly that careful observations, which either arise from or lead to developmental theories, are a necessary precursor to measurement. Once a theory becomes sufficiently well developed to generate confirmable hypotheses, it becomes possible to devise tools and techniques which will measure the variables which are of central importance to the theory. As Levy (1973) has cogently argued, measurement should always develop from such observation and theory, but should never be thought of as a substitute or as an end in itself.

* Discussed in Chapter 2, p. 17—Ed.

This chapter is concerned with measurement. In particular, it is concerned with the objective measurement of cognitive development and the range of behavioural attributes, skills, abilities, aptitudes, attainments or traits (call these variables what you will) which characterise the cognitive domain.

We are also concerned with development. *Development* is a term that can be used in two senses. The first refers to growth along one dimension. Thus we may refer to an individual's development in spatial ability, in vocabulary or in general intelligence. The latter is only unidimensional at a high order of generalisation, but it is nevertheless possible to consider such general development. The second sense in which the term *development* is used is when it refers to the movement of an individual through an invariant succession of qualitatively different stages. Here, a certain level of achievement or performance at one level is a necessary but not sufficient condition for progression to the next stage. Where such a concept of development is used, a description of an individual's level of development should specify not only the highest level or stage he has reached, but also the breadth of his performances within stages.

The major part of this chapter will be devoted to considering the measurement of development in the sense of quantitative growth along one dimension. Before proceeding to this topic, however, some consideration will be given to attempts which have been made to measure stage-like development. Later in the chapter we shall see that the principles of objective unidimensional measurement may equally well be applied to the measurement of stage-like development.

The measurement of the developmental stage reached by an individual

Developmental theories frequently postulate step-like stages, differences between individuals on different steps being qualitative as well as quantitative. For instance, Piaget (e.g. Piaget and Inhelder 1969) postulates four major stages in the development of intelligence. The 'sensorimotor' stage up to the age of about two years is sequentially superseded by the 'preoperational' stage, the stage of 'concrete operations', and finally the fourth stage of 'formal operations' in early adolescence. As the child develops from one stage to another, he integrates structures of thinking developed at a lower stage into higher-level structures. One cannot develop the higher-level structures unless the lower-level structures are present. Such hierarchical dependence is characteristic of developmental theories of this type.

If the range of items within a test covers more than one developmental stage, the resulting person × item matrix may be expected to approximate to a simplex (Guttman 1955) or a 'twisted pear' distribution (Jensen 1970). A perfect simplex is illustrated in Table 1. In this matrix, persons who pass a given item (score 1) can pass all easier items, and those who fail a given item also fail all harder items.

In view of the likelihood of Piagetian items covering a number of developmental stages forming a simplex scale or something closely resembling a simplex, a number of attempts have been made to reconcile the Piagetian and psychometric approaches. Bentler (1971, 1973) has developed procedures for measurement when test items and responses span qualitatively different levels of development. Symposia edited by Dockrell (1970) and by Green, Ford and Flamer (1971) have considered the problem of the integration of developmental theory and techniques of measurement and present the position as it appeared in the late 1960s. More recently, Modgil (1974) has produced a reference work listing and reviewing studies in this area. The impression received from such reviews and symposia is that while advances have been made in developing Piagetian tests, some scepticism exists about the practicability of measuring developmental stages using standardised

TABLE I   *A perfect simplex*

	Items				
Person	1	2	3	4	5
1	1	1	1	1	1
2	1	1	1	1	0
3	1	1	1	1	0
4	1	1	1	0	0
5	1	1	0	0	0
6	1	1	0	0	0
7	1	0	0	0	0
8	0	0	0	0	0

tests (see, for example, comments by Elkind, Nivette, Ayers and Sticht in Green, Ford and Flamer 1971). In commenting on a recent symposium on reasoning, moral judgment and moral conduct in retarded and non-retarded persons (Stephens 1974), Kohlberg (1974) expressed the opinion that 'Piagetian tasks do define a domain irreducible to psychometric concepts'. On the other hand, Hunt (1974), another discussant, argued strongly in favour of ordinal scales of development, preferably criterion-referenced rather than norm-referenced.

A number of attempts have been made to produce tests which assess Piagetian development. Certain tests measure ability at only one developmental level, such as the tests of conservation by Goldschmid and Bentler (1968), or tests of formal operational thinking described by Ward (1972) and by Ward and Pearson (1973). On the other hand, Tuddenham (1971) has developed tests which cover more than one developmental stage, in this case the preoperational and concrete operational stages. This results in total scores which might well be scalable to estimate a subject's ability on a single higher-order trait (such as 'g'), or as Tuddenham (1971) puts it, 'the merit of the subject's performance' (p. 67). However, Tuddenham is also concerned to identify the pattern of scores across the various parts of the test, for it is these that indicate the Piagetian level reached by the child. Hence the search for simplex scales in which the patterns of scores within the test are easily interpretable. This is an essential feature of such scales for—paradoxically—the scale constructor is clearly far more interested in the developmental stage reached by an individual, as represented by his pattern of responses, than he is in the individual's total score or ability on the overall trait.

Simplex techniques, however, do not enable objective estimates to be made of ability within a stage: décalage must be ignored or treated as error. This is one of the major problems in measuring stage-like development. It will be suggested later in this chapter how such difficulties might be overcome. The following section, however, will consider the problems of measuring unidimensional development of the conventional type, such as is found in many intelligence and attainment tests.

The need for objectivity

Most cognitive tests in common use are norm-referenced. That is, it is necessary to compare an individual with a reference group or population in order to obtain an estimate of his ability. Let us make explicit what is wrong with these norm-referenced tests. How are they defective as measures of development? Or, to put the question in a more positive way, what do we require of developmental measures that cannot be provided by norm-referenced tests? Four major requirements for objective developmental measures are as follows:

1.   Sample-free estimates of an individual's ability.
2.   Test-free estimates of an individual's ability.
3.   Ratio scaling—or at least interval scaling—of abilities.
4.   The construction of measurement scales which are able to span the entire age and ability range for which a test is designed.

A brief consideration of existing norm-referenced measures of cognitive development will indicate that none of them possess any of these features! Firstly, all norm-referenced tests by definition require the performance of the person being measured to be compared with a reference population. The estimate of ability will vary according to the population or sub-population the individual is being compared with. Secondly, different tests give different ability estimates due to having non-identical standardisation samples and, just as importantly, because they have different items. It would surely be odd if, when measuring a child's temperature, we could only express this in terms of the average temperatures of, say, older, younger, feverish or hypothermic children, together with a further qualification to the effect that the measurement was obtained on an alcohol or a mercury thermometer. Yet such is the situation in cognitive measurement. Certainly one may wish, for purposes of interpreting a temperature reading, to know what the mean and standard deviation of temperature is in the population. In particular, one may wish to know what level of temperature indicates illness, or what level is dangerous, thus using the readings in a criterion-referenced way. Such requirements are perfectly valid and compatible with objective measurement, but the underlying measurement scale is quite independent of such influences. A third requirement of objective measurement of development is that of obtaining ratio or interval scales of measurement. This is a goal which has already been achieved in the physical sciences, scales being used which have absolute zeros and equal intervals between points on the scale. Sometimes, as in the case of temperature scales, the absolute ratio scale is linearly transformed to give more convenient scales for certain purposes, this time with an arbitrary zero, but still retaining equal interval properties. It cannot be seriously held that any cognitive scales have such properties, although for research purposes they are often treated as if they are interval scales. The difference between two Mental Ages of 2 and 3 years cannot be interpreted as being the same as that between 15 and 16 years, or more ludicrously, between 81 and 82 years. Similarly, a difference of fifteen points between IQs of 95 and 110 does not have the same meaning as that between 130 and 145. Such scales are best considered as ordinal, placing individuals in order of ability but with no assumptions being made regarding equal intervals between the scale points. The final point is related to the previous one. It is a common feature of both longitudinal and cross-sectional studies of development that individuals are compared who span a wide age and ability range. It is difficult for differences to be objectively compared or for developmental growth to be objectively assessed if one is constantly looking over one's shoulder at various reference populations and if apparently equal amounts of difference in scores at different points on the scales are not interpretable as indicating equal differences between individuals.

If it were possible to construct scales of development that were independent of any reference group; independent of the particular items employed in the test; where scores and differences between scores (inter- or intra-individual) could be interpreted as falling on a ratio or an interval scale; and where a single scale covered the full range of ability and development on which all individuals could be measured; if these conditions were met, the measurement of development would be scarcely recognisable in comparison with previous techniques.

A measurement model which enables these advances to be made will be outlined in the following section.

A model for item-free and norm-free measurement

The measurement model which will be outlined below was first described by Rasch (1960, 1966a, 1966b). The model is conceptually simple and makes only three assumptions:

1.   Where a person responds to a test item, there is a corresponding probability of a correct response.

2.   The outcome of the encounter between the person and the item is determined by only two parameters, the difficulty of the item (D_i) and the ability of the subject (A_s).

3.   Given the values of D_i and A_s, all answers are stochastically independent: given that a subject has correctly responded to an item, he is no more likely to get other items right than are other subjects of the same ability who got the first item wrong. Item difficulties are therefore independent both of the difficulties of other items in the test and of the abilities of the subjects taking the items. The abilities of persons are similarly independent.

These last two assumptions will now be discussed in greater detail. With only two parameters used to denote item difficulty (D_i) and person ability (A_s), and for items which can be scored in binary fashion as right or wrong, then the O_{si}, odds of success of a subject s with an item i, can be expressed as the ratio of the parameters (Wright 1968):

$$O_{si} = \frac{p_{si}}{q_{si}} = \frac{A_s}{D_i},$$

where p_{si} is the probability of success for subject s on item i, and q_{si} is the probability of failure. Thus, as ability increases, so the odds of success improve, and as difficulty increases, so the odds of success diminish. A subject may, therefore, be said to have an ability equal to the difficulty of an item on which he has an even-odds chance of success. Thus the difficulty of an item can be thought of as its ability to produce a correct response from the subject. This symmetric relationship between ability and difficulty, in which both are measured on the same scale, is a major feature of the Rasch model. The probability of success can be expressed as:

$$p_{si} = \frac{\exp{(a_s - d_i)}}{1 + \exp{(a_s - d_i)}},$$

where a_s and d_i are the logarithmic forms of the ability and difficulty parameters. It has been found in practice to be most convenient to work with such logarithmic forms.

In addition to the earlier papers by Rasch, Wright and Panchapakesan (1969) have described the estimation procedures and Wright has written a computer program which has been used to analyse data reported in this chapter. The sets of item and person parameters are simultaneously estimated, using an iterative procedure to converge on a maximum likelihood solution. Thus, although conceptually simple, the estimation procedures themselves are complex and a computer is an essential tool for this task. As in all psychological tests, there are inevitable standard errors of measurement for the item and person parameters. These also are estimated by a maximum likelihood method. This enables standard errors to be estimated for *every* item difficulty and person ability, rather than for the test as a whole, as is the case with traditional methods.

The final assumption, that the difficulty and ability estimates are independent of other item difficulties and of the abilities of other subjects, contains a number of implications. Firstly, if a given item, called item A, is twice as difficult as item B, it will be so irrespective of whether the subjects used to estimate the item difficulties are of high or low ability. Consider the item characteristic curves (ICCs) in Figure 1.

Here, the probabilities of getting an item correct have been plotted against the ability levels of subjects. Subjects at point X on the ability scale will find item B easier than item C. The same relationship is found between the items for brighter subjects at point Y. However, although subjects at X find item A the hardest, this finding is reversed for subjects at point Y, who find item A to be the easiest. In other words, item A is a better discriminator than items B and C. Some models of measurement (e.g. Birnbaum 1968; Lazarsfeld and Henry 1968) allow for different ICC slopes by incorporating guess-rate or discrimination parameters. The Rasch model does not incorporate such parameters and requires equal or near-equal discrimination between items, or, in other words, parallel ICCs. This may at first sight appear to indicate a lack of sophistication in the model. It is, however, the very basis of its ratio scale properties, for if items do not have constant relationships between them, independent of the abilities of subjects, estimates of item difficulty and consequently of subjects' abilities must be tied to the group of subjects who were used to calibrate the items and the test.

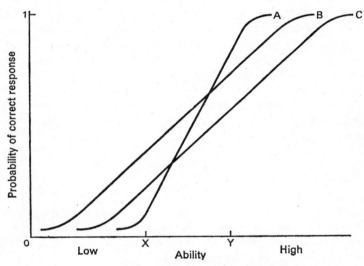

FIGURE I   *Item characteristic curves for three hypothetical items.*

In practice, it would be virtually impossible to find groups of items to form a test which had absolutely identical ICCs. The fit of items to the model can be evaluated, however, using a chi-square test for goodness of fit between observed data and its expected values. One such test of goodness of fit has been outlined by Wright and Panchapakesan (1969). Similar tests of fit have been employed by Andersen (1973) and Hambleton and Traub (1973).

Relatively few applied studies employing the Rasch model have yet been published. The British Intelligence Scale (BIS) is probably the largest and most wide-ranging project to employ Rasch scaling techniques at the present time (Elliott 1974, 1975a). Some twenty individually administered scales of abilities will be produced, covering an age range from two to sixteen years. The use of Rasch scaling in this project has been described by Murray (1975), but results are not due until 1977. To the author's knowledge, only one other test has previously been produced using Rasch methods (Woodcock 1973) and this was in the relatively narrow field of testing reading skills. Another application in the field of item banking, with particular reference to examinations at the secondary school level, has been conducted by the National Foundation for Educational Research (Willmott and Fowles 1974). Apart from these applied studies, only a small number of articles have appeared in journals. Brink (1972) compared the Rasch and Guttman models and concluded that a perfect Guttman simplex scale, not allowing for repeated measurement of a particular level of ability, does not possess the precision that may be possessed by a Rasch scale. A further comparison, this time of methods for selecting test items, was made by Wilmut (1975) between the Rasch model and a more conventional method using discrimination indices. Wilmut concluded that the advantage of the discrimination index method was its simplicity, but admitted that statistically the Rasch method is more rigorous. In two other studies, Anderson, Kearney and Everett (1968) and Tinsley and Dawis (1975) gave various tests, of general intelligence and analogies respectively, to samples of adults and tested the results for goodness of fit to the model. Both studies concluded that the item difficulties and the calibration of ability scores were indeed independent of the samples on which they were based.

Claims such as this are not altogether easy to accept, particularly if one is oriented towards conventional test construction with its norm-dependence both of item difficulties and person abilities. An illustration will be made, therefore, of what Rasch scaling can do.

The model applied

The data employed in the analyses which follow were obtained at the tryout stage of the BIS project. The data to be collected in the standardisation phase of the project are expected to be more extensive and more complete, and consequently the present analyses are for illustrative purposes only. Four major requirements for measures of development were listed earlier. These are that such measures should be independent both of reference population and of test items, that scores should fall on ratio or interval scales, and that they should cover the full range of ability which we wish to test. Each of these four requirements will be considered.

1. Sample-free ability estimates

The Reading scale from the BIS will be used in this example. It is used because the data for this scale are more complete than for other scales. Although this may not be thought to be a good example of a scale of cognitive development, the principles of analysis are general and applicable to such scales. A trial version of a word recognition test was carried out on a group of 128 children aged between eight and eleven years. Forty items were selected which fitted the Rasch model— not a difficult task with such homogeneous item content. Their item facilities (i.e. proportion of correct responses) ranged from 0·16 to 0·82. Two sub-groups of children were then selected, sixty-six who scored between 6 and 20, and sixty who scored between 22 and 36. One of the advantages of Rasch scaling is that ability

TABLE 2   *Ability calibrations for low- and high-scoring children*

Total score	Calibration from low scores (6-20)	Calibration from high scores (22-36)	Standard error of measurement
1	−4·28	−4·18	1·03
2	−3·53	−3·44	0·74
3	−3·06	−2·97	0·62
4	−2·71	−2·63	0·55
5	−2·43	−2·35	0·50
6	−2·19	−2·11	0·47
7	−1·97	−1·90	0·45
8	−1·77	−1·70	0·43
9	−1·59	−1·53	0·41
10	−1·42	−1·36	0·40
11	−1·26	−1·20	0·39
12	−1·10	−1·05	0·38
13	−0·95	−0·91	0·38
14	−0·81	−0·77	0·37
15	−0·67	−0·63	0·37
16	−0·53	−0·50	0·36
17	−0·40	−0·37	0·36
18	−0·26	−0·24	0·36
19	−0·13	−0·11	0·36
20	0·00	0·01	0·36
21	0·13	0·14	0·36
22	0·26	0·26	0·36
23	0·40	0·39	0·36
24	0·53	0·52	0·36
25	0·67	0·65	0·36
26	0·81	0·78	0·37
27	0·95	0·92	0·37
28	1·10	1·06	0·38
29	1·25	1·21	0·39
30	1·42	1·36	0·40
31	1·59	1·53	0·41
32	1·77	1·70	0·43
33	1·97	1·89	0·45
34	2·18	2·10	0·47
35	2·43	2·33	0·51
36	2·71	2·61	0·55
37	3·07	2·95	0·62
38	3·53	3·41	0·74
39	4·29	4·15	1·02

estimates can be obtained for all raw scores on a test even when no person in the calibration sample obtains some of the scores. The reason for this lies in the fact that the patterns of successes and failures on items differ between individuals. Thus difficulty estimates can be obtained for all items, provided not all persons pass or fail a given item. The ability estimates for all raw scores can then be calibrated from the item difficulties. In the example, there is no overlap whatsoever in the scores of the sub-groups and yet, in Table 2, it can be seen that they produce virtually identical ability calibrations.* This is what is meant by sample-free ability estimates, that the estimates of ability we can get from the test are unrelated to the ability of the people who were used to calibrate the test. Of course, this contrasts completely with conventional ability scaling. In the present example, and using conventional methods, percentiles or standard scores could only have been given for the raw scores which either group actually obtained. The finding given above, that provided one uses items which fit the Rasch model the same ability estimates are obtainable from widely differing samples, has been amply confirmed with numerous sets of data. We have, in fact, never found it to be disconfirmed.

2. Item-free ability estimates

Let us stay with our forty-item reading test and the same sample of children. In the previous example, the *sample* was split into two completely distinct groups. This time, let us split the *items* into two completely distinct groups, namely the twenty easiest and the twenty hardest items. These two subtests can be separately calibrated to provide ability scores, the two calibrations being given in Table 3. Each child in the sample can then be separately scored on the easy and the difficult subtest. Bright children getting a maximum raw score on the easy subtest cannot, of course, be given an ability score. Neither can dull children who get a zero raw score on the difficult subtest. Thus our sample of 128 children is reduced to 107. We can now test whether or not the ability estimates for each subject are the same on the two subtests by using a subjects × subtests analysis of variance. Table 4 gives the results of the analysis of variance. Although the mean scores are not significantly different, there does seem to have been a slight tendency for the easy subtest to underestimate children's scores and vice versa for the difficult subtest. The difference between the means is very small, however, and is well within one standard error of measurement (approximately 0·6) of the subtests.

Such a split of a scale into totally separate halves is scarcely the type of procedure one would expect to see adopted in practice, but it provides a severe test of the model's capability of providing the same ability estimates irrespective of items used in the subtests. Under normal testing conditions, however, where a child's ability is 'centred' at or near the average difficulty of a set of items, there is an even closer degree of correspondence between ability estimates from different

---

* The abilities given in Table 2 are expressed in natural logarithms. This will be dealt with later in the discussion. The ability calibration cannot, of course, include zero or maximum raw scores.

TABLE 3   *Easy vs. difficult test calibrations*

Score	Ability on easy test (mean item diff. −0·98)	Ability on hard test (mean item diff. +0·98)	Standard error of measurement
1	−4·07	−2·10	1·03
2	−3·30	−1·35	0·76
3	−2·82	−0·88	0·64
4	−2·45	−0·52	0·58
5	−2·15	−0·22	0·54
6	−1·87	0·04	0·51
7	−1·63	0·28	0·49
8	−1·39	0·50	0·48
9	−1·16	0·72	0·47
10	−0·94	0·93	0·47
11	−0·72	1·14	0·47
12	−0·49	1·36	0·48
13	−0·25	1·58	0·49
14	0·00	1·82	0·51
15	0·28	2·08	0·54
16	0·59	2·38	0·58
17	0·96	2·74	0·64
18	1·45	3·22	0·76
19	2·22	3·98	1·04

TABLE 4   *Summary of analysis of variance*

Source	d.f.	Mean square	F	
Between subjects	106	2·916	8·87	$P < 0·001$
Easy vs. difficult subtests	1	0·826	2·51	$P < 0·05$
Residual	106	0·329		
Total	213	1·619		

Mean ability scores for all subjects:
Easy subtest: −0·046
Difficult subtest: 0·078

sets of items. Two subtests were formed from the Reading scale by assigning odd-numbered items to one subtest and even-numbered items to the other. When the children were scored on both subtests, there was no difference between the ability estimates derived from the two subtests ($F = $ o·o1; *d.f.* 1,127).

These findings, together with others from different BIS scales, lend strong support to the view that Rasch ability estimates are free of item effects under normal testing conditions and will tolerate fairly serious departures from the principle of centring items upon the ability of an individual.★

3. *Ratio or interval scale measurement*

Earlier, when the Rasch model was described, it was stated that abilities and item difficulties were both expressed on the same scale of measurement. This scale, in its basic form, relates to the odds of success when people encounter items. Since, according to the Rasch model, odds of success—varying from zero to infinity—are a function of only two parameters, these parameters can also be expressed on a scale varying from zero to infinity. If a person has zero ability, he has zero odds of success on any item. If an item is infinitely difficult, then again all individuals have zero odds of success on it. In practice, one never observes either items or individuals at the absolute extremes of the scale, but it is possible to conceive of such hypothetical cases.

The unit of measurement, as in the case of physical ratio scales such as weight or length, can be fixed arbitrarily at some convenient value. In the case of the computer estimation procedures reported earlier, as in Table 2, the unit of item difficulty is fixed at the mean of all item difficulties in the set of items being analysed. It could just as easily be fixed at the difficulty of the easiest item or at any other convenient point. This is illustrated in Table 5, which lists hypothetical raw scores on a test.

TABLE 5   *Hypothetical ability estimates*

| | Ability estimates | | | |
| | Set A | | Set B | |
Raw score on test	Ratio scale	Interval scale	Ratio scale	Interval scale
1	0·05	−3	1·0	0
2	0·14	−2	2·7	1
3	0·37	−1	7·4	2
4	1·0	0	20·1	3
5	2·7	1	54·6	4
6	7·4	2	148·0	5
7	20·1	3	403·0	6

If the abilities of persons were all perfectly equally spaced according to raw score obtained on the test—this event being extremely unlikely—one may obtain ability calibrations like those in the table. If we set the unit of measurement to be the ability of those persons who get a score of 4 on the test, we might produce an

★ Murray (1975), however, has reported finding significant differences between ability estimates when conducting tests of the model which are even more severe than the one outlined above. Such findings underline the need to ensure that the test one uses is not grossly inappropriate for a child, just as one ensures that a thermometer is appropriate for measuring temperature within a particular range.

ability calibration such as in Set A. It can be seen that subjects with a score of 4 have twenty times the ability of subjects with a score of 1, in the sense that their odds of getting *any* item right in the test are twenty times better. A similar difference in ability exists between subjects who score 2 and 5, 3 and 6, or 4 and 7. Looking at the table another way, one might say, for example, that a person with an ability of 7·4 has even odds of passing an item whose difficulty is 7·4. Such a person would have odds of about 7 to 1 in favour of passing an item whose difficulty is 1. As a matter of convenience, one may perform a $\log_e$ transformation of the ratio scale to an interval scale (*e* having a value of approximately 2·7). Here, the relationships between intervals on the scale have been preserved, but the scale now has an arbitrary zero.

Instead of setting the unit of measurement of the ratio scale to the ability of the middle score-group of the test, one might equally well set it to the ability of the lowest score-group, as in Set B in Table 5. Such a decision would obviate the need to express abilities as being below 1 on the ratio scale or as being negative on the logarithmic interval scale. The meanings of the scales are, however, exactly the same as in Set A, provided, of course, that the item difficulty estimates have been commensurately adjusted.

As item difficulties are placed on the same scale of measurement as the abilities of persons, the above discussion on ratio and interval scales applies equally well to them.

One outcome of our capacity to define a natural zero and to place abilities on a ratio scale is that we should be able to plot growth curves of ability over age more objectively than hitherto. Thurstone (1925, 1927, 1928) first suggested the possibility of the absolute scaling of abilities, although his scales were essentially norm-referenced. His work has generated little research over the years, although given some attention by Burt (1951) and more recently by Eysenck (1973). Just as Thurstone, in his extrapolation of mental growth curves, found that they reached a zero point at or a little before birth, so it should be possible to set zero ability at or a little before birth—which after all seems to be a sensible point of origin— and to plot the growth of various abilities, using Rasch scales, over age.

4. *Wide ability and age ranges*

The basis for the development of single scales covering very wide ability and age ranges lies in the ratio properties of Rasch scales. Provided the items which are used in a test all fit the model through having similar ICCs, it is possible to place several separate sets of items, which have certain items in common, on the same difficulty scale. The reason for doing this is usually because one wishes to construct a scale whose items have too big a difficulty range to be administered and calibrated on one sample of subjects. For item-banking purposes, one may also wish to replenish or replace existing items without having to recalibrate and restandardise all the items in the test.

As will be realised from the previous section on the ratio and interval scale properties of Rasch scales, the logarithmically transformed interval scale has a simple linear property, in that a shift of one unit at any point on the scale has the same meaning in terms of odds of success. If a group of items within Set 1, for example, also appears in Set 2, it is likely that they will have two different difficulty estimates due to fixing an arbitrary zero in the interval scale (or, to put it another way, due to fixing an arbitrary unit of measurement on the ratio scale). Such a case is shown in Table 6. Both sets of calibrations can be brought on to the same scale, however, by adding a constant to the difficulties in one of the two sets. The differences between the linking items still retain their interval properties which are the same—given some error of estimate—in the two sets of items. In the

TABLE 6   *Linking two sets of items to form one scale*

Item	Difficulty in set 1	Difficulty in set 2	Final difficulty
1	−2·9	—	−2·9
2	−2·6	—	−2·6
3	−1·5	—	−1·5
4	−1·0	—	−1·0
5	−0·4	—	−0·4
6	0·1	—	0·1
7	0·3	—	0·3
8	0·7	—	0·7
9	0·9	−3·1	0·9
10	1·6	−2·6	1·5
11	2·1	−1·8	2·2
12	2·7	−1·2	2·8
13	—	−0·3	3·7
14	—	−0·1	3·9
15	—	0·3	4·3
16	—	0·9	4·9
17	—	1·1	5·1
18	—	1·7	5·7
19	—	2·3	6·3
20	—	2·8	6·8
Mean difficulty of items 9-12	1·82	−2·17	

example, the mean difference in the difficulty estimates for the four linking items in the two item sets is 3·99. This constant is added to the difficulty of every item in the second set in order to place the items in both sets on the same difficulty scale. This process can, of course, be repeated a number of times to construct scales with very large difficulty and ability ranges.

Thus the conceptually simple Rasch model allows the construction of scales which might allow, for example, the direct comparison of five-year-olds with sixteen-year-olds on certain tests. Such wide-ranging scales will also allow individual progress to be objectively monitored over a long period of time without any recourse to norms unless this is desired.

The construction of wide-ranging ability scales should not be taken to imply that any person tested on such a scale would be required to take all the items. Clearly, many items would be quite inappropriate for any given individual, being too easy, too difficult, or both. The Rasch model allows the tester to use as many or as few items as he wishes in assessing an individual. Procedures are currently being developed which will enable a test to be tailored to the abilities of the individual (Wright and Douglas 1974; Murray 1975). The design of the best test for a particular purpose and for a particular individual will, it is hoped, lead to maximum economy in administration time and minimum error of measurement, together with providing the tester with a degree of flexibility in decision-making which is scarcely possible using traditional methods (Elliott 1975b).

Measuring development: some concluding remarks

The use of Rasch scaling, and the need to ensure that items within a test conform to the model, requires us to ask some rather refreshing questions about a test. Are the items homogeneous in content? Do all subjects understand what they are expected to do? Are the types of response required of subjects homogeneous, or are there qualitative differences in the acceptability of responses? Are the difficulties of the items reasonably appropriate for the subjects? And what is it that we want to measure?

It is this last question which is particularly crucial in relating theories of development to methods of measurement and leads us back once again to the problems of measuring stage-like development which were referred to earlier. The problem with existing tests, apart from their lack of objectivity which has already been considered, is that they often do not provide information in which developmentalists are interested and ignore qualitative differences in response.

For example, the problem often arises in assessing performance on a subscale that a given child or different children make qualitatively different responses to test items. In response, for instance, to the question, 'How are an apple and an orange alike?', two common but qualitatively different responses are 'Because they have skins and pips' and 'Because they are fruit'. One way of dealing with such data in past tests has been to treat them quantitatively by giving the responses 1 or 2 points respectively, as in the Wechsler scales. This assumes that both responses represent different levels of development on the *same* latent trait. But suppose we do not wish to make this assumption. Let us suppose that the responses represent levels of functioning on two qualitatively different traits. We could call these concrete and formal operational thinking, after Piaget, or the following of sub-ordinate versus superordinate rules of equivalence, after Bruner (1966). We would have to make the assumption in this case, based on the psychological theory, that a child who made a superordinate or formal response was capable of making a response at the lower subordinate or concrete levels. Let us define two scales, one on which the child is scored one point if he makes a response at the superordinate level only, and the other on which he receives a point for a response at either the superordinate or subordinate levels. Thus, one set of items could produce two ability scores—one score indicating ability to group things according to subordinate rules, the other score indicating ability to group things according to superordinate rules. This, I suggest, is the kind of approach we really require when we want some assessment of children's levels of thinking, for the fact that a child can respond at a given level with one type of item is no guarantee that he will respond at this level with other types of item. Differences in item difficulty will result in a spread of total scores within a defined stage of development.

The scores which an individual obtains on such a test would therefore represent the various developmental levels measured by the test. Inevitably, a person's scores at a lower level would be greater than or equal to his scores at a higher level. The scores should indicate not only which developmental levels were fully reached or not reached at all, but should also provide an objective assessment of performance within a level. The Rasch model would appear to be ideally suited for this purpose. In principle, there is no difference between the use of the Rasch model for the measurement of development within stages which form part of a structural hierarchy, and its use in the more traditional field of the measurement of traits or abilities which do not in theory form part of such a hierarchy.

A very necessary precursor to the construction of tests is a theory of whether all responses to the test items are only quantitatively different or whether they represent qualitatively different behaviours. If the latter is the case, the structural hierarchy should be defined, if this is postulated by the theory, together with the response types which represent each level of the hierarchy. If the items are homogeneous in content, and if we have succeeded in defining homogeneous response types at each level, we would expect the items in the test to fit the Rasch model for each level. Failure to define unidimensional response types may be expected to lead to the test fitting the model badly at one or more levels.

Three major scales are currently being developed, as part of the British Intelligence Scale project, which are based on specific hierarchical theories of cognitive development, and which are designed to measure performance at various developmental levels (Pearson 1975). Two scales, measuring children's understanding of number and formal operational thinking in later childhood and adolescence, are based on Piaget's theories. The third, involving reasoning about hypothetical social situations, is based on Kohlberg's (1969, 1971) theory of stages in moral development. It is intended that all these tests will be scored at various levels and that Rasch ability estimates will be obtainable for each developmental level.

This chapter has attempted to show how the measurement of development, whether of a single trait or of a hierarchical structure of traits, is possible using Rasch's model for item and ability scaling. However, much applied work in this field is still required, although the next few years should see the publication of a number of such ability scales; their advantages in being norm-free, item-free, covering wide ability ranges, and placing abilities on ratio or interval scales, should go some way towards a long-needed reconciliation between psychometric and developmental theories.

Acknowledgements   I am most grateful to David Murray for data computation and, together with Lea Pearson, for helpful comments on an earlier draft of this chapter.

6. Perception and cognition: where do we stand in the mid-seventies?

For Piaget (1969), the fundamental epistemological question concerns the extent to which objective knowledge derives from perception. His solution to the problem is to deny that any direct lineage can be traced between cognition and perception, arguing that the extent to which they share a common structure reflects their origin in the same sensorimotor roots. By contrast, the literature on the perceptual capacities of infants prompted Charlesworth (1968) to suggest that a useful working hypothesis for developmental psychologists would be to consider perception as *preceding* instrumental behaviour in establishing cognitive structures. Today, the literature is unanimous in declaring even the very young infant a 'competent, active, perceiving, learning and information-organising individual' (Stone, Smith, and Murphy 1974). Yet, despite this general consensus, little progress has been made in connecting the perceptual precocity of infants to a wider theory of cognitive growth.

The grounds for a distinction between perception and cognition

According to Piaget, the development of objective knowledge entails the progressive differentiation and coordination of action schemes, which are defined as 'a sensorimotor concept, the motor equivalent of a system of relations and classes' (Piaget 1953, p. 385). Coordinated action schemes form higher-order structures which mediate direct perceptual experiences. The structure of action is described in terms of Poincaré's logic of groups, a group being 'a closed circle of operations which return to the point of departure' (Piaget 1954, p. 105). It is because schemes function in accordance with logical rules that the infant acquires objective knowledge of space, time, causality and objects. Appreciation of the group structure of space leads the infant to an awareness of the reciprocal relation between the movements of an object and the correlated movements which would return it to its point of departure and hence leave it invariant.

Having established the group structure of space, the infant becomes able to distinguish between a change of place of an object and a change of state. A change of place of an object can be reversed by a movement of the observer, whereas a change of state of an object cannot be reversed by the observer taking up a new position. Since the infant below nine months of age is said not to distinguish between his own actions and independent events, the distinction cannot be made. So an object which changes its position is not understood to retain its identity and an object which disappears is not understood to continue to exist. The first reversible groups are constructed at about nine months of age, when the infant comes to organise action into a means-end relationship in goal-directed behaviour.

So Piaget's basic reason for wishing to distinguish perception from cognition rests on the argument that the infant only comes to appreciate the objective properties of reality by imposing more and more complex sequences of action into experience. The logic of action frees the infant from the subjective and egocentric standpoint of direct perception.

Perception and cognition as poles on a dimension of cognitive development

At first sight, the grounds for a distinction between perception and cognition seem compelling. Piaget (1969) lists fourteen differences of which the following three are probably the most important for the purposes of this chapter:

1.   Perception is tied to objects of which it provides information, whereas cognition functions in terms of mediating conceptual frameworks.
2.   Perception is limited by conditions of spatial and temporal proximity of the stimulus information being processed.
3.   Perception is egocentric, whereas the essence of cognition is that it provides knowledge freed from the standpoint of the observer.

Wohlwill (1962) has criticised Piaget's account of the functional independence of perception and cognition. He proposes that perceptual and cognitive processes can be related along three dimensions. As one proceeds from perception to cognition, the amount of redundant information required decreases, the amount of irrelevant information that can be tolerated increases, and the spatial and temporal separation over which the total information in the experiential field can be integrated increases. Together, these yield a single dimension of specificity ranging from approximative processes such as the judgment of perceptual constancy to the accuracy of processes such as mathematical reasoning.

It is tempting to retain a distinction based only on the immediate nature of perceptual processes and the mediate nature of processes termed cognitive. However, this escapes the crux of the problem, which lies in the nature of the logical processes common to perception and cognition. Even apparently immediate perceptual processes require separate events to be connected over time. Bruner has stated the implication of this quite clearly: 'The principal characteristic of perceiving is a characteristic of cognition generally. . . . A theory of perception needs a mechanism capable of inference and categorizing as much as one is needed in a theory of cognition' (1957, p. 123).

The most explicit account to make use of this principle is that of Bryant (1974). He argues that young children are heavily dependent on logical processes in perception to categorise experience. According to Bryant, these processes are prior to rather than consequent upon the acquisition of logical processes in cognition. He argues that young children rely on external frames of reference in relation to which they make deductive inferences about perceptual continua such as size, number and so on. The external frame of reference acts as the mid-term (*B*) in a deductive inference of the form *A*:*B*, *B*:*C* therefore *A*:*C*. As children grow older, they abandon external frames of reference in favour of more flexible internal frameworks, such as number systems which allow for the precision usually associated with conceptual judgments.

If this argument is applicable to properties of objects such as number and size, might it be applicable to objects themselves? Could it be that logical mechanisms in perception allow the infant to structure the world in a stable fashion long before the opportunity arises to act on the world instrumentally? In the next few pages, evidence will be reviewed which suggests that perceptual mechanisms are capable of specifying objective information directly.

Perception as an active process

The first example to be considered will be that of the perceptual constancies. The infant is said to discover the constancies at about nine months of age by correlating information from the sense of touch with changes in the retinal image as the object is displaced in the visual field (Piaget 1954). Quite a body of evidence now suggests that infants register the real size and shape of objects long before nine months of age (Bower 1966; McKenzie and Day 1972; Day and McKenzie 1973). These studies suggest that the important cues mediating appropriate responses in the presence of objects of varying retinal size and shape are derived from motion parallax. Pictorial cues of the type contained in photographs were not effective in eliciting appropriate responses. Infants seem to respond on the basis of complex invariant aspects of input. Recently, Bower (1974) has demonstrated appropriate manual responses to objects of different diameter in infants as young as eight days of age and Bruner and Koslawski (1972) have shown that infants of eight weeks of age make appropriate hand and arm movements to objects of different sizes. In some crucial respect, the space of hand and eye appear to be mapped on to each other before the infant has had experience of the hand in the visual field.

Thus, if a group structure is to be used to describe visual perception, it seems to be functional long before eight or nine months of age and is probably innate. In fact, such a model of perception has been proposed by Hoffman (1966), who argues that transformations of the retinal image, with respect to a frame of reference centred on the observer, can specify directly invariant properties of objects such as size and shape. Paillard (1974) has suggested that the structure of the body, together with its links with the invariant direction of gravity, can act as the basic frame of reference in relation to which perceptual judgments can be made. Whatever its structure, the principle that an egocentric frame of reference can act to specify invariant properties of objects is an important one which will now be pursued in the context of the perception of object permanence and identity.

The 'screen effect'

Object permanence is said to be discovered at about nine months of age when the infant will retrieve an object hidden at a single location (Piaget 1954). This action implies a reciprocal awareness that an object can also be hidden by covering it. Michotte (1950) was the first to argue that the permanence of an object which disappears from the visual field can be specified directly by the visual system. He drew an analogy with the figure-ground phenomenon in visual perception. Even though the ground is hidden by the figure, it is perceived as existing behind it. The visual system specifies the continued existence of the background directly. (N.B. According to Salapatek and Kessen 1966, the distinction between figure and ground is made from birth.)

When a stationary object is slowly covered by a moving screen, adults perceive the sequence of events as one object hidden by another. While Piaget (1969) does not deny that such effects take place in adults, he maintains that they are based on the sensorimotor acquisitions of nine months and onward. Prior to this age, such a disappearance sequence is said merely to specify the merging of one object with another (Piaget 1954).

Bower (1967, 1971) has performed experiments which suggest that infants as young as three months of age expect an object to go on existing after perceiving such a disappearance. The ability is subject to spatial and temporal constraints, typical of processes designated as perceptual. For instance, the maximum period of occlusion was fifteen seconds, after which infants did not behave as though they expected the object to go on existing. The speed of disappearance was another constraint which became more flexible as the infants got older.

The elements of an explanation are suggested by a close examination of the conditions of disappearance. The important factor may have been that the object was stationary when it was covered by the moving screen. That is, its position defined with respect to the stationary infant remained invariant. Even when the object had been removed before the screen moved away, infants expected an object to be at that place (Bower 1971). So the child did not merely recognise a qualitatively similar object which appeared after the first had disappeared.

The basic criteria for the individuality of an object are expressed in the statement that an object can only be in one place at one time. To be known with certainty to retain its individuality through time, it would seem necessary that the object should be experienced continuously and yet this is impossible. The infant requires some means to connect the momentary positions occupied by the object one to another. This can be accomplished by means of a mediating spatial framework which remains a continuous aspect of experience, a function fulfilled by the egocentric spatial framework. The egocentric framework is perfectly adequate to connect the separate momentary positions of a stationary object since a stationary observer can specify the invariance of a stationary position.

The identity of the object can then be deduced from the fact that it has occupied a stable position over time. The basic structure of a deductive inference is therefore spatial, since momentary experiences of an object are connected solely by virtue of their relation to the mediating spatial framework. As Quinton (1973) puts it: 'A position is the permanent possibility of an object'.

Identifying a moving object

In real life, however, objects and observer move in relation to each other. Thus far, we have only considered how a perceptual system might specify permanence for a stationary object using the self as the basic frame of reference. While the system is perfectly adequate to cope with a stationary object, it cannot cope with movements of the object or of the observer. As Piaget argues, movement introduces the necessity to distinguish a change of place from a change of state. That is, the object that occupied position p_1 at time t_1 now occupies position p_2 (defined with respect to the self) at time t_2. The infant has to decide whether this is a single object that moved with respect to the self or a qualitative replica at a new position.

Whenever an object moves, the position code locating it with respect to the self must be brought up to date. This ensures that the object always occupies a permanent position defined with respect to a stable space. However, updating would require a belief that the object *will be* the same object after it changes position. The deductive process outlined above entails no such belief. The identity of the object can only be deduced perceptually when successive momentary positions can be connected by means of a spatial frame of reference that remains invariant through time.

The problem of updating can be overcome if the infant can establish some external spatial framework which remains invariant with his own movements. Then, since the framework remains invariant with respect to the observer, it can substitute for the self as a means of connecting separate experiences over time. An object that changes one stable position p_1 for another p_2 (defined with respect to the invariant visual frame) can be deduced to have moved and hence retains its identity. In other words, the external frame of reference specifies simultaneously an infinity of stable positions that the object can occupy, thereby removing the necessity to make the distinction between a change of place and a change of state.

This argument takes us one step closer in tracing the relation between perception and cognition. The fundamental point is that the criteria for identifying an object are spatial, the mechanism is one of deductive inference and the problem of movement necessitates an external frame of reference. In fact, it is not until infants are about six months of age that they will track a visible moving object without error. Prior to that time, infants will look along a repeated path of movement or to momentary stationary positions of an object, even when they see it moving off in another direction (Bower and Paterson 1972). This type of error in the face of a completely visible object suggests that infants do not yet adopt an external framework as their primary frame of reference.

Yet infants seem to perceive movement in relation to the background prior to six months of age (Harris, Cassel and Bamborough 1974). It seems likely that infants have not yet coordinated egocentric and external frames of reference and it is in this context that the role of action is paramount. It is possible that coordination comes in gaining control over posture. Lee and Aronson (1974) have demonstrated that standing in infants is under the control of visual framework cues. Cessation of tracking errors for a visible object at six months may coincide with adoption of the seated posture. Gaining postural control may act to coordinate the background with the egocentric frame of reference and thereby introduce the infant to the background as the appropriate frame of reference to monitor changes of position of the object. Once the infant comes to rely on the background, the problem of updating is overcome and the infant should no longer make errors in visual search, at least when the object is visible.

One interesting consequence of this argument is that it helps to explain the problem of 'décalage' in development. This is a term adopted by Piaget and extended by Bower (1974) to explain why particular types of error may be overcome in one context yet reappear in another. In this case, errors are overcome when one motor system is involved, for example the system controlling eye movements, yet reappear when another motor system is involved, for example the system controlling hand movements. Infants of nine months of age will make errors when retrieving a visible object, after the object has been moved from an initial location (Butterworth 1974; Harris 1974). So there is evidence that infants make errors in manual search when errors in visual search have been overcome. However, this need not indicate that one motor system has access to conceptual knowledge of which the other is deprived.

It is more parsimonious to consider motor systems to be multiply embedded, one within the other (Gibson 1968). The process of coordinating internal and external frames of reference can be quite specific to the particular system in use. Held and Bauer (1967) and Hein (1974) have shown that motor systems can independently come under the control of visual frameworks. It may be that since visual search precedes manual search, coordination of frames of reference may be complete for visual search in advance of manual search. In both cases, the mechanism for object identification would be a perceptual deductive inference, but conflict between frames of reference would occur if they remain uncoordinated for a particular motor system.

The 'tunnel effect'

In the previous section, the visibility of the object or its movements was stressed because identification can take place directly with respect to a perceived frame of reference. There is ample evidence that infants do not have general conceptual rules for identity in visual or manual search when the object and its movements are hidden.

Michotte (1950) described a phenomenon in adult visual perception which he called the 'tunnel effect'. Even though no visual information specifies it directly, adults often report perceived continuity of movement when observing an object pass through a tunnel. A number of studies have adopted this paradigm to establish whether infants might perceive movement in the same way (Mundy-Castle and Anglin 1969; Gardner 1971; Bower 1972; Nelson 1971, 1974). Most of these studies showed that infants will visually extrapolate the trajectory of an object. The ability is subject to spatial and temporal limitations such as the visual angle subtended by the tunnel and the time for which the object remains hidden (Gardner 1971).

The fact that the ability is not based on general conceptual rules linking movement to identity is demonstrated by two phenomena. Firstly, anticipation is not usually immediate but is acquired over several trials, even by infants over nine months of age. Secondly, if the path of movement is reversed, infants have to reacquire the pattern of anticipation over the next few trials (Nelson 1971, 1974). The data suggest that infants may first establish the contingencies of events at the disappearance and reappearance points and then deduce that movement must have taken place along a particular trajectory. Mundy-Castle and Anglin (1969) noted that infants would track along the apparent trajectory for an object that appeared recurrently at each of two locations. By varying the conditions of stimulus presentation, the trajectory of movement inferred by the infants could be altered appropriately.

A separate but perhaps related explanation for extrapolation of a trajectory has been proposed by Ball (1973). He argues that infants perceive events at either end of the tunnel as a causally related sequence. Movement is transmitted between the object that disappears at the entrance and the object that appears at the exit. Such a mechanism would link objects that are quite distinct. In fact, Bower (1971) argues that infants under three months of age do not take into account a change in the distinctive features of an object that passes through a tunnel, which suggests that some such process may be at work.

Infants over three months backtrack to the exit as though expecting the original object to emerge. While infants do differentiate between objects on the basis of features (see Bond 1972), information from features alone is not sufficient for judgments of the fundamental identity of an object to be made. As was argued earlier, the criteria for such a judgment are spatial.

Manual search

Thus the infant appears to be in possession of perceptual mechanisms for identifying a stationary or moving object before nine months of age. However, when the object or its movements are hidden, both visual and manual search are prone to error. There is no need to postulate a décalage to account for this. Nelson (1971) showed that infants make errors in visual search for hidden objects at an age when manual search errors are also known to occur. For example, early on in a sequence of trials in which an object moves through a tunnel, infants look to the entrance, where the object disappears. Analogous errors occur in manual search (Gratch and Landers 1971; Bower and Paterson 1972).

For the most part, the evidence suggests that infants pass through a stage in the development of manual search, between the ages of nine months and one year, when they will search either at the original location (*A*) or at the final location (*B*) for an object hidden successively at *A* and *B*. In cross-sectional studies, manual search errors take the form of half the infants in a sample searching at *A* and the remainder searching at *B* (Evans and Gratch 1972). Furthermore, a delay seems to be necessary between hiding the object and allowing retrieval before errors will occur (Harris 1973; Gratch, Appel, Evans, Le Compte and Wright 1974). Although infants can cope successfully with delays as long as seven seconds at *A*, any delay at *B* produces the typical conflict between *A* and *B*.

No new principle is required to explain errors in manual search since they seem also to reflect a conflict between an egocentric and visual frame of reference. However, errors can be eliminated if the movement is made to take place with respect to some invariant landmark in the immediate visual field (Butterworth 1975). Identification then becomes possible with respect to a perceived spatial framework, since all the necessary information to enable the infant to deduce that a single object has changed location remains in the visual field.

From object percept to object concept

It was noted that a delay between hiding the object and allowing search is important for error to occur. This suggests that a memory retrieval problem may subserve error, although this can be compensated by structuring the immediate visual field in such a way that the infant can *recognise* that it remains invariant through time. The perceptual problem for the infant is to connect momentary positions through time. The corollary of the definition that an object can only be in one place at one time is that an object can be at an infinity of possible positions at different times. Such a definition frees the object from the constraints of directly perceived space and places it in the conceptual realm. How might the transition from perceived to conceived object occur?

In principle, the transition should be very simple. It requires only that the external frame of reference should be interiorised for spatial constraints to be eliminated. That is, it can be argued that it is not the interiorisation of action which forms the basis for the object concept, but the interiorisation of the invariant consequences of action. In practice, nothing is known about the way in which such a process might take place. Following the earlier line of argument, it seems possible that the adoption of the upright posture may play a part in introducing the infant as a unified motor system to the background as the appropriate frame of reference. A represented object against a represented ground would then be freed from the constraints of a perceived frame of reference.

Social objects

In Chapter 7 in this volume, John and Elizabeth Newson argue for the social origins of symbolic functioning. The theory offered in this chapter would be incomplete if no attempt was made to relate it to the social precocity of the infant. In fact, no new principle is required to encompass the behaviour of infants to social objects described by the Newsons under the heading of 'intersubjectivity'.

If the egocentric frame of reference forms the primary structure mediating the process of deductive inference, it would be no accident that the infant should be so sensitive to other people. The first frame of reference encountered by the infant to bear an invariant relation to the self would be another person. The infant is required only to recognise the match between self and other (the mid-term in the inference) to place his own actions in correspondence.

Some studies suggest that infants as young as two weeks of age can match movements of parts of their face to the corresponding actions of another person (Maratos 1973; Moore and Meltzoff 1975). Recently, Scaife and Bruner (1975) found that infants of three months of age are able to follow the line of regard of another person to locate a position in space. As yet, nothing is known about the particular cues which make these behaviours possible and this problem requires further research. However, the principle that a process of deductive inference might subserve them would seem a useful one in generating a theory which can account for the perceptual behaviour of infants to both animate and inanimate objects.

Conclusion

The aim of this chapter was to consider the problem of the relation between perception and cognition. The argument was couched in terms of the perceptual precocity of the infant, since the debate on the origin of cognitive processes rests ultimately on the means at the disposal of the infant for achieving a stable reality.

On reviewing the evidence, it was suggested that the continued existence of an object could be specified directly by the visual system. It was proposed that the basic process subserving object permanence and identification is one of deductive inference. This process need not be conscious, indeed it is likely to be unconscious and automatic. Nor is it dependent on previous experience, since on this account egocentric space has the status of an '*a priori* hypothesis', in relation to which conclusions about the identity of a stationary object can be reached. As McDougall (1928) argued, even the simplest mind responds to an object with the awareness of 'something there'.

The developmental problem comes with movement. This requires the infant to externalise the continuity of experience afforded by an egocentric frame of reference. This is achieved by establishing an external framework which remains stable despite changes in posture. In this respect the theory is in agreement with Piaget in emphasising the role of action. The importance of action lies in generating the flux of changing stimulation from which the invariant system of reference can be extracted. However, even this process depends on a pre-existing ability to perceive invariance through change.

To avoid a conflict between egocentric and external frames of reference, instrumental activity must come to be monitored in terms of the external reference frame. The infant must become skilled in directing action to objects. The present account implies that it is the process of coordinating frames of reference which results in the long sequence of stages in sensorimotor development, rather than the acquisition of a notion of invariance which only later comes to be fed back into perception. In a very real sense, development in infancy can be construed as a mapping of the self on to the world. Even though the infant is in possession of the correct criteria for determining object identity, application of the criteria can only result in conflict unless frames of reference are congruent in specifying a stable space, in relation to which an object can move.

Returning to the problem of the relation between perception and cognition, it is apparent that the real basis for a distinction lies in the freedom of conceptual thinking to span spatial and temporal intervals which are insurmountable by the processes of direct perception. The transition from object percept to object concept does not require any new logical process to be acquired. What changes with development is the frame of reference to which the same basic logical capacity is applied. In this case, the transition is from an external to an internal frame of reference. In all probability the internal frame is a representation of the invariant external frame in relation to which perceptual judgments were made. The transition from percept to concept therefore constitutes a loop from organism to environment, which then feeds back to the organism to form a new and more general level of functioning.

The implication of the theory that has been advanced is that, at root, cognitive structures have their origin in perceptual processes. This should not be taken to mean that cognitive structures do not extend and refine these basic processes, but that perception and cognition are functionally interdependent in categorising reality.

D

7. On the social origins of symbolic functioning

Piaget's standpoint and the approach presented here

One of the most important debts which developmental psychology owes to Jean Piaget derives from his steadfast insistence that it is *symbolic functioning*, via the establishment of cognitive structures, which provides the key to our understanding of what is important in human psychological development. And Piaget goes on to assert that symbolic activity must clearly be recognised as a function which in some sense emerges, as a result of the child's activities, at a distinctive point in the human infant's natural psychological development: 'At the end of the sensorimotor period, at about one and a half to two years, there appears a function that is fundamental to the development of later behaviour patterns. It consists in the ability to represent something (a signified something: object, event, conceptual scheme, etc.) by means of a "signifier" which is differentiated and which serves only a representative purpose: language, mental image, symbolic gesture and so on' (Piaget and Inhelder 1969).

Obviously, for the purpose of constructing a comprehensive theory concerning the course of subsequent cognitive growth, it was necessary to begin somewhere. But instead of beginning, classically, with thought, Piaget takes as his starting point motor activity, initially of a simple reflex kind, which the child is said to display in the presence of objects. This leads him to emphasise sensorimotor activity, involving the manipulation by the infant of inanimate objects. He goes on to suggest that thought is the 'interiorisation' of such actions: 'In order to know objects, the subject must act upon them, and therefore transform them: he must displace, connect, combine, take apart, and reassemble them' (Piaget 1970).

Knowledge, then, originates in activity: originally overt activity of the infant, shown in the physical manipulation of objects. And this leads later to the performance of operations which, as a result of internal processes of organisation (equilibration), are not self-evident in the infant's observable behaviour. The primary emphasis is, however, on active interaction between the organism and his environment.

It needs to be stated here that the theoretical position which will be outlined in this chapter will represent a shift of emphasis rather than an absolute disagreement with Piaget's philosophical standpoint. For instance, we would not quarrel at all with his proposition that '. . . objective knowledge is not acquired by a mere recording of external information but has its origin in interactions between the subject and objects . . .' (1970, op. cit.). To this statement we merely wish to add that the object with which the human infant interacts most often, and most effectively, particularly in the earliest stages of development, is almost invariably another human being. In this sense the Piagetian standpoint needs to be qualified and elaborated in certain important respects, but in general terms can be accepted as a useful overall conceptual frame of reference. We would also fully agree with Piaget when he asserts, in opposition to empirical behaviourists, that knowledge arises neither from outside the organism nor from within it. As he puts it: 'The main point of our theory is that knowledge results from *interactions* between the subject and the object, which are *richer* than what the objects can provide by themselves' (1970, op. cit.).

To align Piaget's position with our own, it is necessary to enlarge the concept of 'object' to include human beings. Yet human beings are not quite like other objects, in as much as they have the power to communicate with others of their kind and hence to share with them a common culture: an articulated framework or structure of knowledge which is, in a sense, understood only because it is *mutually* understandable. The argument is, then, that knowledge itself originates within an interaction process (highly active on the part of the infant) between the infant himself and other, more mature, human individuals who already possess shared understandings with other communicating beings. Furthermore, these shared understandings are embedded in a uniquely human way of conceptualising the world in spatial and temporal terms. In short, the child only achieves a fully articulated knowledge of his world, in a cognitive sense, as he becomes involved in social transactions with other communicating human beings. Knowing, and being able to communicate what it is that we know, need to be viewed as opposite sides of the same coin.

The infant's knowledge of objects

Piaget's view that the infant's knowledge somehow originates from an internalisation of the actions he performs in coordinating hand and eye movements, so as to grapple with inanimate objects, was supported by observations he made upon his own children. He describes their reactions when objects were made to disappear from view by covering them, dropping them silently or hiding them inside containers. One of the infant's most important 'constructions' is said to be that which leads to the discovery of the notion of a permanent object at between nine and twelve months of age. Thus: 'During the first months of existence, there are no permanent objects, but only perceptual pictures which appear, dissolve, and sometimes reappear' (1970, op. cit.). At this stage it is suggested that the object is only conceptualised as a result of the actions involved in looking for it: 'One real example is an eleven-month-old child who was playing with a ball. He had previously retrieved it from under an armchair when it had rolled there before. A moment later, the ball went under a low sofa. He could not find it under this sofa, so he came back to the other part of the room and looked for it under the armchair, where this course of action had already been successful' (1970, op. cit.). It should be noticed, in passing, that in this account the infant in question clearly has the capacity both to hold in mind an accurate knowledge of certain relevant spatial locations like 'under the armchair', and to sustain an intention to retrieve an object, such as a ball, when it is no longer in view. However, on the basis of numerous similar observations of strategies used by babies to retrieve hidden or lost objects, Piaget asserts that the achievement of object permanence at around this age represents a major mental achievement: it contributes to a veritable 'Copernican revolution' which babies accomplish in the course of the first twelve to eighteen months. It is this evaluation that has stimulated many further studies aimed at verifying that babies do react towards the disappearance or reappearance of objects in the way he describes.

However, our purpose is to do more than study babies' reactions; it is to explain how they themselves become *agents*, directing their own actions. This is a distinction not always made in conventional experimental psychology. Among psychologists working in the experimental tradition, Bower is outstanding. In a recent monograph (Bower 1974), he has surveyed a wide range of experimental studies which have a bearing upon the way infants behave in the presence of what adults would regard as objects. Bower draws attention to a respectable array of carefully recorded evidence, showing that the human infant is capable of extraordinarily complex feats of behavioural adjustment to external events and circumstances, often from the moment of birth. One surprising finding is that, even within the first two weeks of life, infants are able to reach out and grasp for visually presented objects with a considerable degree of accuracy: 'The hand opens before contact and closes on contact, but too quickly for the contact to have released the hand closure' (Bower 1974). To demonstrate these responses it is necessary to support the infant in an optimal posture, relieving him of the muscular burden of head control while allowing free movement of the limbs; but when this is done, objects presented at a suitable distance will frequently be attained with delicately appropriate and coordinated hand and arm movements, on a visual cue alone, and without the necessity for practice in hand-eye coordination which Piaget, among others, has assumed to be necessary.

More strikingly still, Bower has fitted certain infants with polarising spectacles so as to be able to study their reactions to a 'virtual object' (i.e. an object which appears visually to be solid and three-dimensional, but which is in fact produced by stereoscopic techniques). When such a virtual object is substituted for the real object, it is claimed that the infant reaches for it as before, but is then 'upset' to find there is no normal tactual feedback. Bower also asserts that accurate reaching reactions become strangely difficult to elicit from babies after the age of four weeks and only reappear, in the babies he has followed up, around the age of twenty weeks.

Bower's claims, particularly those concerned with the reaction to the virtual object, need to be verified by workers in other laboratories before they can be interpreted unambiguously. There is, as might be expected, much scope for interpreting the behavioural evidence of 'upset' when observing babies of this age, who are only able to sustain their attention for short time spans and are very easily distressed when manipulated for experimental purposes. His work is, however, part of a more pervasive trend among contemporary developmental psychologists to observe and record the behaviour of very young infants and to subject their recordings to detailed and systematic forms of analysis.

Bower's contribution is but one example of a host of recent investigations which have begun to suggest that the human infant is a much more complicated organism than previous generations of developmental psychologists have led us to believe. The well-known experiment by Bruner and Kalnins (Bruner 1968), showing that infants can adjust their sucking behaviour so as to bring a picture into clear focus, provides a similarly dramatic demonstration of the intrinsic 'cleverness' of the human neonate, and particularly highlights visual sophistication.

Clearly, findings of this kind (and there are similar findings about the accuracy of visual scanning activity in new-born babies) suggest that infants at birth are already possessed of the necessary sensory, motor and neural equipment to make it possible for them to respond appropriately towards real objects in a three-dimensional world. In consequence these results would seem to refute those empiricist theories which have led some psychologists to assume that babies require prolonged experience with objects before they develop such skills. At the same time we need to treat with caution the suggestion, both implicit and explicit in Bower's writing, that the human infant is somehow inherently possessed of the 'knowledge' that seen objects are tangible. Behaviour, however complicated, carries no necessary implication that the organism is capable of appreciating the ends towards which its own behaviour is directed. However accurately a guided missile is able to seek out its target, we do not generally feel it necessary to credit the missile with having *knowledge* about the target, in the sense of conceptualising the target as an object, out there, about to be destroyed. Adult human beings do, however, share with one another the capacity to make such conceptualisations, and it seems reasonable to ask how the infant is brought to the point of sharing them.

To do him justice, Bower does devote the final chapter of his monograph to a more considered discussion of cognitive development as such. He also provides an excellent summary of experimental observations upon children's reactions to the disappearance and re-appearance of objects or their apparent transformation. At two months an infant can track slowly-moving visual targets, even if they pass behind an obscuring screen and re-emerge at the opposite side. A little later he will be able to backtrack visually if the emerging object is radically different from the one which went behind the screen. Between two and four months there seems to be some evidence to suggest that he will respond with a decelerated heart-rate (surprise?) when an object, after being momentarily screened from him, proves to have vanished. Not until about six months will most babies attempt to remove a cloth cover deliberately; that is, with intent to retrieve a hidden object. Even at a year, infants who observe an object hidden in the experimenter's palm and then placed under a cloth will, after the hand is removed and shown to be empty, still not think to look for the object under the cloth, despite the tell-tale lump to be seen in full view.

One conclusion arising from this review is that the search for definitive evidence that object permanence is suddenly achieved, at one particular instant in the child's mental progress, is unlikely to prove successful. Each method of demonstrating that the child will respond appropriately to a disappearing or re-appearing object seems to give rise to a different operational definition of what is meant by the achievement of object permanence. Cumulatively, these demonstrations merely make it increasingly obvious that the human infant is sensitive to a vast number of happenings or events: and that these leave residual memory effects, in the sense that they can be shown to influence his subsequent observable reactions. How early this can be seen will depend to a very great extent upon our social skill in drawing a baby's attention to objects as salient entities within the compass of his attention, and upon our experimental ingenuity in detecting his differential responses in subsequent encounters.

All this does little to provide us with satisfactory evidence for the dramatic arrival within the baby's mental experience of some entirely new level of awareness directed towards objects as such. Perhaps the most secure evidence that the baby can represent objects to himself, in the sense that we ourselves do, would be a demonstration that he is able to communicate with some other person about 'objects' in a reliable and consistent way. In short, we need to be very cautious about arguing that objects exist as entities for babies until we have evidence that babies can share with us a certain mutual understanding of event sequences in which we and they are caught up. Human knowledge about the environment— as opposed to mere reactivity towards it—depends upon some measure of agree-ment between interacting persons about how reality is being construed. It is in this sense that the child's knowledge about objects, and his ability to communicate what he knows, are fundamentally inseparable. At all events, the accounts of both Bower and Piaget seem to place far too little emphasis on the fact that the human infant is also surprisingly *socially* active almost from the moment of birth. Further-more, he approaches the business of intentional action in a manner which makes sense to himself in the same way as to others, rather than merely reacting to circumstance.

The primacy of social responsiveness in human infants

Moving, three-dimensional, self-deforming and noise-producing objects have a basic attention-demanding function for the human infant which far exceeds the effect of any static object, however brightly coloured or 'novel' it might otherwise be in terms of such factors as shape or size (Schaffer 1971). This is a part of the reason why the human face of his mother clearly begins to exert a compelling fascination from the moment when the infant is capable of bringing it into clear focus (that is, more or less from birth). The patterns of reaction whereby the infant can demonstrate such interest also need to be carefully noted. And when these are examined in slowed down video-recordings of an interacting mother-baby pair, it turns out firstly that the different sensorimotor components of the infant's activity are highly synchronised with each other, and secondly, that his action sequences are temporally organised so that they can mesh—with a high degree of precision—with similar patterns of action produced by his human care-taker. The fact is that, from a very early age indeed, infants appear to be capable of taking part in dialogue-like exchanges with other human beings. Thus, when the adult talks to the infant, the infant displays all the complex gestural accompaniments that one normally expects of attentive listening; and when the adult pauses, the infant can reply with a fully articulated, gesturally animated, conversation-like response. Prolonged social interchanges comprising an alternating succession of passive and active role-taking apparently occur with an effortless spontaneity; and this seems to 'come naturally' not only to the mother, who obviously has a long history of conversation experience, but to her infant who is in most other respects conceptually and socially quite inexperienced. Clearly, observations of this sort add strength to the argument that the infant is somehow *innately primed* to participate in complicated social rituals.

The reciprocal nature of this phenomenon implies, as Colwyn Trevarthen has pointed out (Trevarthen *et al.* 1975), that the movements of eyes, head, mouth, limbs and voice are based in rhythmic synchronies and patterns which are common to human social interaction regardless of age, race or social custom. Such patterns represent cultural universals which man also shares with many animals lower in the phylogenetic chain, and they thus have very deep biological roots. Indeed, it is probably because these rhythmic coordinations of behaviour are so ubiquitous and pervasive that they have been completely taken for granted, and hence over-looked, in the behaviour of very young infants. Trevarthen's approach might be described as that of a behavioural embryologist: he tends to emphasise the great complexity of genetically-based behavioural systems with which the human infant is endowed. He seems inclined to stress the inborn nature of the ability to take part in complex social interaction rituals, and he describes the phenomenon as 'innate intersubjectivity'.

When Trevarthen uses the term 'intersubjectivity', he is referring to a specific kind of sociability which mediates communication between two human subjects. It is his view that infants are inherently responsive to those patterns of temporal movement which typically govern the episodic behaviour cycles characteristic of most living organisms, or at least of those which are phylogenetically advanced enough to engage in social forms of communication. Thus, for instance, the ways in which the eyes of both infant and adult move within the head seem to him to depend upon genetically pre-programmed timing mechanisms which govern the step-like jumps or 'saccades' which are normally made in looking behaviour. The human baby both responds *to*, and responds *with*, actions which are synchronised in accordance with basically shared rhythms.

Beyond this, however, the looking behaviour of neonates—when viewed in slow-motion action replays—is very delicately coordinated with certain hand and arm movements, and even with facial and mouthing movements, all of which are integrated together in such a precisely coordinated rhythmic sequence that the total response can be most aptly designated 'pre-speech'. The forms of stimulation which optimally call forth such complex conversational reactions from very young infants are themselves not simple. It may be true, for instance, as other students of neonatal behaviour have pointed out (Condon and Sander 1974), that human speech conforms to a basic rhythmic pattern of vocalised sound which calls forth precisely synchronised motor movements in new-born babies. But these and other phenomena, such as social smiling, may best be viewed as only part of a more general complex responsiveness to the social approaches we make to babies: reciprocal social responsiveness which is the end product of a biological selection process aimed at the important biological goal of making human communication with babies feasible.

Susan Pawlby, from our own Unit, when interviewing mothers about their early attempts to communicate with their babies, at the pre-verbal level, found that some of them talked spontaneously about trying to get on to the same wavelength. The analogy is an interesting one. As every schoolboy knows, effective communication between a transmitting and a receiving station demands that both stations are at least tuned to the same basic carrier frequency before any transmission of information can take place. The motor action sequences which human beings characteristically employ (intonational pattern, hand gestures, facial movements, etc.) are temporally patterned in ways which are far from random but also in ways to which, as human beings, we are selectively highly responsive. It is obviously dangerous to stretch analogies too far, but it may well be that all information exchange implies a certain basic compatibility in the temporal response characteristics of the communicating individuals.

In two-way communication it may also be essential to arrange that transmission and reception periods alternate according to some rule or device which ensures that one transmitter remains silent while the other is operating, since there would otherwise be gross interference between competing signals on the same wavelength. Trevarthen has not been the only observer to point out that babies seem to be natural conversationalists (Schaffer 1974), in the sense that they are innately skilled in turn-taking. They look attentive when we speak to them and wait for an appropriate pause or hiatus before they in turn make some gesture, or vocal or pre-vocal response. Opinions differ as to how much the baby's actions are under the puppet-like control of the more experienced partner in such communication sequences. Schaffer (op. cit.) and Shotter (1973) have suggested that it is the skill of the mother which mainly accounts for the alternating form of the dialogue which can be observed; but even so, it may still be the case that infants must be biologically primed in certain very specific respects for it to be possible for mothers to select points for action in the situation so as to give such convincing simulations of the dialogue form which appears to be a feature of all interpersonal communication, regardless of culture.

This brings us to a further reason for wanting to introduce a term such as 'intersubjectivity'. Typically the form of control which a mother exercises in trying to establish communication with her baby is one which makes a great deal of use of his own spontaneous actions. These first appear as coordinated segments of apparently goal-directed activity. As Bower's work shows, the baby's behaviour seems to be 'aimed at' objects and events in the world surrounding him which other human beings would also naturally expect to notice or to find interesting (Bower 1974). This means that it is possible, almost from birth, for the interacting adult to take his or her cue from the spontaneous actions performed by the baby and to weave these into the form of a dialogue with him. Thus mothers and babies begin to conduct 'conversations' concerning objects and events to which both partners are attentive, even though there is as yet no evidence for verbal understanding on the baby's part. Since, however, the baby plays a very active and self-directed role from the outset, the course of the ensuing dialogue is never strictly under the sole control of either partner. Whatever communication takes place emerges as an intersubjective product of their joint collaboration. The word 'intersubjectivity' therefore usefully draws attention to the general principle that human cognitive understanding arises from a process of *negotiation* between two or more human beings; and it suggests that it may not be sensible to seek the roots of those shared understandings which constitute human knowledge within the action patterns of any one individual viewed in social isolation. (It is in this sense that the word is used by the French philosopher Merleau-Ponty when discussing socialisation from the sociological standpoint; see O'Neill 1973.)

Mother-baby interaction sequences

While paying respect to the inborn predispositions of the human infant, con-temporary developmental psychologists are increasingly becoming interested in the functional significance which should be attached to this precocious social activity of normal babies and, more particularly, in how this may be related to the overall course of cognitive and symbolic development. In practice, most mothers are apparently very skilled in sustaining the interest and attention of their babies, both towards themselves and towards significant objects and events which are encountered in the course of everyday life. Mothers also often act as mediators between the baby and outside events. They tend to provide, quite unself-consciously, forms of feedback which are dramatically attention-compelling because they are contingently geared—in a very delicately timed way—to actions which are spontaneously made by the infant himself. Even in the most straight-forward adult-and-baby encounters with objects, the adult's visual monitoring of the baby's activity may be highly critical. Note how, in practice, one is able to elicit simple visual following behaviour in a supine four-week infant using a dangling ring. In this superficially simple task, the test demonstrator will carefully attend, not just to the general state of arousal of the infant, but to his precise focus and line of regard. Having 'hooked' the attention of the infant upon the ring, one then begins gingerly to move it across his field of vision in such a way that the infant's eyes continue to hold the object with successive fixations until eventually the head follows the eyes in that coordinated overall movement pattern which denotes successful tracking. If the test object is moved too suddenly, or is left static too long, the visual attention of the infant will flag and the attempt will have to begin all over again from scratch. In this instance, what is in fact happening is a highly skilled monitoring by the adult and a consequent adjustment of the dangling object, moment by moment, depending on the feedback which is being obtained from the spontaneous actions of the infant. It might even be argued that one is dragging from the infant a complex response which he would be unlikely to give to an object which was moved by mechanical means across his visual field. The resulting action sequence of the infant is therefore a combination of his own activity and *an intelligent manipulation of that activity by the much more sophisticated adult partner*. The adult, by being contingently responsive to the infant in a way which only another human being could be, manages both to hold the infant's attention and to shape the course of his ongoing activity pattern; and, incidentally, the infant is provided with a sustained looking experience which might not otherwise have occurred.

Confronting a baby with a humanly presented object thus turns out to be complicated even though the baby is required to give his attention only to the movement of a single object. The situation obviously becomes much more difficult to analyse when the baby is called upon to divide his attention between the person presenting the object and the object itself. Yet it is this kind of activity, in which a baby begins to switch his visual attention from his mother to other objects and back again to his mother, which provides her with an extremely rewarding set of social signals and makes her feel that communication between herself and her infant is at last a real possibility. However, visual switching activity also appears to be something more complex than an automatic response to external events. Again it seems to emerge as a product of collaboration, in which the mother as a sophisticated adult capitalises upon the spontaneous actions of her child so as to entrain them into sequences which are potentially useful both as communication gestures and in alerting the baby's attention to events which can become foci of shared reference.

Switching eye direction between contact with another person and contact with shared objects of reference is clearly of enormous significance as a means of sustaining social rapport between any two human beings; and the fact that most babies become proficient in this art at around the age of six months provides us with yet another example of their staggering social precocity. Closely linked with this is the whole question of how babies become able to imitate actions which they see others perform; and here, once more, it can be argued that facility in imitation develops out of a collaboration between two partners in which the adult provides the infant with forms of feedback which are closely linked to the spontaneous actions of the infant himself. Mothers seem to stage-manage the situation in such a way as to draw out of the infant sustained patterns of action which mirror the adult's own actions. A case can be made, then, for saying that the infant's capacity to imitate (and hence to empathise with others) itself develops within the context of spontaneous social exchanges which almost invariably occur between the infant and those who seek to communicate with him in human terms (Newson and Pawlby 1975).

Problems of recording and analysis

Within the two-way interaction games which ordinary mothers spontaneously play with their babies, a very large number of actions which the baby makes are interpreted as communication gestures in the sense that they are incorporated into the dialogue. From the baby's standpoint, these particular actions are apparently rendered significant by the quality and timing of the mother's gestural and vocal reciprocations. The effect is to highlight or 'mark' certain events as having special significance, and hence to *punctuate* the contribution which the baby is making according to a pattern of meaningfulness which is, to some extent, being imposed by the more sophisticated partner. The mother's intonational gestures, often accompanied by dramatic alterations of facial expression, clearly have a powerful effect in alerting the baby's attention to the significance of his own actions.

The attempt to give a detailed sequential description of the alternating flow of communication gestures which typically takes place poses certain methodological problems. One of the most obvious is that the two-way communication process takes place so rapidly, even with very young babies, that it is only possible to look at it in detail by making simultaneous audio-visual recordings which can be slowed down and then replayed as many times as is necessary in order to establish precisely what has taken place during the interchange. Ideally, one needs to encapsulate on the permanent record the signalling actions of both partners, the direction and quality of their changing attentiveness, and the overall setting within which the interaction is taking place. One also needs to be able to relate the activities of each partner to those of the other in an accurate time sequence. And all this is only a minimum technical requirement which must precede the evolution of coding schedules designed to be sensitive to the meaningful content of whatever communication is taking place. Various research workers both in the UK and elsewhere are currently preoccupied with such problems, and it is as yet too soon to report any consensus as to the most appropriate strategies for coding and analysis.

Although it is also too early to offer a review of published findings deriving from this particular research approach, some general comments arising from attempts to undertake practical research studies may be of interest. It seems, for instance, that the roles of observer and participant in relation to adult-infant interaction sequences are quite distinct and separate. As a participant, or actor, one inevitably pays maximal attention to the communication gestures of the other partner, i.e. the baby, and one cannot be simultaneously aware of all the subtleties of one's own communication gestures—particularly the non-verbal ones—without putting the smooth functioning of the communication process at risk. This is analogous to thinking too much about the mechanics of the walking process and tripping over one's own feet. This does not imply, however, that a participant may not be able to function as an observer when viewing his own behaviour in retrospect, and indeed there may be considerable advantages in securing this kind of cooperation from mothers. This consideration leads us to yet another reason for invoking the notion of 'intersubjectivity'. In a sense, it is only possible to chart the course of a communication interchange by oneself engaging in such activity as a 'communicant' or practitioner of human communication skills; that is, as one who has already been initiated into human culture. Thus while the analysis of temporal event sequences lends itself appropriately to computer processing, the identification of the significant events must remain the province of the empathic human observer. Indeed it may even be the case that, at the pre-verbal level of communication, the mother herself will sometimes be the only person who can identify certain communication gestures which her baby is currently making, because only she shares a history of common communication experience with that baby (Newson and Shotter 1974).

Further theoretical implications

Evidence is now accumulating which strongly suggests that communication at the pre-verbal level provides the foundation upon which verbal language can be built. In other words, the representational function which makes language possible seems to develop out of what Werner and Kaplan have called the *primordial sharing situation*: 'In this situation the human infant is "sharing" rather than "communicating" an experience (the object of reference) with another person, usually the mother. That is, the primordial sharing situation is a sensorimotor affective "pre-symbolic situation in which there is little differentiation in the child's experience between himself, the other (typically the mother), and the referential object". The precursory components for symbolization, however, are present. Together, the mother and child are sharing the same thing. What is still necessary is that the child must differentiate and integrate the primordial sharing situation—himself, from objects of reference, from his means of symbolic communication, from his communicants (others)—so that his symbols represent his objects of reference in a communicative fashion to both others and himself' (Langer 1970).

In practice, it certainly seems to be necessary to make a fairly fundamental distinction between face-to-face exchanges involving adult and child, and exchanges during which one of the partners (usually the adult) is offering comments upon the elsewhere-directed actions which the other partner (usually the child) is performing. The rules governing social interplay in these two rather obviously different situations do not seem to be the same. It appears to be the case, for instance, that active participation in face-to-face conversational episodes is possible at a much earlier age; and this is in tune with the idea, well supported by observational study, that manual manipulatory competence generally comes surprisingly late in the developmental timetable, as compared with visual exploratory skill. It is, however, the interplay between the child's person-oriented gestures and his object-related actions which is likely to prove a most fruitful area for further research. Very young babies can pay sustained attention to another person and will often respond to people while largely ignoring inanimate objects; it is only during the second half of the first year that they seem to become capable of sustained absorption or play with objects. It may be significant, therefore, that it also takes time for infants to reach the stage where they can alternate their attention appropriately between persons and things. Yet when this does become possible, it opens up a whole new field of collaboration: the child's attention can be drawn not just towards the objects themselves, but towards the fundamental cognitive distinction between objects and the actions which they elicit.

The general proposition that the child's knowledge has its roots in his early social ability receives striking support from yet another source: '*Any function in the child's cultural development appears on the stage twice*, on two planes, first on the social plane and then on the psychological, first among people as an *intermental category* and then within the child as an *intramental category*' (Vygotsky 1966). It is of particular interest that Vygotsky invokes the term 'intermental', which is hardly distinguishable from the term 'intersubjective' as we have used it in this chapter.

Summary and conclusion

Human cognitive competence is predicated upon the fundamental assumption that most of the actions we perform are readily intelligible to other human beings, as are theirs to us. Yet this is obviously not the case with the new-born child, who is quite unable to respond to communications which adults take for granted as 'basic', such as the gesture of pointing towards some object which is clearly visible in his field of view. The child gradually achieves such competence, but only—we now believe—as a result of being positively involved in numerous experiences of reciprocal activity with other human beings. His early experience, being largely socially mediated, very frequently involves being caught up and swept along in exchanges with other communicating persons, who intuitively engage him in alternating-role sequences such that his own natural and spontaneous actions and reactions are assigned a precise function within the context of an apparently meaningful exchange. Through such dialogues-of-action, the infant becomes thoroughly familiar with the role of a skilled communicator, participating in forms of communication long before he is able to understand the full content of what is being communicated.

Involvement in such activity provides what seem to be the optimal conditions for arriving at genuine shared understandings with his partner. The situation is such that the child is under very little constraint, and can freely experiment in his role as actor. At any moment within the dialogue he can ad lib or enlarge upon the part he is being called upon to play, since nearly any variation of his own action or reaction can be compensated for by being incorporated into the ongoing dialogue, which remains understandable in human terms throughout. He is thus massively and repeatedly involved in non-verbal dialogues whose form is governed by some underlying structure of meaning. At the same time, however, the content of any given communication is by no means wholly imposed by the more skilled partner; it arises out of the combined activity of both individuals. Thus the basic human ability to structure knowledge in such a way that it can be shared—the ability to commune with others—derives initially from mothers' 'natural' inclination to treat their babies as if they already had understanding.

The term 'intersubjectivity' has recurred throughout this chapter. In using it, attention is being drawn to a fundamental proposition: that the origin of symbolic functioning should be sought, not in the child's activities with inanimate objects, but rather in those idiosyncratic but shared understandings which he first evolves during his earliest social encounters with familiar human beings who are themselves already steeped in human culture.

Note   A version of this chapter was first read as an invited paper to the Annual Conference of the British Psychological Society at Nottingham in April 1975, and it was subsequently published in the BPS *Bulletin* under the title 'Intersubjectivity and the transmission of culture'.

D. *Graham*

8. Moral development: the cognitive-developmental approach

The main concern of the cognitive-developmental approach to moral development is with cognitive factors and with moral awareness and thinking. It does not deny that other aspects may be important, but its focus of interest is upon the cognitive aspect. This approach also stresses that moral development takes place in an orderly way which cannot wholly be accounted for by the specific experience of the individual as viewed from outside. Common to this approach has been the notion of stages of development, each characterised by its own particular qualities. There is no implication of discontinuity between stages. Each stage, as it were, merges into the next.

Piaget's pioneering work

Piaget's book, *The Moral Judgment of the Child* (1932), represents his attempt to apply the notion of stages of development, which he had already used in other ways, to the development of moral judgment. Piaget, like Kohlberg later, is primarily concerned with moral judgment rather than behaviour or affect, although no doubt he would have expected to find some relationship between these. According to Piaget, development takes place as a result of interaction between the child and the (social) environment.

1.   First of all, Piaget concerns himself with children's conceptions of the 'rules of the game'—in particular the game of marbles. He says, in fact, 'The little boys who are beginning to play are gradually trained by the older ones in respect for the law: and in any case they aspire from their hearts to the virtue supremely characteristic of human dignity, which consists in making a correct use of the customary practice of a game. As to the older ones, it is in their power to alter the rules. If this is not "morality", then where does morality begin? At least, it is respect for rules and it appertains to an enquiry like ours to begin with the study of facts of this order' (op. cit., p. 2).

     In the development and practice of children's application and understanding of rules, there are, Piaget proposes, three stages: (i) The stage of 'motor behaviour' when the only rules or 'regularities' the child observes are purely individual habits. The 'motor rule' thus arises out of habit, but does not include any of the obligatory nature of the social rule. Nevertheless, the 'motor rule' would seem to be necessary for the later development of social rules. (ii) The 'egocentric' stage in which the child becomes interested in the rule-regulated behaviour of older children, but does not appreciate the *social* nature and function of rules. Piaget remarks, 'Egocentrism in so far as it means confusion of the ego and the external world, and egocentrism in so far as it means lack of cooperation, constitute one and the same phenomenon. So long as the child does not dissociate his ego from the suggestions coming from the physical and from the social world, he cannot cooperate, for in order to cooperate one must be conscious of one's ego, it is necessary to liberate oneself from the thought and will of others. The coercion exercised by the adult or the older child is therefore inseparable from the unconscious egocentrism of the young child' (op. cit., p. 87). The coercive rule depends upon the unilateral respect of the child for the authority of the adult. Fair comment might perhaps be that the authority of the adult is likely to rest on his *power* to dispense rewards and punishments. (iii) Finally, children reach a point where they have mastered the rules of the game as such. We have here mutual respect and a concern for reciprocity, together with a degree of autonomy in the sense of the child's understanding of the nature of the decision-making, and of the mutual obligations between himself and others. Thus we find Piaget virtually distinguishing three stages in the application and appreciation of the rules of the game—an amoral stage; a stage at which rules are seen as coercive, sacrosanct, with binding power in their own right; and a stage at which rules are seen as the product of agreement and are thereby modifiable by mutual consent. The major distinction is between a 'heteronomous' attitude in which binding power rests with 'authority', and an 'autonomous' attitude which involves mutual consent.

2. Piaget believes that 'moral realism' is characteristic of childhood up to the age of about nine years. The aspect of moral realism which has attracted most attention is the notion of 'objective responsibility' versus 'subjective responsibility' or intention. If an offence is judged in terms of 'objective responsibility', the seriousness of the offence is estimated in terms of the seriousness of the consequences rather than in terms of the intentions of the actor. Piaget claims that 'the notion of objective responsibility diminishes as the child grows older' (op. cit., p. 120), although he admits that some children of only six years of age do in fact judge in terms of intention rather than in terms of consequences. Piaget seems to think that adult constraint contributes to an attitude of 'objective responsibility' because at least some adults apply their sanctions so as to suggest that it is the damage done rather than the intention which matters. But he is also careful to point out that 'those parents who try to give their children a moral education based on intention, achieve very early results, as is shown by current observation' (op. cit., p. 130). Thus, according to Piaget, in at least one way parents may have a real positive influence. Piaget has not always been allowed credit for this kind of observation.

Piaget believes that his studies of moral realism suggest an advance from judgment in terms of consequences to judgment in terms of intention. He suggests that moral realism results from the nature of the child's mental development, *together with* the way in which children are treated by adults. Moral realism is thus associated with unilateral respect or heteronomy, and is also associated, in Piaget's view, with *intellectual* realism as shown in the child's tendency to draw things as he *knows* they are rather than as he sees them.

3.   Piaget's third concern is with *justice*. Here, he is mainly concerned with punishment. One may regard punishment in a *retributive* way, as the dire and proper consequences of wrong-doing; or one may regard punishment as a question of reciprocity—of seeing that the transgressor puts right, or atones *appropriately* for, any wrong he commits, or at least is held responsible for the consequences of his misdeeds. Piaget himself found that the proportion of 'expiatory' punishments recommended by children decreased from six to ten years of age. Piaget may be criticised here for not being more definite in what he meant by 'reciprocity'. This seems to cover a whole range of punishments from 'an eye for an eye and a tooth for a tooth' to simply seeing that the offender appreciated the fact that he had broken the rules of mutual obligation.

Much has been made of Piaget's idea of 'immanent justice'. A belief in 'immanent justice' means that the believer feels that punishment for wrong-doing emanates from the world itself, and such a belief is, according to Piaget, widely held by younger children. Piaget believes that the belief 'originates in a transference to things of feelings acquired under the influence of adult constraint' (p. 260). Thus adult constraint is again the villain of the piece. Belief in immanent justice disappears as the child realises the relativity of adult justice, and acquires an attitude of cooperation rather than one of subservience.

Piaget does not find the *same* developmental stages in these three areas, but the major point he wishes to make is that there is progression from a 'heteronomous' to an 'autonomous' basis for moral judgment. Whereas Freud's theory emphasises —indeed overemphasises—the importance of the child's subservient relation to his parents, Piaget's theory emphasises the importance of the child's interaction with his peers, although, as we have indicated, he allows that the attitude adopted by the parents may be important. In general, however, Piaget does seem to underestimate the positive influence of parental precept and example in the development of moral judgments and attitudes. At the least, it would appear reasonable to suppose that discipline imposed from without by parents and other adults may provide the basis in control of behaviour, for the adult self-discipline and 'autonomy' upon which Piaget lays such stress. Piaget himself writes, 'Adult authority, although perhaps it constitutes a necessary moment in the moral evolution of the child, is not sufficient to create a sense of justice' (p. 319). In any event, adult authority may contribute substantially to aspects of morality other than justice. Justice is not the *only* thing that matters.

Studies deriving from Piaget's work

Piaget's claim that, with increasing age and social interaction with peers, the basis of judgment shifts from a consideration of *consequences* to a consideration of *intentions* has received a good deal of support (see Graham 1972). Kugelmass and Breznitz (1968) suggest that intentionality increases slowly from the age of eleven years to the age of fourteen years, quite quickly from fourteen to seventeen years and then again less rapidly. Kugelmass and Breznitz very reasonably suggest that the cognitive ability to abstract principles is here crucial. Turner (1966), as reported by Lunzer and Morris (1968), claims that in Piaget's story about the two children, one of whom broke many cups with good intentions while the other broke only one cup but that deliberately, we have in the first case good intentions coupled with disastrous results, and in the second case bad intentions coupled with less catastrophic results. Turner holds that there must be an intermediate stage in development, in which the subject would say that the first child was *really* good and the second *really* bad, but would be unable to *retain* this judgment and would say that the 'good' child was *worse* than the 'bad' child because of the consequences when both children were judged together. The implication of the relevance of *cognitive ability* cannot be denied. A developed intelligence is necessary for the development of effective moral principles.

There has also been support for Piaget's ideas on immanent justice (see Graham 1972), although it seems that cultural relativity may be important here.

As a matter of fact, more recent research relevant to Piaget's moral theory has mostly been concerned with 'intentionality'. Schleifer and Douglas (1973) used Piaget's 'intentionality' stories to study the effect of training. They wished to see whether the effect of training would last over time and generalise to rather different material. In their first experiment, they selected a population of six-year-old children who did not spontaneously make 'intentional' judgments on Piaget's stories. As they observed, all the pairs of Piaget stories contrasted good intentions plus a large amount of damage with bad intentions plus a small amount of damage. For their follow-up test, Schleifer and Douglas modified several pairs of stories so as to *match* bad intentions and extent of consequences. Training consisted of correcting 'low-level' ('consequences') responses and explaining why they were wrong, and also of discussing the general principles involved in *intentions*. In one group of subjects, an adult explained and discussed, while in a second group, a child of the same age as the subjects did so. Nearly all the subjects showed the effect of training in making more judgments in terms of intentionality. This advance was maintained after four weeks. One would have liked some evidence that similar, more extended training would have had effects persisting over a longer period.

In their second experiment, with children of five and a half and three and a half years of age, Schleifer and Douglas used films as visual equivalents of Piaget's stories. At these ages, both controls and trained children showed an increase in intentionality, although the trained children showed more advance.

Schleifer and Douglas incline on the whole to agree with Turiel (1969) that the effect of training is to advance the child's cognitive level rather than to bring about specific learning effects. With Turiel, they think that the operative factor is probably the presentation of alternative points of view which stimulate thinking about the issues involved. Similarly, Jensen and Larm (1970) found trained subjects superior in *explaining* their choices, and think that this indicates that they really understood the concept. They also found training by discussion superior to simple reinforcement.

Jensen and Hafen (1973) take up Piaget's suggestion that the change from immature to mature judgment (between three and nine years of age) results mainly from social interaction with peers. Young children were read pairs of stories describing an act which caused damage. They were asked to say which was the worse of the two acts. Two groups were involved. In the first group, children were rewarded when they chose the action where damage was intended. In the second group, children took part in a discussion of their choices. *Both* types of training increased the likelihood that children would take account of intentions in their judgments. Such experiments, however, while illustrating that different procedures may both have a reinforcing (short-term) effect, is scarcely relevant to the wider, long-term implications of Piaget's thinking.

Costanzo, Coie, Grumet and Farnill (1973) remark that Piaget seems to imply that children in the 'preoperational' stage do not use intention as a basis of judgment. They remark that since Piaget's stories 'covary two parameters at once, it is impossible to decide whether these children make their choice on the basis of the consequences because intentionality is considered irrelevant to the choice or whether outcome is seen as simply the more salient and identifiable cue for their moral discriminations' (p. 155). This is a good point. Costanzo *et al.* ask the question, 'How far do emergence from moral realism and the ability to take the social perspective of another reflect the same underlying cognitive processes?' This would appear indeed to be a crucial question. Costanzo *et al.* found that older children attributed more importance to intentions in respect of *harmful* consequences, but that there was little age difference in respect of *beneficial* consequences. They suggest that the *child himself* (the 'perpetrator') may well be evaluated by young children according to consequences with little attention to intentions.

In a very relevant article, Chandler, Greenspan and Barenboim (1973) argue that previous studies have suggested that children concentrate on consequences up to the age of about nine years. These authors argue that, in such studies, verbal presentations have made consequences *more salient* than intentions. In their own experiment, the authors used children of approximately six years of age. They presented their children with issues similar to those used by Piaget, and found that their children often *did* take account of intentions, *especially* when the dilemmas were presented over video-tape.

Glassco, Milgram and Younis (1970) remark that when specific change in judgment occurs, it may be that only superficial or verbal levels are affected. As they very justly say, when training fails, it may be because the training was not the right kind of training. They seem to imply that to demonstrate the effectiveness of training contradicts the stage-developmental position. This is not necessarily so. Stage-developmental theory claims that development follows a certain sequence of stages—*not* that it cannot be advanced or retarded by, or is independent of, environmental events (reinforcements).

King (1971) studied the ability of children to distinguish intentional action from accident, and the ability to identify unconscious intentions in the behaviour of other people. Subjects were children of four and a half, six and a half and nine years of age. The oldest group was significantly superior to the two younger groups in respect of unconscious intentions. Here, the two younger groups showed no significant difference. However, one may perhaps have some doubts concerning the assessment of 'unconscious intention', however reasonable the results may appear. More obviously, the ability to discriminate between intention and accident increased with age, as we should expect.

Armsby (1971) claims that the stories used by Piaget do not adequately discriminate between the intentional and the accidental. Consequently, he used stories in which an *intentional* act was clearly contrasted with an *accidental* act. Armsby found, with children of from six to eight years of age, that there was an age progression in the proportion of judgments in terms of intentions. He noted that these children quite frequently responded to his stories in terms of intentions. (His stories were given on paper rather than verbally, so as to minimise the possible effect of memory.) Armsby also found that his children *did* consider the amount of damage resulting from an accident to be important.

Gutkin (1972), again, points out that in Piaget's stories good intentions *plus* much damage are contrasted with bad intentions *plus* little damage. In his studies, Gutkin varied both intention and damage. A scalogram analysis of his results suggested that the development of appreciation of intentions goes through four successive stages: (i) attention is paid *only* to the amount of damage; (ii) the amount of damage is still important primarily, but *some* consideration is given to intention; (iii) intentions become of primary importance, but some account is still taken of the amount of damage done; (iv) intentions become the sole criterion. It may be suspected that even in persons for whom intentions are *normally* the only criterion of judgment, in extreme cases the extent of damage may also be significant.

In general, research on the development of 'reciprocity' concepts versus 'expiatory' concepts supports Piaget, despite apparently contradictory findings by Durkin (1959a, b, c). As children get older, there would appear in general to be more feeling against fighting (unless under closely controlled conditions), and against physical retaliation. Piaget's view of this would be that fighting and retaliation constitute an unstable form of equilibrium and should tend to give way to a more *mutual* way of settling disputes: 'What is regarded as just is no longer merely reciprocal action, but primarily *behaviour that admits of indefinitely sustained reciprocity*' (op. cit., 323). It thus appears that what Piaget means by 'reciprocity' is not simply a matter of an eye for an eye. In fact, Piaget's use of the terms 'equality', 'equity' and 'reciprocity' is by no means clear. It is interesting that Aronfreed (1968) believes that children whose parents use 'induction' methods of discipline have more strongly internalised consciences than those whose parents use 'sensitisation' techniques. Sensitisation techniques sensitise the child to the consequences of his actions for himself (e.g. punishment for wrong-doing). Induction techniques sensitise the child to the consequences of his actions *for others*, and involve the use of reasoning and appeal to principles. Similarly, Hoffman (1963) found the use of *reasoning* to be particularly associated with the development of internal standards.

In an interesting study by Stuart (1967), an attempt was made to investigate the relation of 'decentration' to moral judgment. For Piaget, centration involves a concentration on some one striking aspect of the object or question, to the relative neglect of other features; decentration reflects the ability to take account of different aspects or points of view. If a child centres on the *height* of water in two beakers of different diameter, he will not be able to see that there may be the same amount of water in both beakers. In decentring, he is able to take account of both height and width. Stuart in fact used graphic representations of figures from different points of view in his assessment of centration. His subjects were children of from seven to nine and from eleven to thirteen years of age. Stuart did find decentration related to moral judgment (though also to age and intelligence). This is a highly interesting and provocative finding.

Rubin and Schneider (1973) likewise take up Piaget's point that the young child cannot decentre and that this leads to the egocentric thought and immature moral judgment of the preoperational child. The child is unable to take the point of view of the other, and centres entirely on his own view. It should then follow that the child who cannot decentre must fail to consider the interpersonal and reciprocal aspects of moral relationships. Rubin and Schneider hypothesise that there is a positive relationship between the capacity for decentring and the amount of altruistic behaviour to be expected from the young child. More specifically, Rubin and Schneider hypothesise that there should be a positive relationship between communication skills (absence of egocentrism) and moral judgment and altruistic behaviour (in seven-year-old children). Moral judgment was assessed by Lee's (1971) modification of the Kohlberg scale. 'Giving behaviour' was significantly correlated with lack of egocentrism and with level of moral judgment. Helping younger children was also significantly related to lack of egocentrism and to level of moral judgment. The authors concluded that there was support for a relationship between decentring (communication skills) and moral judgment and altruism.

A different kind of study by Koenig, Sulzer, Newland and Sturgeon (1973) predicted that lower-class schoolchildren should be cognitively less complex and hence show less advanced moral judgment than middle-class children. In their study they used the Barron-Welsh Figure Preference Test and the Sulzer-Koenig Moral Judgment Test. The median score for cognitive complexity was 4·7 for middle-class subjects and 2·4 for lower-class subjects. It was found that social class was related to *both* cognitive complexity and moral judgment ($P < 0.01$). Complexity and moral judgment were also found to be associated.

Criticisms of Piaget by learning theorists

One of the most pointed criticisms of Piaget has come from the 'social learning' school. Bandura and McDonald (1963) seemed to show that judging in terms of 'intentionality' could be reversed by social learning, and that its emergence in the first instance was probably also due to learning from adult example. Kohlberg (1969) claims that the findings of Bandura and McDonald represent only a super-ficial and temporary phenomenon, and further claims that the effects of learning 'downward' (according to his scheme of stages) is less stable over time than learning 'upward'.

Cowan, Langer, Heavenrich and Nathanson (1969) replicated the experiment of Bandura and McDonald. They concluded that 'neither the present study nor that of Bandura and McDonald could be used directly to affirm or deny Piaget's hypothesis. Most of the present results serve as a basis for more differentiated statements concerning the model's effects, but some of the findings raise questions which cannot yet be answered within the social learning approach' (p. 261). Bandura (1969), in a reply to this article, has said of the 1963 study by Bandura and McDonald, that 'objective and subjective judgments exist together at all age levels rather than forming successive stages that partially overlap' (p. 276). Bandura contends that findings 'consistently demonstrate that moral judgments are more variable within and between individuals, and more modifiable than Piaget's theory would lead one to expect. Furthermore, modelling influences, which receive no mention in Piaget's account of the conditions regulating judgmental behaviour, though they are obviously operative in everyday interactions, emerge as significant determinants' (p. 279). It seems to us that relatively compelling examples of behaviour must constitute part of the social or moral reality of which the child has to make some kind of sense, and that there is good ground for a future accommodation between cognitive-developmental theory and social learning theory. Both are right, both are limited.

The contribution of Kohlberg

Kohlberg (1963) bases his work on that of Piaget, but has extended Piaget's notions in several ways. Kohlberg proposes three *levels* of development: the premoral level, the conventional level and the level of accepted principles. Each level is divided into two stages, so that Kohlberg propounds six stages of development as follows:

Level I   Premoral. At this level, the child is responsive to cultural rules and some evaluative labels, but regards them from the point of view of the pleasant or unpleasant consequences which action may entail, or from the point of view of the physical power to impose their demands, of those who impose the rules.

Stage 1. At Stage 1, the child's orientation is in terms of obedience and punishment. He feels deferential to those in power, and is concerned to avoid trouble. At this stage, he regards responsibility *objectively*, that is in terms of consequences.

Stage 2. Kohlberg refers to this stage as the stage of 'naively egoistic orientation'. What is right is what satisfies one's own needs (and perhaps sometimes the needs of others). The subject is aware that 'values' are here relative to the needs of the particular actor concerned. At this stage, there is *some* concern with exchange and reciprocity.

Level II   Conventional level. The child is here concerned with actively maintaining the expectations of his family and peers, and with justifying their expectations.

Stage 3. Kohlberg calls this the stage of the 'good boy orientation'. The child is concerned with gaining approval and with pleasing and helping others to that end. He seeks to conform to stereotyped images of what role-behaviour and intentions should be.

Stage 4. At this stage, the child is concerned to maintain the existing social authority and order. He is concerned with 'doing his duty' and with showing respect for authority. He respects expectations of others which they have properly earned.

Level III   Principled level. This is the level of principles which the individual himself accepts. The child is concerned with the definition of values and principles without direct regard to any supporting authority.

Stage 5. This stage is referred to as the stage of contractual, legalistic obligations. Duty is defined in terms of contract, avoidance of violation of the rights of others and majority will and welfare.

Stage 6. This is the stage of conscience or principles properly speaking. One's orientation is not to the actual rules and laws of society, but to self-accepted principles which involve appeal to logical universality and consistency.

Assessment of moral level is based on answers to questions relating to a series of nine moral dilemmas, verbally presented.

Studies deriving from Kohlberg's position

Kohlberg reports a distinct pattern of usage of his stages with increasing age in America, although Stage 6 responses remain rare. He also claims that studies in a variety of cultures justify his six stages (Kohlberg 1966). We should expect a fair degree of internal consistency and consistency over time in Kohlberg's measures, and he does indeed claim that (*a*) on average, most judgments fit a single stage, (*b*) there are fair intercorrelations between stories and (*c*) there is a fair amount of consistency over time. In our own studies, we found rather less tendency for judgments to fall in one stage, and for judgments to be spread over a wider range of stages, although it must be admitted that this may conceivably have been because of uncertainties of scoring. McGeorge (1974), however, found significant variation across Kohlberg's situations, and suggests that *two* factors underlie responses, 'an empathic or role-taking factor and one involving concepts of social rules and structures' (p. 116).

Turiel (1969) produces evidence that children are more responsive to efforts to influence them toward the stage *above* that at which they locate most of their judgments. He claims that his children did actually learn to apply a more mature form of moral reasoning rather than simply learning to apply particular answers to particular problems. Very similar findings were reported by Rest, Turiel and Kohlberg (1969), who also indicated that their children *preferred* reasoning at one stage above their own. Rest, Turiel and Kohlberg use Piaget's concept of 'décalage' to refer to the probability that in the course of their development, children *prefer* reasoning at a higher stage of judgment before they *understand* it, understand it before they fully *assimilate* it, and assimilate it before they *use* it. Moreover, as Turiel (1969) remarks, 'a child can conceptualise some issues at a higher level than others' (p. 115). This would be relevant to our own finding that children's judgments were spread over a wider range of stages than Kohlberg originally suggested. McGeorge (1974) remarks that 'presumably stage mixture in response to a single situation is occasioned by the presence of different aspects of morality within that situation' (p. 118). This again would be supported by our own findings. One would also expect, of course, that different children might conceptualise different issues at higher levels. It would indeed be rather surprising if this were not so.

Turiel and Rothman (1972) hold that moral reasoning and action are interrelated, and that, for example, subjects at Stages 5 and 6 are less likely to cheat than subjects at Stages 3 and 4, and subjects at Stages 3 and 4 less likely to cheat than subjects at Stages 1 and 2. Turiel and Rothman conducted an experiment in which subjects were exposed to reasoning at one stage above or one stage below their typical level. Subjects were initially at Stage 2, Stage 3 or Stage 4. The issue involved was whether or not to go on in an experiment in which the subjects were depriving a stooge of tokens. Turiel and Rothman report that 'Stage 2 or Stage 3 subjects persisted in this choice (continuing), regardless of the level of reasoning used to support either of the alternatives. Stage 4 subjects, however, chose to stop only when the reasoning supporting this choice was at the stage above' (op. cit., p. 748).

Turiel and Rothman further comment that 'although most subjects in this study showed preference for reasoning at the stage above, nevertheless they showed little transformation in their own stage of development' (p. 750). This finding would seem to provide some measure of support for the developmental stage view. In this study, it was also found that subjects at Stage 4 decided in favour of 'stopping' when this was supported by Stage 5 reasoning. Turiel and Rothman suggest that Stage 3 subjects tended to keep behaviour and reasoning separate, while Stage 4 subjects tended to integrate them.

Grim, Kohlberg and White (1968) draw attention to 'ego-strength' factors in moral control. It is scarcely surprising that 'ego-strength' factors ('will-power') should be important. Indeed, it might well be argued that psychology has been seriously at fault in not paying more attention to such matters. After all, things like 'will-power' have long been recognised among the general public, and they should not simply be ignored without good reason. Grim, Kohlberg and White, in a factor analysis of results, found three factors: (i) a factor involving task conformity, with loadings on psychomotor measures and teachers' ratings of stable conformity to authoritative social expectations; (ii) a factor involving inner stability and related to cheating/not cheating; and (iii) a factor interpreted as 'restlessness'. Grim, Kohlberg and White note that observed moderate to high correlations between morality measures and attention measures suggest the importance of 'ego-control' factors. They pronounce the further rather obvious observation that moral behaviour is not entirely a product of conscience. These authors stress the importance of a 'slowly developing cognitive-voluntary ability of sustained attention' (p. 250).

They also express the view that fully internalised moral values prohibiting cheating are a late development. This kind of interpretation, they hold, is consistent with the 'voluntaristic' view of William James, who wrote that 'the essential achievement of will is to *attend* to a difficult object and hold it fast before the mind' (James, quoted in Grim, Kohlberg and White 1968, p. 251). The present writer is happy to see some signs of a return to a psychology where 'voluntarism' may be regarded with respect.

We have seen that Piaget stressed the importance of peer groups rather than adults for true moral development. Likewise, Kohlberg (1971) suggests that opportunities for varied role-playing ought to encourage moral development. Selman (1971) used sixty middle-class children of from eight to ten years of age. Controlling for intelligence, he gave them two role-taking tasks and Kohlberg's moral judgment measure. He found role-taking skill positively related to *conventional* moral judgment (Stages 3 and 4). After a year, a re-test of ten subjects who had been low in role-taking and in moral judgment suggested that 'the development of the ability to understand the reciprocal nature of interpersonal relations is a necessary but not a sufficient condition for the development of conventional moral thought' (Selman 1971, p. 79)—as indeed one would have thought. It may perhaps be legitimate to remark that adequate tests of role-taking are difficult to devise, and that those used in Selman's study may not have been wholly adequate. The possible function of role-taking in moral development is one which deserves much more attention.

From a rather different point of view, Fishkin, Keniston and MacKinnon (1973) have investigated moral reasoning and political ideology. During May 1970, seventy-five undergraduates (a rather small number) in eight universities were given the Kohlberg material and also measures of political ideology. These authors found that subjects whose moral reasoning was at Stage 3 or Stage 4 (conventional level) tended to be politically conservative; preconventional subjects (Stages 1 and 2) tended to favour violent radicalism. There appeared in fact to be an exceptionally high relationship between Stage 4 reasoning (law and order) and conservatism, which would, indeed, in Kohlberg's terms, seem to be in accordance with expectation. Fishkin, Keniston and MacKinnon further found that *postconventional* reasoning appeared to be associated with *rejection* of conservative views, without, however, being associated with the ideology of violent radicalism. The implication would appear to be that the postconventional subjects favoured a more individualistic view. It would indeed be interesting to see if the findings of these authors were confirmed by a similar (and preferably extended) study in Britain and possibly also elsewhere.

Fontana and Noel (1973) studied moral reasoning among students, teachers and administrators in the university. They found that administrators more frequently used Stage 4 reasoning ('law and order') than either students or teachers. Those with political leanings to the Right used more Stage 4 reasoning than those who leaned to the Left, while Leftists appeared to show more Stage 2 ('egoistic') reasoning. Teachers tended more frequently to use reasoning at Stages 5 and 6. These results, although none of them are spectacular, lend some support to

Kohlberg's position. Once again, it would be interesting to see whether similar results were found in different cultures.

Again, Kohlberg (1963, 1969) reports that in American society, middle-class children go through his stages faster than working-class children. We ourselves in England confirmed the superiority of middle-class children on Kohlberg's material, although the difference between the classes was rather small when verbal intelligence was controlled for. It would appear likely that such social class differences as cannot be accounted for in terms of differences in (especially) verbal intelligence are due to differences in the 'social perspective' of the two classes arising from their different roles in the occupational structure, and also perhaps to the greater use of verbal and 'induction' techniques of discipline by the middle-class parents.

Criticisms of Kohlberg's position

In his chapter 'From is to ought', Kohlberg (1971) claims that his stages of development represent a *logically* necessary progression, and that they therefore transcend relativity and break through the myth of 'ethical neutrality'. Kohlberg claims that each of his stages of moral thinking represents a more 'integrated' and also a more 'differentiated' way of thinking, that such is the progress of all thinking, including scientific thinking, and that each successive stage is justified in that thinking at that stage is able to handle and resolve moral problems more complex than can be dealt with in terms of any lower stages of thinking. It is not entirely clear in what sense Kohlberg's stages logically follow on from one another (Peters 1971). But even if they did, we should be inclined to agree with Alston (1971) when he says, 'the mere fact that one concept logically depends on another has no tendency to show that moral thinking involving the former is superior to moral thinking involving the latter' (p. 275). We think, in other words, that despite the undoubted interest of Kohlberg's work and the future possibilities of work based thereon, given his definition of what is moral, he has not succeeded in showing that his 'moral stages' have any *absolute* application. It may turn out to be an empirical fact that Kohlberg's stages recur in all societies. But that does not *ipso facto* mean that they reflect the *only* possible concept of morality, nor dispose of 'the myth of ethical neutrality'. We feel inclined to question how far we are entitled to assume that Kohlberg's six stages do indeed represent successive approximations to moral perfection—as such stages of moral development should. The mere fact that there is so much controversy among moral philosophers as to what is 'moral' should warn us to be extremely careful in our assumptions. The present writer, in fact, has a lot of sympathy with those who attempt to distinguish in principle between 'is' and 'ought', and with those who argue that ethical neutrality is not entirely a myth.

Ian M. L. Hunter

9. Memory: theory and application

Memory as problem-solving

In this chapter I shall present a developmental, problem-solving view of memory. Such a view, which I have taken before (Hunter 1964), has relevance for educational psychology, and in recent years has inspired fruitful work in the Soviet Union and in America (see the excellent review article by Meacham 1972). It is also the view adopted by Piaget, whose genius this book celebrates.

We may begin with a meticulous series of studies by Butterfield, Wambold and Belmont (1973), who presented children and adults with the following probe-type, short-term memory task. The subject (S) faces an upright screen containing a horizontal row of small windows. In the first window, at the extreme left, a letter of the alphabet appears for 0·5 sec., then vanishes. A second letter then appears for 0·5 sec. in the next window along. Then a third letter in the third window, and so on until a succession of six letters has been shown. Then in the seventh window, on the extreme right, one of the letters appears again: this is the probe letter and S has now to press the window where that letter appeared earlier. When each letter appears it remains exposed for an automatic 0·5 sec., but the onset of each letter is controlled by S himself, who pushes a button at the base of the panel. Thus the task is self-paced.

A trial starts with the appearance of a black square in the left-most window. To see the first letter, S presses the button which causes the black square to be replaced by the first letter for 0·5 sec. S must then press the button again to see the second letter in the second window; then again to see the third letter; and so on. An automatic record is kept of the pace of working, e.g. the time between the disappearance of each letter and the next push-to-see, and between the appearance of the probe letter and S's pressing one of the windows. S attempts several such trials with different letter sequences and with the 'correct' letter located in different windows.

In this task, adults who are moderately mentally retarded do markedly worse than normal adults; for example, when the correct response is to press the left-most window, the average success rate is about 25 as contrasted with 85 per cent. To say that the retarded have poorer memories than normal is true but less informative than to notice that they deal differently with the task. A normal adult's performance reveals, on analysis, an eight-step sequence. He exposes the first three letters in rapid succession; pauses and rehearses that first triplet of letters; exposes the last three letters in rapid succession; without pause, exposes the probe letter; seeks the former location of the probe letter by searching the second triplet which is still echoing in mind; if he finds the location there, he at once presses the corresponding window; if he does not find it, he now thinks back to the first, rehearsed triplet; if he finds the location there, he presses the corresponding window.

So during the acquisition phase, the normal adult groups the exposures, deliberately rehearses some items and does not rehearse other items. During the retrieval phase, he searches the most recently seen triplet before searching the least recently seen. Throughout, he discriminatingly selects his activities so as to be appropriate to the task. By sharp contrast, the retarded adult moves through the task at a relatively uniform rate and searches for the location of the probe letter in a relatively haphazard way. His performance is indiscriminate, unadapted to the task. But why? Further experiments show that he is capable of carrying through all the necessary component activities and, if taught how and when to apply these, he performs as well as a normal adult.

In one teaching study there were eight moderately retarded people aged thirteen to twenty-one years. The first session was a pre-test on the memory task and the success level could be indicated by saying that, when the correct window was one of the first three, Ss were correct on 28 per cent of trials; when the correct window was one of the last three, Ss were correct on 53 per cent of trials. The second session, a week later, was devoted to teaching the eight-step sequence which normal adults used spontaneously. On a post-test at the end of this session, success rates were now 72 and 81 per cent. The third session, one week later, started with a retest on which success rates were 51 and 75 per cent—a drop from the week before, but still better than the pre-test. There was then further teaching followed by a final test in which success rates were 80 and 87 per cent. In these final tests, the retarded Ss were doing slightly better than normal adolescents and only slightly worse than normals who had been explicitly coached on the eight-step sequence.

On this memory task, then, retarded subjects do as well as normals, after they have been taught in detail how to proceed (if any of the eight steps are omitted from training, success rate is poorer). So the retarded command all the necessary component activities but fail spontaneously to deploy them appropriately. What happens if Ss are now given an altered memory task, e.g. with nine letters exposed rather than six, or with an enforced delay before the probe letter can be seen? Normal people adjust fairly quickly, and almost unawares, but retarded people do not show this adaptive flexibility. Again, they betray their weakness in diagnosing the task's requirements and selecting the appropriate activities. The investigators conclude that with regard to memory training in the retarded 'the appropriate level of analysis for future research is the level of selecting, sequencing, and co-ordinating processes that are in the cognitive repertoire. Trying to train executive function instead of the particular skills for whose success it must ultimately be responsible may save much effort and yield more general theory in the bargain' (p. 668).

Three propositions

The above experimental findings illustrate three propositions basic to the study and management of memory:

1.   Memory is a problem-solving activity which involves, during both acquisition and retrieval, an intricate selection and coordination of many different activities.

2.   Problem-solving is hierarchically organised. Consider how a computer program is designed. A master program is devised to achieve some overall objective by calling in successively appropriate subroutines which, in turn, may achieve their subgoals by calling in various sub-subroutines. The total operation is, at the least, two-tiered with a lower-tier repertoire of subroutines being deployed by an upper-tiered program. Notice that the relevant subroutines need not have been devised originally with the present program in mind. They may have been devised at times, and in contexts, and for purposes that were greatly varied. But irrespective of their origins, if they can be detached from their original contexts, they may now be imported as subroutines for a new program. This new program may, indeed, be devisable only because the subroutines already exist and, in its turn, this program may be used as a subroutine in a newer and more ambitious program.

Since computer programs are merely externalised and unusually explicit instances of human problem-solving procedures, it is not perhaps surprising that all problem-solving activity exhibits hierarchical organisation and is, at the least, two-tiered (see Miller, Galanter and Pribram 1966). For example, in the probe-type memory problem, there are subroutines (rehearsing, identifying letters) and a program, or plan of action, that selects and sequences these subroutines; and both tiers of activity are essential. Likewise, the biographical development of competence throughout the lifespan is hierarchical. There is, for example, a characteristic lag between the attainment of lower-tier and upper-tier activities. Long after a person has acquired component activities necessary for some task, he may lack upper-tier activities needed to diagnose task requirements and devise a plan of action that can be carried through by calling on his existing repertoire of components. This developmental lag, sometimes called 'production deficiency', is widespread at all stages of psychological development and is well exemplified in the probe-type memory task.

3.   In any memory problem, the necessary and sufficient condition for success is the carrying through of task-appropriate activities. If the activities are task-appropriate, success is assured irrespective of whether these activities arise intentionally or accidentally or by some external inducement, such as the way the material is presented, or instructions about how to proceed (see Meacham 1972). For example, our intention with regard to a memory task is important, but it has its effects only by inducing us to act in ways we think may be appropriate.

By itself it is not sufficient, for if it leads to inappropriate activities we do not succeed; nor is it necessary, for otherwise we would remember only those things we had deliberately set ourselves to memorise. To illustrate, Bower (1972) gave university students twenty pairs of object names to memorise at five seconds per pair. One group of students was told to learn by saying each word pair repeatedly throughout the five-second exposure: the average correct recall score was 35 per cent. A second group was instructed to learn by imagining the objects themselves as related together in a vivid scene: their average recall score was higher at 71 per cent. A third group was told *not to learn* the pairs, but merely to imagine the object-pair scenes: their average recall score showed a statistically significant rise to 77 per cent. In the second group, the intention to memorise was presumably getting in the way of task-appropriate activities.

That intention is not necessary for memorising is demonstrated by the fact that children, in the first few years of life, have yet to develop any appreciation of what it means deliberately to memorise something for their future use. Yet young children do commit things to memory by their involuntarily task-appropriate activities. The point is illustrated by Appel *et al.* (1972) who, in a carefully designed investigation, worked with children aged four, seven and eleven years. Each child examined a display of picture cards under two different task conditions that were fully and credibly explained to him. In one, his task was to memorise the pictures for later recall. In the other, his task was to look carefully at the pictures. The child then studied the pictures while, unknown to him, his observable study behaviours were watched and recorded on a time-sample check list. After each study period, recall was asked for.

The eleven-year-olds recalled more after studying for 'memory' than for 'look'; their observed study behaviours were different between the two tasks; and in the 'memory' task, these behaviours were mostly task-appropriate. In sharp contrast, the four-year-olds recalled the same amount after study for 'memory' and for 'look', and their observed study behaviours were identical in the two tasks. In no way did they deal differently with the two tasks (so much for exhorting four-year-olds to memorise things!). The seven-year-olds did not recall significantly more after studying for 'memory' than for 'look', but their study behaviours were different in the two tasks. However, in the 'memory' task, these behaviours were mostly not task-appropriate. These children appreciated that memorising called for 'something special' and they tried to do what they thought might work; but they were not yet able effectively to diagnose requirements and select appropriate activities.

In the light of these three propositions, we can attempt to answer the nicely worded question to which a valuable symposium was devoted in 1971 (Flavell *et al.* 1971): What is memory development the development of? The biographical development of memory comprises the two-tiered development of (*a*) repertoires of activities that can be deployed as constituents by (*b*) repertoires of strategic activities that are appropriate to the memory problems in hand.

Levels of intellectual development

Taking the view that memory is intelligent activity which is special only in that it is applied to the reconstruction of past experiences, we would expect a person's memory to mesh closely with his knowledge-handling activities at large. There are individuals who violate, or appear to violate, this close relation between 'memory' and 'intelligence' since, for one reason or another, they dedicate most of their knowledge-handling resources to the goal of memory: see the cases of Shereshevskii (Luria 1969) and of 'VP' (Hunt and Love 1972). Furthermore, there are always occupational and cultural pressures that may induce people to develop specialised skills. But granted these apparent exceptions, the relation between 'memory' and 'intelligence' is close. Working with children aged three to thirteen years, Piaget and Inhelder (1973) studied how memory activities reflect the level of intellectual development. This work, as Inhelder (1969, p. 362) has pointed out, was 'in the tradition of the great Bartlett (1932)'. This work and its findings are perhaps best introduced by a parable.

'2, 3, 5, 7, 11, 13, 17, 19, 23.' This material is studied and later reproduced by four people at different developmental levels. The first person is a non-reader who can treat the material only as a display of shapes. The second can read numbers but cannot yet order them by numerical size. The third can read and order numbers but knows nothing about prime numbers. The fourth can read, and order, and knows about primes. Throughout the memory task, these four perform in ways that reflect their different available resources. Some months later, the third person is again asked to remember the material, which he has not seen in the interval. But in the interval, he has learned about prime numbers. His delayed recall benefits from this recently acquired knowledge because, in reproducing the material, he now realises that the original was a list of the first nine prime numbers. Because of his shifted level of development, his delayed recall is better than his recall immediately after studying the material.

This parable gives the flavour of the investigations by Piaget and Inhelder, for they presented materials embodying features, such as serial relationships, principles of classification, and causal relationships, which the children would or would not appreciate according to their developmental level. The children's memory performances were found to reflect their grasp of these features. To illustrate, consider the quickly-describable task of remembering horizontal levels (Piaget and Inhelder 1973, chapter 16; Furth *et al.* 1974).

The child inspects a drawing depicting a tilted, clear-glass bottle which is half filled with liquid. The drawing is removed and the child, by sketching and otherwise, reproduces what he remembers. Six- and ten-year-olds typically bring different resources to this task. In particular, most six-year-olds do not yet appreciate that liquid maintains a horizontal level irrespective of the container's orientation. And indeed, most six-year-olds, as contrasted with ten-year-olds, do not correctly recall the liquid level as being horizontal. After a lapse of six months, the six-year-olds are asked for a further reproduction of the drawing, which they have not seen again. Some of the children now remember the liquid as being horizontal.

What is happening here? When the six-year-old first inspects and reproduces the drawing, his activities do not involve an appreciation of horizontal levels. But six months later, he has probably begun to appreciate this property. So, if he vaguely remembers a tilted bottle containing liquid, he may 'improve' his remembering. It should be stressed that this 'improvement' concerns altered recall

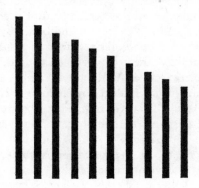

FIGURE 1a   *Ten rods in serial order of length.*

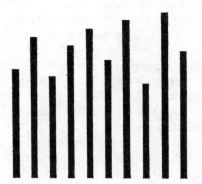

FIGURE 1b   *The ten rods in a non-serial configuration.*

due to applying some recently developed understanding: the 'improvement' may, or may not, be a more accurate reproduction of the original. This point is demonstrated by Altemeyer *et al.* (1969), working with children aged five to six years.

Ten rods of different lengths were glued to a sheet of paper to form a simple serial configuration (Figure 1a). On recall, one week later, only nineteen of the sixty-five children reproduced a serially-ordered display. This was consistent with the finding that most children of this age do not appreciate serial ordering. In delayed recall, six months later, thirty-two of the children reproduced a serially-ordered display. A more refined classification of the reproductions showed that twenty-eight of the sixty-five (43 per cent) 'improved' their second reproduction by making it more serially ordered than their first. As a control, twenty-nine other children took a parallel task in which the presented display was non-serial (Figure 1b). Of these children, twelve (41 per cent) 'improved' their second reproduction to make it *more* serially ordered than their first and thus *less* like the original display.

These 'improvements' resemble the 'rationalisations' which Bartlett (1932) found in adult reconstructions of meaningful material. They also resemble the 'reminiscence' which Ballard (1913) found in twelve-year-olds: these children studied a poem or prose passage that was presented for too short a time to allow complete memorisation, and they recalled the material better after a lapse of two or three days than they did immediately after study. Incidentally, the fact that Piaget's 'improvement' effects are shown by only some of the children studied does not imply that these effects are artifacts of poor experimental design. The effects are genuine, but only demonstrable when the right memory task is taken by a child at the right level and rate of mental development.

These 'improvement' effects have few practical implications. But they dramatically underline the substantive conclusion that a child's memory performances reflect the level of intellectual development he has attained. This main conclusion is supported by commonplace observations. Older children do better than younger on most memory tasks. A person does better on memory tasks involving material about which he is especially knowledgeable. And it is a truism (which is none-the-less important for being a truism) that we most easily commit material to memory when we can most readily translate that material into something we already know.

Production deficiency

I shall concentrate on children's failures to apply categorising activities to memory problems in which they would be task appropriate. I shall not be concerned with how, why, or where the child has acquired his categorising activities; merely with the fact that he has acquired them but does not use them as a means of dealing with memory tasks. Let us begin by citing the work of Mandler (1970) to illustrate the point that categorising can assist memory.

Mandler has explored the following task as done by adults. *S* is handed a pack of one hundred cards on each of which is printed a different word. He is asked to sort these cards into anywhere from two to seven categories. He sorts the cards, deciding for himself the exact number and nature of the categories. Then the cards are shuffled and he does another sorting trial, and another, until his sorting is consistent on two consecutive trials. Thereupon he is asked to recall as many of the words as he can. Mandler finds a highly significant relation between the number of categories used and the number of words recalled. The rough rule is that the use of one more category leads to recalling four more words; for example, in one experiment, *S*s using three categories recalled thirty-eight words on average while

B

Ss using seven categories recalled fifty-two. Mandler has checked that these findings are not due to differences in the total time spent in sorting, nor total number of sorting trials, nor to self-selection on the part of Ss concerning the number of categories used. The findings still hold when Ss are told exactly how many categories to use, and whether or not Ss expect to be asked for recall.

With children and adults alike, categorising can usefully be applied to a great variety of memory tasks, both during acquisition and retrieval. Kobasigawa (1974) worked with children aged six, eight, and eleven years and was particularly interested in categorising at the time of retrieval. The materials were thirty-two cards with an object drawn on each. There were twenty-four small blue cards and eight larger white cards. The twenty-four objects depicted on the small blue cards could be grouped into eight categories with three objects per category:

ZOO	ROOM	PARK	BABY
monkey	table	seesaw	doll
PARK	BABY	ROOM	ZOO
slide	blocks	lamp	camel
BABY	ZOO	PARK	ROOM
ball	bear	swing	couch

FIGURE 2   *Verbal representation of the layout of experimental material in Kobasigawa's study*

these twenty-four pictures were used as 'recall items'. The eight larger white cards were used as 'cue cards'; each of those cards showed an object or scene depicting one of the eight categories to which 'recall items' could be related. For presentation, these cards were pasted on to two display sheets, one of which is represented in Figure 2. The lower-case words represent twelve of the 'recall items', the upper-case four of the 'cue cards', each of which appears three times. The second sheet displayed the remaining pictures in a similar arrangement.

The two display sheets were presented to each of 108 children in exactly the same way. First, a deck of cards containing all the 'recall items' was rapidly shown to ensure that each could be identified and named. Then the first display sheet was shown and S told that the task was to remember the 'small blue pictures'. S was taken through the pictures as follows: 'Do you see that these big pictures (cue cards) go with the small ones? In the ZOO you find. . . ? (E points to the first small picture and waits for S to name the monkey.) With the BABY you find. . . ?' And so on. The sheet was then replaced by the second display, which was treated likewise. Thereupon, both sheets were removed and S asked to recall the 'small blue pictures' under one of three recall conditions which differed in the extent to which they structured the child's retrieval activities.

In Free Recall, S was merely asked to remember as many of the small blue pictures as he could. In Recall With Cues Available, he was additionally shown a deck of the eight cue cards and told 'When you try to remember the small blue pictures, you can look at these cards if you think these cards help your remembering.' The deck was then placed face down in the child's hands. In Recall With Directed Use of Cues, S was shown the eight cue cards, one at a time, and told 'There were three small blue pictures that went with this. Can you remember these?' The question was repeated with each cue card.

The mean numbers of items correctly recalled are shown in Table 1 (to the nearest whole number). Clearly the recall procedure affected the amount recalled, and the younger children profited most from having their recall organised for them. They 'knew' the items, but did not apply the categorising activities that would bring them to mind. Strategic weakness was also evident in the youngest children's use of the cue cards. When these cards were available for optional use, most six-year-olds did not use them as aids to recall, and Ss who did look at a cue card

TABLE 1   *Mean numbers of items recalled in Kobasigawa's study*

	6 years	8 years	11 years
Free	11	13	15
Cues available	10	15	20
Directed use of cues	20	21	21

recalled only one item from that category before moving to the next cue card. Other experiments using picture cards are reported by Flavell (1970) and Appel et al. (1972) and show failures to apply task-appropriate categorising during acquisition. Herriot, Green and McConkey (1973) report attempts to help retarded people make better strategic use of categorising, and Moely and Jeffrey (1974) report similar attempts with normal children aged six to seven years.

In the Soviet Union, Smirnov (1973) has investigated memory performances that touch more directly on daily problems and range from professional actors memorising their roles to school children studying and remembering descriptive materials. The categorising with which he is concerned is the division of prose passages into meaningful groupings, and in one investigation with children aged seven, nine and eleven years he finds that production deficiency is prevalent. A few of the very youngest children cannot form the meaningful groups at all. But most of the children, who can form these groups when specifically asked, do not spontaneously form them while studying the passage and recalling its contents.

Memory development

Each of us, from birth onwards, acts upon the world in which we find ourselves. That world acts back upon us and, in the process of this ongoing dialectic, we build repertoires of information-handling activities, such as perceptual skills, motor skills, and bodies of understanding about objects, people, events and, not least, ourselves. These repertoires are the spectacles through which we view our world, the frames of reference by which we relate our experiences together, the co-ordinates by which we integrate our actions upon the world, and the apparatus by which we detect and deal with problems—including memory problems.

In our early years, all this 'just happens' so far as we are concerned. We make no distinction between 'memory' and other 'faculties', and little appreciate that we ourselves are causal agents in our dealings with the world. But we begin vaguely to discern links between our treatment of material and whether we remember it, and we clarify which activities work or do not work as a means for securing later recall. We slowly, and never exhaustively, discover how to solve memory problems by deploying our repertoire of information-handling activi-ties. We find it sometimes helps to break the material into segments, to try to relate it to something we already know, or to describe it to ourselves by gesture patterns, words or pictorially imagined scenes. We try these potentially helpful techniques and find they sometimes work, sometimes not. By such explorations we build understanding of ourselves as handlers of knowledge.

Children's lack of appreciation of their own memory activities is illustrated by Moynahan (1973). The materials were display cards on each of which were pasted eight pictures of common objects. On some cards the pictures were cate-gorised, e.g. a block of four animals and a block of four fruits. On other cards the pictures were uncategorised, each picture coming from a different category, e.g. chair, hand, spoon, seesaw, house, bracelet, hammer, moon. In the recall task, a child was shown a card and asked to name each of the eight objects; the card was removed and the child asked to recall as many objects as he could. Each child did this recall task with several cards. With children aged seven, nine and eleven years, mean recall scores with uncategorised cards were 3·2, 4·1 and 4·5 respectively: with categorised cards, 5·4, 6·4 and 7·1. There was a strong link between cate-gorising and recall and indeed every individual child recalled more from the categorised cards.

Did the children themselves appreciate this link between categorisation and recall? Many of the younger children did not, as shown by a prediction task. Each child was shown a pair of eight-picture cards, one categorised and one uncategorised. He named all the pictures and was then asked which card would be easier to remember if the cards were removed and he had to remember as many things from it as he could. The pair of cards remained in view throughout. The eleven-year-olds predicted fairly accurately, but the seven-year-olds predicted only slightly better than chance. Half of the children took the prediction tasks after having taken the recall tasks and so after having opportunity to notice their higher success with categorised cards. Yet these children did not predict significantly better than children who took the prediction tasks before the recall tasks. Small wonder that such children, when asked to memorise a display of potentially categorisable pictures, do not spontaneously think to categorise them as an aid to memory.

It is a long voyage of discovery, this many-sided exploration of our own information-handling activities. At each stage, we may learn from those who have progressed further on this journey than we, and assist others who have progressed less far. On this journey, we discover many strange things; for example, that skills are often multi-purpose. We can detach them from their original contexts and use them to subserve new purposes. Thus, once we have constructed, at around the age of seven or eight, the logical use of the word 'because', we may further discover that, in some of the word-memorising experiments in which psychologists involve us, we can use this construction to link seemingly unrelated words into because-type sentences and thereby aid our memory performance.

As we continue our voyage, we gain progressive competence in diagnosing the requirements of memory tasks and meeting these by appropriate deployment of our current repertoire of resources. We also find ourselves facing yet higher-order memory problems. Throughout our adult years, for example, we increasingly encounter problems of retrieving material we know we know. This problem may sometimes arise from neurological impairment, but mostly it reflects the greater difficulty of selecting from among a larger population of 'memories'. A particular book is easier to find in a library of ten volumes than in one of several hundreds; and in using the larger library we need to devise new classificatory systems for retrieval. So too with the enlarging library of our internally-stored knowledge.

Another higher-level memory problem is: What, of the material we encounter, ought we to conserve for future use, and in what form? This level of problem often faces university students and professional people. Suppose, for example, we read a chapter in this book and find it interesting. Should we deliberately contrive to keep anything of it in memory and, if so, what and how? Verbatim passages, or our precis of the chapter, or our critique of its shortcomings? Should we make notes and file them, taking steps to remember the 'address' of the file? Should we photocopy the text and shelve it, deluding ourselves that we now 'possess' the chapter's contents? Such problems require us to conjecture our future knowledge requirements. These problems are not made less challenging by the further realisation that our solutions will determine our future knowledge resources and that, if we adopt some consistent style of solution to such problems, we will profoundly influence the long-term direction of our own knowledge development. There is no end to the problem of being intelligent about memory.

Part Three

K. Wedell

10. Programmes for cognitive growth

The use of the word 'programme' in the title of this chapter needs some introduction. To the European it suggests a specific educational package, consisting of
deliberately graded stages, and directed at specific educational or other needs. On
the other side of the Atlantic the word is used in this sense, but also more generally.
In this latter sense, 'programme' may refer to the general curriculum offered to
children in a school. In the context of this chapter I will be using the word in its
more limited meaning, although the programmes to be discussed may vary in
their specificity. Furthermore, even a specific programme may, in the context of
its use, represent only one instance of a general educational orientation that characterises other aspects of the education offered.

The word 'cognitive' does not require an introduction—even if, as will
become apparent, its definition may be elusive. However, it is necessary to mention
those aspects of children's needs which programmes of cognitive growth are not
intended to meet. Cognitive needs are probably most clearly seen in distinction to
emotional needs, in spite of the fact that these interact in the case of the individual
child. Similarly, cognitive function is seen as distinct from sensory or motor
function, although some of the programmes which will be mentioned emphasise the
interaction between these functions. Whether perceptual and cognitive functions
can be distinguished is an important question to students of Piaget, which is dealt
with at length by Butterworth in Chapter 6 of this volume. It is also a question
of much complexity and controversy, and most of the programmes to be considered
here themselves do not make the distinction in any clear sense.

Programmes for cognitive growth are usually directed at children with
retarded intellectual development. Their objective is to foster the cognitive
development of the child, and hopefully to accelerate the pace of his development.
As Bereiter and Engelmann (1966) pointed out, unless a programme can accelerate
a child's development it will not overcome the child's retardation in the area at
which it is directed. The child's development may progress, but relative to his
age expectation he will continue to be retarded. Expectations about the possibility
of acceleration differ with respect to the various categories of children with special
needs. For this, and for other reasons which will be discussed below, it is necessary
to distinguish between these main groups of children:

1. *The socially deprived or disadvantaged.* These are the children whose retarded
cognitive development is ascribed mainly to the absence of environmental stimuli

for cognitive growth. It was with reference to these children that Bereiter and Engelmann made their point about acceleration mentioned above. Programmes for socially deprived children are dealt with in the chapter by Chazan and Cox, and will not be further considered here.

2. *Children with specific learning disabilities.* The definition of this group of children has presented considerable problems, since the criteria used are largely negative. These are children whose intellectual and educational problems are not primarily thought to be of emotional origin, or caused through environmental deprivation. In so far as their intellectual problems are specific, and therefore not representative of their general level of cognitive functioning, this group of children is defined in terms of a further negative criterion—namely that the children are not mentally subnormal. The implication here, again, is that development in the specific area of deficiency may be accelerated, to achieve a level of functioning commensurate with the child's other abilities.

However, while specific learning disabilities may be more easily recognised when a child's general level of functioning is average, similar discrepancies can be found, if they are looked for, in many mentally subnormal children. Consequently some have applied the term 'learning disabled' to certain subnormal children, often with the implication that specific deficiencies have had a retarding effect on other aspects of their cognitive development, resulting in generally subnormal functioning (e.g. autistic children). Expectations about the prospects for accelerated development vary for these children, but are certainly implied in some of the programmes to be considered.

3. *The mentally subnormal.* From an educational point of view, the main characteristic of these children is probably that there is little or no expectation of acceleration in cognitive development. They are distinguished by the fact that development is expected to tail off at less than mature levels by the time the individual reaches adulthood. This, in turn, has interesting implications for the application of programmes of cognitive growth. Since normal levels of functioning are not expected, educational emphases are switched from more general objectives to more specific ones. Self-help and occupational skills are emphasised, although not of course to the total exclusion of other educational objectives. As we shall see, most programmes of cognitive growth make assumptions that the intellectual development aimed for will generalise, and consequently facilitate the acquisition of more specific skills. The assumptions about the subnormal reduce such expectations, and the more specific educational objectives are symptoms of this. Even where some programmes are applied in the education of subnormal children, the emphasis is often on the acquisition of the relevant elements of the programme for their own sake, rather than on their scope for generalisation.

The content and organisation of programmes reflects both the educator's conceptualisations of children's needs, and also the factors causing them. Programmes appear to fall into three main categories, and these will now be considered in turn.

1. *Programmes which emphasise the organic basis of cognitive function*

These programmes are based on the assumption that all functioning depends on the physical integrity of the organism, and that, correspondingly, malfunctioning reflects organic disturbances. Few would question these assertions so much as the corollary which is drawn, namely that organic defects may be modified by programmes directed at behaviour.

The links between behavioural and organic features are illustrated in the programmes for retarded children put forward by Delacato and his associates (1963). These workers propose that the child, in his development, recapitulates the course of human phylogenetic development. The retarded child is seen as having stopped at certain levels of neurophysiological development, and therapeutic programmes are directed at moving him on from these levels. The achievement of speech is regarded as representative of the highest levels of neurological development, and as associated with the establishment of unilateral hand preference. A central feature of these programmes is, therefore, the establishment of asymmetrical patterns of motor skills, such as the alternating movement of arms and legs in crawling. The objective is to establish 'asymmetrical' neural functioning, which in turn would facilitate cognitive growth.

Not surprisingly, these assumptions have been questioned. Research reported by Delacato *et al.* (1966) supports the effectiveness of their measures, but research by others (e.g. Robbins 1966; Kerschner 1968) has either failed to validate the programme, or actually contradicted it. For example, Robbins (1966) found that after four months of training, a group of seven- to eight-year-old children showed less lateralisation of motor skill than at the start.

Another worker developing programmes based on similar assumptions is Ayres (1965). Her approach is based on physio-therapeutic concepts, and she traces poor motor organisation to inadequate inhibition of infantile motor reflexes. Here again, the proposition put forward is that cognitive growth can be mediated by neurological improvement resulting from motor activities.

Both these approaches use the progress of normal development as the pattern on which the sequence of components of the programme is built. The components are identified because they are thought to be present in the developmental sequence, and it is assumed that the sequence also implies a causal dependence between each stage and the next. It will become evident that this assumption occurs quite frequently in the thinking underlying programmes of cognitive growth. But the question as to whether the sequence of stages in normal development necessarily provides a model relevant to educational practice for individuals with abnormal development, is frequently not even asked.

2. *Programmes emphasising functional analysis*

This category of programmes is directed at analysing the functional components of children's performance, without any major emphasis on extending this backwards to neurophysiological levels. These approaches tend to use models derived from experimental psychology and also from psychometrics, but in a developmental context. In these programmes, interest is therefore found in the development of information-processing functions such as perception. Children's performance in educational tasks is seen as dependent on the adequate prior development of perceptual and language functions, and consequently poor educational achievement is held to be the result of inadequate development of these functions. It is interesting to note that this line of argument also contains some features of task analysis. In other words, the choice of functions appears sometimes to be influenced by the fact that they are seen as components of the 'target' tasks of achievement in basic educational skills, and sometimes by the fact that they are seen as developmentally antecedent. The distinction between these two points of origin appears not always to be clearly appreciated, and, of course, does not necessarily lead to different programme elements in any case. Functions such as 'auditory discrimination' would, for example, be included in a programme whether this was based on a task analysis of the reading process, or of the normal cognitive development of the child. Clear divergences between programme elements selected on the basis of these two types of analysis would only become apparent as the level and complexity of the target tasks was increased.

An example of an approach which merges developmental and task-analysis models is that of Kephart (1971). Kephart's interest was mainly directed at perceptual motor functions. He was concerned with the process by which a child achieved the concept of a stable environment. He conceived this in terms of the child's achievement of the 'perceptual-motor match'—organising his responses appropriately within the spatial dimensions of his environment. Kephart's views in this respect coincided to some extent with those of Piaget (Piaget and Inhelder 1969). However, he was less concerned with the way in which the child developed his *concept* of space, than with the use he made of this in functioning adequately in his everyday behaviour. Kephart held that the child built up his concepts of the spatial aspects of the world around him through movement. He regarded movement as being the spatial 'connection' between objects in the child's environment. Kephart regarded the child's knowledge of the spatial coordinates of his own body—front, back, up, down and left, right—as the basis on which his spatial judgments were built. He spoke of this in terms of the establishment of the child's 'body image', an essential feature of which was the 'body midline' which served as a reference point between 'right' and 'left'. Effective left-right discrimination was seen as an essential component not only of competence in everyday behaviour, but also of educational performance, where letter orientation represented a critical element.

Kephart's extensive programmes of perceptual-motor training thus have a wide range of general cognitive and educational objectives beyond the more immediate ones of motor competence. Validation studies of the effectiveness of Kephart's programmes have largely been carried out with reference to educational criteria, and these will be mentioned later.

Another well-known set of programmes has been devised by Frostig (Frostig and Horne 1964). The functions with which she was concerned were also derived partly from developmental and partly from task-analysis models. Her earlier work was particularly influenced by a task-analysis view of the pencil and paper aspects of education in the classroom. This led her to construct a battery of perceptual motor tests, designed to distinguish some of the component skills involved. Her battery includes tests to measure 'eye-motor coordination', 'figure-ground discrimination', 'form constancy', 'position in space' and 'spatial relations'—all regarded as components of performance in the basic educational target tasks. With this as a basis, she then produced programmes of activities intended to improve children's performance in each of these functions. She also advocated the importance of language development, particularly as a means of helping the child to conceptualise some of the relevant dimensions of discrimination involved. Frostig's more recent work has developed in the direction of greater emphasis on movement programmes.

More recently movement programmes have also been devised as a medium for developing children's language, particularly with reference to sentence structure and the logic of classes. Workers such as Cratty (1972) have devised programmes involving children in individual and group activities in which they 'act out' relational and classificatory distinctions. Movement here is used as a means of making abstract concepts more real to children.

Over the last few years, an increasing amount of research has been directed at evaluating the effectiveness of these various programmes. This has raised, implicitly rather than explicitly, the question as to whether the developmental or the task-analysis model is the more relevant. Clearly, if the developmental model is regarded as the more important, a programme can be regarded as effective if children improve in the activities included in the programmes. For example, if right-left or figure-ground discrimination are necessary elements in the sequence of a child's development, then all that needs to be demonstrated is that children given the programmes show improvement in these functions. The only further requirement would be that this improvement generalised to performance on similar tasks in the same category. If, on the other hand, emphasis were placed on the task-analysis model, then programmes would have to be validated against achievement of those target tasks on which the task analyses were based. Since educational performance tended to be regarded as the basic objective of the programmes, level of educational attainment—usually in reading—was frequently used as a criterion for validation.

Validation studies have been reviewed by Cruickshank and Hallahan (1973), Myers and Hammill (1969), Cratty (1970) and Wedell (1973). The degree of experimental rigour with which these studies were carried out varied, and was particularly examined by Cruickshank and Hallahan in their review. In studies where adequate controls were applied, the findings often failed to show the programmes to be more effective than specific teaching or the other experiences offered to the control groups concerned. 'Specific teaching' referred, for example, to straight reading instruction. The relative effectiveness of programmes tended to vary with the level of target achievement expected of the child. For example, there are some indications that, where early reading levels are taken as a criterion, perceptuo-motor programmes show some superiority in effectiveness. Similarly, when aspects of social competence rather than educational achievement are used as criteria, some studies have also shown programmes to be more effective.

The issue as to whether programmes are based on a developmental or a task-analysis model thus does become one of central importance for the judgment of their effectiveness. If 'cognitive growth' is an implied objective of the programme, then it would be expected that the effect of the programme would generalise to relevant aspects of a child's performance, including, at the appropriate stage, educational achievement. Validation studies tend not to have been carried out on children who are chronologically or developmentally at a pre-academic level, since it is so much more difficult to specify appropriate criteria. The simplistic notion of using tests of general intelligence, which was applied to validation studies of compensatory education programmes, tends not to have been carried over to the evaluation of these programmes.

Wedell (1975) argues for a more general evaluation of the effectiveness of programmes and suggests the use of behaviour-observation measures as evaluative techniques. If these programmes are relevant to general cognitive growth, this ought to be reflected in children's problem solving and general behavioural competence in everyday life. Similarly one would suggest assessment with reference to Piagetian stages of reasoning, since these would also supposedly be within the area of expected generalisation. If programmes did not show transfer to specific educational target tasks, they could still be justified on the basis of these other types of criteria.

3. Programmes emphasising behaviour-shaping approaches

Behaviour shaping is mainly associated with behaviour modification techniques, and consequently tends to be applied to very specific target areas. To this extent, it might not be thought relevant to the topic of cognitive growth. The principles involved have, however, been applied to educational settings (Ward 1975).

In contrast to the functional-analysis approach, where the desired attainment was approached through the mastering of component skills, the gradations of the shaping approach are based on approximations to the target task itself. An approach which would seem to fall into this category is that used by Cruickshank et al. (1961) in their study of brain-injured children. Their method of helping children who were hyperactive and distractible was to provide an educational setting whose organisation and structure supported the children initially to whatever extent was necessary to achieve controlled behaviour and educational progress. In their study of a group of seven- to eleven-year-old children, a classroom was especially modified to reduce extraneous distraction. Study materials were constructed to emphasise those task features to which the children were required to attend. The children's day was designed to provide maximal organisational support. All of these and other 'props' were then gradually withdrawn, until the children were able to manage without them. Functional-analysis models were also applied in this study, but the main characteristic seems to have been this gradual shaping of the expected levels of behaviour and achievement. Although Cruickshank and his co-workers do not specifically describe their approach either in terms of 'cognitive growth' or of 'behaviour shaping', their study does seem highly relevant in this context. Attention is clearly a crucial element both indirectly, as a facilitator for cognitive growth, and directly, as an aspect of it. Cruickshank and his co-workers carried out a follow-up evaluation of their educational methods, using as a comparison group children with similar problems who received conventional special educational help. When the control and experimental group children were reassessed on a number of indices at the end of the school year, the experimental group showed consistently greater improvement, but this was statistically significant on only two measures—figure-ground discrimination and social maturity. The authors would have liked to follow the children up over a longer period, but this was not possible.

Three approaches to the construction of programmes for cognitive growth have now been outlined, and it is notable that these have been directed, explicitly at least, at information-processing functions rather than at the products of these functions—namely concepts.

It is of interest to speculate why programmes of cognitive growth have been slanted in this way. As far as children with specific learning disabilities are concerned, the supposition has always been that they are of 'average general ability' apart from the area or areas of their specific disability. Consequently, the term has tended to be applied to those children who showed that they were able, in many respects, to build up conceptual frameworks appropriate to their age—presumably through effective application of their remaining abilities. Indeed, one of the main ways in which the children showed that their cognitive difficulties were in fact limited was that they could recognise their own areas of deficiency. 'Why can't I make my hands do what my eyes see?' is the sort of statement that illustrates this point. It is assumed that the children have been able to develop their power of reasoning, and consequently were often also in a position to compensate for their deficiencies by finding ways round them. Inhelder (1968), for example, found that dysphasic children showed a discrepancy between their levels of 'figurative symbolism' and of 'operativity', and that this enabled them to compensate for their handicaps in language with their asset of operational reasoning.

While this may be true of children whose problems were mainly limited to 'executive' processes, it was less likely to be true of children with deficiencies of 'receptive' functions, such as perception. It is well known that disturbances of input functions are more handicapping than those of output functions, since the former are liable to distort or reduce the information on the basis of which the child builds up his concepts about the world around him. The child with developmental expressive language delay is considerably less handicapped than the child with receptive aphasia. Similarly, the child who has difficulty in discriminating the relevant spatial features of the model which he is trying to copy, is more handicapped than the one who cannot make 'his hands do what his eyes see'. It is with reference to children such as these that one might have expected aspects of Piaget's research to be applied. In such instances, one would like to know what the child's view of his environment in fact is. What, for example, are the concepts of causality which the children have built up, or what is their awareness of perspective? Very little work has been carried out on these questions among these children. The fact that investigations of this kind would possibly be fruitful, was indicated by the results of a study of size constancy among cerebral palsied children (Wedell et al. 1972). This study involved a group of children who were selected because they had had limited experience of independent mobility. The study compared the size judgments of children with greater and lesser experience of independent mobility, and the results suggested that those with lesser experience showed less constancy in their judgments. Those with almost normal experience of independent mobility, approximated in their size judgments to a comparison group of non-physically handicapped children.

If limitations of experience as specific as these may effect the development of children's concepts of their environment, one might suppose that deficiencies in information-processing functions such as perception would have an even greater effect. One could even postulate that some of the apparent confusion shown by severely disturbed children, for example those manifesting so-called autistic behaviour, was a reflection of a failure to establish concepts of their environment which were sufficiently structured to provide a basis for appropriate response. In another context, suggestions of this kind were put forward by Wedell (1973).

Investigations of the stages of reasoning postulated by Piaget have, of course, been carried out on mentally subnormal children. Woodward (1970), for example, studied the development of severely subnormal children and found that they were severely retarded in the attainment of the various sensorimotor stages. In earlier studies, Inhelder (1968) had also shown that the subnormal achieved levels of reasoning at later chronological stages, and that the highest levels they attained were paralleled by the degree of their subnormality. It appears that the sequence of development in the subnormal is similar to that in ordinary children—the difference is represented by delay. While such a parallelism seems likely in the early stages of development, one would question how strictly it applied to chronologically older individuals—particularly if one began to investigate the quality of reasoning implied by subnormal patients' competence in some of the more specific aspects of their performance.

The emphasis on enquiring into the individual's conception of the problem with which he is presented, has had a major influence on approaches to intellectual assessment, not only of the subnormal. The paucity of information derived from the use of the simple 'pass-fail' approach to assessment is now generally appreciated by psychologists, and the Piagetian studies have contributed to this. It is worth considering the reasons why Piagetian stages of reasoning have not been so widely applied as objectives in the construction of programmes for cognitive growth for the children we have been considering in this chapter. There is no doubt, of course, that these stages have made a major impact on teaching approaches for nonhandicapped children in infant and junior schools. As is well known, and as Chapter 12 indicates, the various aspects of the concrete operational stage have been quite explicitly used as objectives in the teaching of number.

A number of experiments have also been carried out to investigate whether children's levels of reasoning can be raised from one stage to the next (see Modgil 1974 for a summary). The outcome of these studies has generally been to demonstrate that higher levels of reasoning can be achieved with respect to specific tasks, but that the extent of generalisation is limited. Within the context of Piagetian research, the issue has been related to the question about the extent of maturational determinants of development. Where generalisation of the effect of training has been found, it has been hypothesised that the individuals concerned were in any case on the verge of transition to the next level of reasoning. Clearly, such an argument can begin to be circular. Bryant (1974) has suggested that, in some respects, the problematic aspects of the tasks used to assess Piaget's levels of reasoning reflect the amount of information available to the child, rather than his capacity to make rational use of the information. The present chapter is not an appropriate context in which to pursue this question.

Conclusion

Programmes for cognitive growth have been considered in three main groups, according to the models on which they are based. Decisions about the application of these programmes were found to be related to expectations about consequent acceleration in cognitive development. These, in turn, were found to vary according to the generality of children's intellectual retardation. In the case of children with specific learning disabilities, educational approaches were based on the assumption that areas of poor function could be improved to the levels of non-impaired functions. In the case of mentally subnormal children, continued progress at a constant but slower rate was expected up to a stage of development below normal maturational levels. Correspondingly, educational and social training objectives tended to become more specific with older groups of retarded children, since expectations about their capacity to generalise the effects of training were limited. In this way, the concepts of potential acceleration and generalisation were linked. This accounted for the fact that decisions about applying programmes for cognitive growth were dependent on the age and type of intellectual handicap of children. Whether it is justifiable to take these factors into consideration in planning special educational curricula is, of course, open to question, and this has been an issue in special education for some time (Gulliford 1975). Furthermore, current economic stringencies have forced educators to pay more attention to whether their approaches are having demonstrable effects. This has resulted in a trend towards setting up more specific objectives. It is not surprising that programmes for cognitive growth are currently surrounded with controversy.

K. Lovell

11. Understanding scientific concepts

Introduction

Tyler (1967) has made a number of suggestions for improving science education. One of the points he makes is that the primary contribution of research in this connection resides in formulating conceptual frameworks, models and parameters for models, in order that we may better understand the educational processes and so be helped to plan and conduct educational programmes more effectively. Now the central theme of this chapter is that the understanding of scientific concepts is closely linked to, and dependent on, intellectual growth. And in order to avoid any criticism that could be levelled by Tyler, use will be made of Piaget's developmental theory of intellectual growth. This framework will enable us to consider the kinds of concepts, and the types of thought strategies, that are available to the pupil at different stages in his intellectual development.

To say that the understanding of scientific concepts is fundamentally due to intellectual growth in no sense lessens the need for good and sustained teaching, and for relevant experience more generally. Nor does it imply that we can ignore the climate of the home, and the manner in which pupil attitudes to, and achievement in, science are thus affected. Put in another way, it can be said that intellectual growth is a necessary, but not sufficient condition for the elaboration of scientific concepts. Again, although the Genevan theory of intellectual growth will be employed, it must be realised that it is a developing framework and that whilst it is the most useful framework that we have at present from the viewpoint of our topic, it remains incomplete and imperfect in many ways.

It will be appreciated that the term 'logical thinking' has often been used synonomously with intellectual functioning more generally. One needs to be careful here as it obscures the nature of many problems in science. If we take a reasoning task to be logical in the strict sense such that deduction from given premises *alone* is sufficient for its solution and no further empirical knowledge is required, then many problems in science have a logical component but cannot be solved by strict logic alone (cf. Osherton 1974). For example, inductive reasoning is often required and a knowledge of facts are needed. Thus when we meet in the Piagetian model, the term 'logical thinking', the term often implies intellectual functioning in a wider sense. Many of the tasks used by the Genevan school certainly have a logical component, but they also have components which are not strictly logical. This is also the case in many scientific problems.

Some basic points in Piagetian theory

Piaget has been concerned with the growth of the intellect or of the very general ways of knowing. These have to be actively constructed by the child through his interactions with objects, persons and events. Once built, these general ways of knowing are never forgotten in mental health. Thus the individual never forgets that if $A > B$ and $B > C$, then $A > C$. Moreover, Piaget distinguishes these very general ways of knowing or reasoning, from particular knowledge which is primarily obtained from specific aspects of the environment and for this purpose all manner of teaching may be used. Moreover, it is the quality of the intellectual structures which governs the way in which particular knowledge is assimilated. Furthermore, the latter knowledge may be forgotten at any time and have to be revised.

Again, the central mechanisms of intelligence seem to be derived from the individual's actions on objects in the early months of life. These actions are internalised from around twenty-one months of age onwards with the help of, but not deriving from, language, thus yielding implicit mental actions. These emerge as reversible and integrated structures around seven to eight years of age. It is this action—which early on is overt and later mainly, but not always, covert—which transforms one reality state in another. Thus for Piaget to understand a state one must know the transformations that bring the state into being.

The role of language in the elaboration of logical thought is not well understood at present. However, in the Genevan view language, at least to pre-adolescence, develops partially independently of cognition yet interacts with it. With the advent of more advanced thinking strategies in adolescence, such as Piaget's notion of formal operational thought, language may play a greater role in the growth of thought, although we do not know this for certain. From the point of view of understanding science (or other subject matter) it seems that even if language plays only a modest role in the growth of thinking in childhood, it certainly is an important symbolic vehicle that carries thought.

Finally, we should note that Piaget makes a useful distinction between physical knowledge and logical-mathematical knowledge (Piaget 1970), although he also makes the point that these are almost indissociable and are looked upon more as a continuum than as a dichotomy. In the case of physical knowledge the individual abstracts, or 'takes from', things to which his knowing is directed. Whether or not a lump of iron sinks or floats in water can be determined by trial, and generalised empirically. On the other hand, logical-mathematical knowledge is not derived from objects themselves but from physical and/or mental actions performed on objects. Thus the concept of density, as such, cannot be discovered empirically or built by empirical generalisation. It has to be constructed or invented by the individual's own cognitive activity in combination with empirical experience. In the case of logical-mathematical knowledge the pupil has to keep a constant check on the coordination of physical and mental actions to avoid contradiction. That is to say, he reflects on his coordinating activity in an autoregulatory manner. It must not, of course, be thought that physical knowledge is a mere recording of phenomena, since it always involves assimilation to logical-mathematical structures, as when the different weights of similar sized objects are compared and they are ranked according to their weights.

The first five years of life

During the first twenty-one months or so of life the infant slowly becomes aware of his world through an increasing recognition of his own actions and through his perceptions, and during the same period he puts an elementary organisation on reality by constructing those broad categories of action which enable him to delineate the self from the non-self, and to build his first elementary notions of time and space. By the end of the period the emergence of implicit mental actions enable the child to solve simple problems in familiar situations without actually putting his physical actions to the test. At the same point in time new behaviours are seen emerging, indicating that he is now able to represent the world to himself even in its absence. True, these behaviours do not emerge simultaneously, but they become increasingly in evidence if not all at once. Thus we see the child employing deferred imitation, attempting simple graphical representation in the form of scribbling, engaging in symbolic play, and using language. And with the advent of language he has a more flexible and permanent model of the outside world.

From around twenty-one months to the fourth birthday the child is building up his powers of representation and reworking, so to speak, with the aid of language and other forms of representation, all that he did earlier without them. Further, his thinking shows two characteristics. First, his notions seem to lie between that of the individual object and that of the class of objects. For example, when walking in the fields with an adult he does not regard a rabbit as an instance of a class, but says 'rabbit', suggesting a notion between the individual instance and a class of instances. Second, the child tends to use transductive thinking or arguing from particular to particular. Thus if mother is combing her hair she must be going out, since that sequence of events followed one another on a number of earlier occasions. Such thinking will lead him to the correct answer at times; on other occasions he will be seriously wrong in his predictions.

At four to five years of age the child's thinking is still semi-logical, although soon after he enters school at five years of age (in the UK) changes set in which allow him to give, somewhat more often, what adults call sound reasons for his actions and beliefs. Indeed, for the next two years or so logical thought remains isolated and sporadic. The inconsistencies of his thoughts are reflected in a number of ways, only a few of which are indicated here. First, there is difficulty in imagining an ordered sequence of events and there may be an actual reversal of their order at times. Second, a succession of quite unrelated events may be given as the cause of a particular event. Third, there is great difficulty in holding in mind more than one relationship at a time pertaining to a given object, person or situation. The child entering school can certainly assert 'This rod is heavy', 'That rod is light'.

But he has great difficulty in using the statement 'This rod is short but heavy'. This disability leads to many problems, for he is unable to compare relationships. He tends to 'centre' on one dimension of an object, or one aspect of a situation, and thus fails in the conservation problems.

Although the child's thinking to this point is not yet systematised, he has nevertheless been interacting with persons, objects and situations, so building up a great amount of particular knowledge of the world around him. This knowledge is abstracted directly from the situation, and is of the form of physical and social knowledge. Such knowledge is of limited value from the strict scientific viewpoint, although it is laying the foundations for his later knowledge of the world. On the other hand, it has been known for a long time that before the third birthday, the average child grasps that *men* and *women* are *people*; also that *apples* and *potatoes* are *food*. By four to five years of age the next stage in the growth of generalisation hierarchies occurs, for he can understand the *apple–fruit–food* relationship. Even more steps can be understood by older children, although there is much individual variation in respect of the age at which any one stage emerges. However, the point being made here is this. In these examples only generalisation is involved, for all the terms are at the same level of abstraction or dissociation from reality. It is the latter, and not the former, which is critical to concept formation in science or, indeed, in any subject area, as Braine (1962) has reminded us. If a five-year-old has a dog called Rusty, he finds it impossible to move through the relationship *Rusty–dog–species* (that is, an object, a class, and a class of classes), although he can easily move through the generalisation hierarchy *dogs–housepets–animals*. The distinction between generality and abstraction must not be overlooked. The relation between degrees of generality are transitive; if *dogs* are *housepets* and *housepets* are *animals* then *dogs* are *animals*. But this is not the case in respect of the membership relation between levels of abstraction; for if Rusty is an instance of a *dog*, and *dog* an instance of a *species*, it does not follow that Rusty is a species.

The relevance of concrete operational thought to understanding scientific concepts

By seven to eight years of age the pupil can, in essence, look in on and monitor his own thinking and so becomes aware of the sequence of action taking place in his mind; while at the same time he can carry out reversible operations thus appreciating that for every operation (i.e. a mental action which is part of a related network) there is an opposite one that cancels it. Moreover, whereas around twenty-one months of age he reached a first level of abstraction, for he separated the self from the not-self, now he can attain a second level of abstraction, for he can distinguish his experiences from the organisation or categorisation that *he* imposes on them. Pupils can now increasingly master the following: hierarchical classification, seriation, substitution or equivalence, symmetry, multiplication of classes, multiplication of series, one-many equivalence in classes, one-many equivalence in series.

The period of concrete operations lasts for around five years in very able pupils, longer in pupils of average ability, although from around twelve years of age we begin to see the emergence of new skills in very many pupils. However, from seven to eight years of age onwards the pupil begins to elaborate the basic concepts of science. In general terms we can say that he can increasingly elaborate those concepts which involve the building of exact relations between mental actions that bear directly on things, real or imagined. That is to say, he can systematise the relations between the objects and events of his world, and build such basic concepts of science as class, series, number, length, weight, axes of reference, area, time, temperature and so forth, all of which result from the coordination of mental actions that bear directly on reality. The pupil can thus build first-order relations, and while these are fundamental to science, they are quite inadequate to handle the more complex concepts required by science. Further, these concepts do not come all at once. Indeed, Piaget's theory, although a developing one, is still unable to explain in a satisfactory manner the problem of horizontal décalage. For example, even at the time of the emergence of concrete operational thought, two issues arise which the theory does not resolve at present. First, tasks which have the same structure, such as conservation of discrete and continuous quantities, are not of equal difficulty. Second, there is the differential difficulty in elaborating the structures themselves; for example, conservation comes before transitivity. And more generally, Inhelder (1968) concedes, 'The general succession of stages seems to be confirmed by all authors, but the relationship between different tasks and substructures, apparently requiring the same mental structure, is still far from adequately explored; what is more, the experimental findings on this point are difficult to interpret.'

As we saw earlier, the advent of concrete operational thought permits the child to carry out hierarchical and multiple classification, also seriation and multiple seriation. These fundamental skills are required for the organisation of intuitive data, and with the coming of these skills the child can systematise the relations between objects, or events, of his world, thus laying the basis for science. Among the early investigators of classification were Hazlitt (1930), Thompson (1944) and Annett (1959), but the most important work in this field is that of Inhelder and Piaget (1964). In spite of difficulties that still remain, it is clear that from around seven to eight years of age onwards the child enters the domain of classes and relations, thus enabling him to organise the events of his world in ways that were not possible before.

At around the same time children move from a perceptual to a conceptual space in the sense that they can now represent spatial relations to themselves in thought. The child can now elaborate a frame of reference and use axes of reference, understand sub-division and the interaction of a sub-unit thus grasping measurement in respect of segments (lengths) and regions (areas), and construct and interpret the graphical representation of data (Piaget and Inhelder 1956, 1960). The notion of measurement is, of course, of crucial importance, for it has widespread application throughout science, mathematics, and in everyday life.

Other first-order invariants are also constructed, as for example in the case of weight, although in this case the elaboration is more complex and is more affected by experience than the Genevans at first thought. And by nine years of age the child can carry out temporal operations, whereas up to this age he had only the ability to use certain time-words and to tell the time. Accordingly, his temporal perspective was shallow to this point. Thereafter he develops the ability to co-ordinate instants and intervals, seriate events in order of succession, use a time scale and fit smaller units within larger ones, and use some unit of time as a standard of measurement for all other periods (Lovell and Slater 1960; Piaget 1969). Note carefully, however, that the child's concept of time at this age extends only to intuitive data in the sense of there being imageable or perceptual happenings or events. It will be well into secondary or high school before 75 per cent of pupils will correctly answer, with sound reasons, the question 'In springtime when we advance the clocks by one hour, do we get one hour older?'

The elaboration of the concept of time, together with the ability to carry out the mathematical operations of multiplication and division, permits the pupil to relate, precisely, duration and distance covered. A ten- to eleven-year-old can grasp that forty metres in ten seconds is four metres per second, for he can relate the problem to an intuitive notion of a moving object. By this age he can also tackle problems involving equal distances and unequal times or vice versa; although he fails to calculate speeds when both times and distances are unequal, since this involves proportionality (Lovell, Kellett and Moorhouse 1962; Piaget 1969).

The concept of volume is an interesting one. It can be used in three senses:

1.   The amount of space inside, say, a box, or internal volume.
2.   The amount of space which, say, a box occupies, or 'occupied' volume.
3.   The amount of water displaced by an object when the latter is immersed in water, or displacement volume.

The first two meanings are acquired from nine years of age onward, and by eleven years of age pupils can, using unit cubes, be led to understand the method of calculating internal and occupied space using cuboids. But displacement volume is more difficult. If we ask pupils a number of questions involving the amount of water displaced by objects of similar dimensions but having different weights, the effect of change of shape of immersed object (e.g. Plasticine) on the amount of water displaced, and the effect of size and shape of a full container on the amount of water displaced by a given object, then around 10 to 15 per cent of ten-year-olds, and around 50 per cent of fourteen-year-olds will show a good grasp of displacement volume. There are reasons for this as we shall see later. Even a few university science graduates have difficulty with displacement volume. But the relatively late grasp of displacement volume—even later than the Genevans originally proposed—has important implications for science teaching, although it is possible that more could be done in school to foster this under-standing.

Shayer (1972) has carefully examined the evidence produced by Inhelder and Piaget (1958) in respect of pupil responses in the period of concrete operational thought. He categorised individuals' performance into: investigating style, 'the reason is' relationships, and the use of model as theory. Such categories (or lack of them) are of great importance to the science teacher. In the early part of the period the pupil 'will investigate what happens in a haphazard way; argue that "this goes with that" (association only); order a series (e.g. length or weights) but is unable to do so as part of a perception of a relationship in an investigation; is unable to use any model as theory'.

During the latter part of the period, when the thinking is more flexible and extends to greater areas of experience, the child 'will find out what happens, including the use of seriation and classification as tools of perception; can use ordering relations to partially quantify associative reasoning, e.g. "as this goes up, that goes down", "if you double this you must double that"; can use seriation and the multiplication of two seriations as perceptual strategies; can understand the rules of a simple model but not in relation to the experiment in hand'.

The ability to classify is basic to science education and some of the newer elementary school science programmes in the USA have placed some emphasis on this skill. However, we know little of the effect of these newer programmes on the thinking of children. Allen (1968) worked with children of above average IQ from upper-middle-class homes. The experimental group had been exposed to the Science Curriculum Improvements Study and the control group to a more traditional-type programme. On testing at around $8\frac{1}{2}$ to $9\frac{1}{2}$ years of age on tasks involving grouping, flexibility in classification and class inclusion, no significant differences were found between the groups. The results of such comparative studies must be interpreted with caution. For example, can we be sure that the SCIS programme was well implemented? Moreover, the findings could not be generalised to less able and less advantaged children.

The move to more advanced strategies and concepts

The Genevan school does not say much about the move from concrete to formal operational thought. Indeed, there is a period between, say, eleven years and the onset of formal operations about which little is known, but during this period new intellectual skills appear to be emerging which seem to be necessary, but not perhaps sufficient, for formal operational thought.

First, there is a slow improvement in the ability of the pupil from eleven years of age onwards, to handle purely logical tasks as defined at the onset of this chapter. For example, the work of O'Brien (see Shapiro and O'Brien 1970) used written problems such as 'If the car is shiny it is fast. The car is shiny; is it fast?' (Modus Ponens). At eleven years of age some 85 per cent can handle the Modus Ponens Form, 60 per cent the Contrapositive Form, 12 per cent the Inverse Form and 10 per cent the Converse Form. Thereafter the ability to handle the task in its various forms improves so that between twelve and fifteen years of age the correct response rate for the corresponding forms would be around 95, 65, 35 and 10-15 per cent. In another strictly logical problem provided by Matalon (1962) it was also shown that up to about eleven years of age children tend to treat an implication as if it were an equivalence. Thereafter pupils slowly begin to realise that there is not enough evidence to decide the answers in the Inverse and Converse Forms of the examples provided by O'Brien. In short, there is an improvement in the ability to tolerate a lack of closure or to weigh the evidence.

Another skill which seems to be necessary for more advanced strategies of thinking is that which permits the pre-adolescent to begin to handle multiple-interacting systems. Following Lunzer (1973) we will say that if the solution to a task depends only on one system of covariants (e.g. lengths *or* weights *or* speeds) it is said to be a simple system. It is also a simple system if there are a number of objectives involved in the task, providing each objective involves only *one* independent system of variation (e.g. lengths, weights, speeds, acting independently). But if the solution to a task involves more than one system of covariation (e.g. length, weight, speed, acting together) the system is said to be complex or multiple interacting. One can imagine that some motor mechanics can handle complex systems in respect of the car or lorry, but perhaps have a limited capacity for formal operations.

A third skill evolving in the eleven- to fourteen-year-old period is the ability to move to the next level of abstraction so that now an intuitable referent is no longer as necessary as it was in earlier years. Consider again the tasks considered earlier in respect of the concept of displacement volume. The main difficulty for the pupil lies in the fact that he must attain this third level of abstraction. Success in the three tasks will not be realised until volume and surface area (the latter may well change under a transformation) have been abstracted or dissociated from the objects themselves; weights and volumes of objects placed in water have also to be abstracted from the objects themselves; weights and volumes of objects placed in water have to be abstracted from the size of the containing vessel. No doubt teaching and relevant experience plays some role in aiding this abstraction, but it is in great measure due to the emergence of new skills.

The relevance of formal operational thought to the understanding of scientific concepts

At the level of concrete operational thought the pupil can make some extension of the real in the direction of the possible providing he is dealing with information that is simple and familiar, as in the outcome of a story. But with the onset of formal operational thought the young person can elaborate a hypothesis, deduce the consequences if it were true, and then note if his new observations are consonant with the hypothesis. Inhelder and Piaget (1958) argue that the essence of this new advanced strategy is the ability to invert the direction of reality and possibility. In other words, the pupil has the power to display a combinatorial ability allowing reality to be analysed into a set of hypotheses. One can see immediately that some tasks involving hypothetico-deductive thought involve an ability to tolerate lack of closure and/or the ability to handle multiple interacting systems. It will, of course, be realised that hypothetico-deductive thought is in evidence for solving problems in, say, history or literature or economics, and not just in science.

Another way of looking at formal operational thought is to regard it as second-order operations. As we said earlier, concrete operations permit first-order relations. But hypothetico-deductive thought necessitates, so to speak, second-order relations. As Lunzer (1968) pointed out, if the pupil appreciates the significance of holding constant the variables he is not considering at the moment, then while testing one hypothesis he must also be aware of alternative hypotheses and their consequences. That is, he must be aware of the hypotheses in question and the implications that follow, and at the same time be aware of the second-order relations between hypotheses. In a word, at the level of formal operational thought the pupil can coordinate and structure relations between relations. This opens the way to a formal analytic understanding, rather than an intuitive grasp of, say, transpiration, electron or isobar, for in an analytic sense none of these can be derived directly from mental action on first-hand reality. Rather they are constructed concepts, devoid of concrete referents. This understanding of second-order relations or concepts is aided by the increasing power of abstraction that has been developing in the years immediately preceding, and which was mentioned earlier.

Levels of abstraction seem to be limited to three, for at this level we are no longer dealing with first-hand reality. On the other hand, the order of the concepts within the third level of abstraction may be any number, depending on how complex it is. For pupils at school the major difficulty seems to be the move from first- to second-order relations or concepts, and not to a higher-order concept within the third level of abstraction. Consider the concept of temperature (t), which is a first-order relation. Next consider heat ($Q = m\theta$) where θ is a temperature difference, or the more general case $Q = mc\theta$. This is a second-order concept; while entropy $\left(\phi = \int \dfrac{mc\theta}{T} \right)$ is also a second-order relation but of a higher order than $Q = mc\theta$. Now entropy is a more complex concept than heat, and more difficult for the pupil, but the major move, and most difficult step, is from t to Q. Thus the logical order in which concepts are taught does not necessarily indicate their relative difficulty.

The writer has indicated elsewhere (Lovell 1974) in more detail the difficulty for the pupil in moving from an intuitive grasp to a formal analytic understanding of the concept of momentum. There is some evidence that around one half of eight-year-olds, admittedly of above average measured IQ (mean IQ 115), have an intuitive notion of momentum. Such a grasp depends only on first-order relations. But to have a good understanding of momentum at, say, the level of GCE 'O' level Physics, unpublished research by D. J. Williams at Leeds indicates that the pupil has to have the ability to handle the following, which are given in order of difficulty:

1. $p = mv$ and simple calculations by rule.
2. $\Delta p = F \times t$ (where t = time) and simple calculations by rule.

3.   'Σp = constant' type problem (excluding the class $\Sigma p = o$) with the notion of inverse proportion so that if mv = constant then $m\alpha\frac{1}{v}$.

4.   '$\Sigma p = o$' type problem but with only an intuitive idea of directional property and not vector p.

5. $\Delta p = F \times t$ with an understanding of $\Delta p \alpha F$ at constant t, and $\Delta p \alpha t$ at constant F.

6. $\Sigma p = o$ in terms of $F_1 = -F_2$, with a grasp of $\Delta p = F \times t$ and vector p.

7.   Vector p revealed as in problems involving Σp = constant in rebound and in calculations of Δp in rebound.

Again, at the level of concrete operations the pupil has intuitive notions of force, work and mechanical energy, which relate to concrete referents. For example, he can appreciate that water at the top of the waterfall has position energy or that it can do work in virtue of its position. At the bottom of the waterfall it has movement energy. But at the level of second-order relations precise relations exist between force, work and energy, and no concrete referents are necessarily involved.

Within second-order relations there is also a gradation of difficulty, but there have been few studies of this in science as yet. One such study was by Archenhold (1975). He showed that there was little difference in respect of the difficulty of understanding work done in a uniform field, in a non-uniform field, and in work done as change in potential energy. But a grasp of electrostatic and gravitational potential is considerably more difficult. Incidentally, this study clearly suggests that some pupils work examples (presumably recognising the example type) without a good understanding of the concepts involved.

There is evidence that pupils' familiarity with, and the ability to manipulate, first-order concepts affect capacity to elaborate second-order concepts. Thus earlier teaching and experience are important. It follows that pupils may have more difficulty in elaborating second- and higher-order concepts in one field than in another, due in part to past experience and familiarity with the kinds of ideas involved, and to the somewhat irregular development of the varying skills necessary for the elaboration of the concepts.

Earlier reference was made to the concept of volume. Brainerd (1971) looked at the relationship between understanding volume and understanding density. He found that over the age range eight to fifteen years the relationship shows some non-linearity although the departure from linearity is not great. Moreover, the data suggests that the same underlying cognitive skill is found in both concepts, and that an adequate volume concept invariably precedes an adequate density concept.

It is worth noting in passing that while first-order relations or invariants are rather isolated constructions (cf. Pinard and Laurendeau 1969) so that training on one gives limited transfer to another, it has been suggested (cf. Brainerd and Allen 1971) that there may be greater transfer of training effects to dissimilar concepts in the case of second-order relations. In other words, the coordination of first-order operations among themselves might introduce greater generality into the cognitive system. Such a prediction has yet to be confirmed by research.

Shayer (1972) also categorised pupils' responses to the tasks set by Inhelder and Piaget (1958) at the level of second-order operations. In the early part of the period he found the pupil will: 'Show more interest in looking for *why*: see the point of making hypotheses if simplified to one variable, but cannot perform the simplification systematically himself; be able to establish causative necessity; use or perceive metric proportion in a concrete situation; make simple deductions from a model if the use of the latter is explained.' During the latter part of the formal operations period the pupil will: 'have an interest in checking a "why" solution; know that in a system of several variables he must "hold all other things equal" while investigating one possible variable at a time; formulate general or abstract relations; use direct and inverse proportionality both for perceiving and formulating relationships; actively search for an explanatory model or extend one that is given'.

It will be apparent that formal thought is required before the pupil can acquire a well-developed analytic understanding of many concepts in physics, chemistry and biology; e.g. moment of inertia, mole, photosynthesis. In the form of proportional reasoning it is very important in applications of the ideal gas laws, in atomic theory and in the calculation of reactants and reaction products. On the other hand, as Karplus (1973) points out, atomic theory has some aspects of a language that, providing it is learnt, can be used in simple situations using concrete operational thought; e.g. the conservation of atoms in a reaction. Moreover, some questions set at secondary or high school level can be answered by either concrete or formal operational thought. Again, some current schemes of work ask pupils to set up experiments and to 'investigate variables', the pupils having to select their own materials and procedures. Since various alternatives have to be considered, together with the relationships between variables, the pupil must be able to guard against premature closure and bring formal operational thought to bear.

So far we have mainly considered concepts in the physical sciences. The same arguments apply in the biological sciences although far fewer studies have been carried out here. A recent study made by one of the writer's students has shown the great difficulty twelve- and thirteen-year-olds have in handling the ratio surface area/volume in biological topics because problems of proportionality are involved. Again, a current study involving twenty-seven concepts in the area of reproduction, growth and transport amongst GCE 'O' level Biology candidates illustrates the difficulty which pupils have in biology questions which demand formal operational thought (see also Shayer 1974).

A recent publication by the Geneva school (Piaget 1975) has explored in detail the development of the relation between physical causality and operational thought. In essence the volume argues that, at every level, the development of the understanding of causality proceeds by interacting with the development of operational thought. The two developments interact and help one another. There is only a one-way action on special and temporary occasions and in alternating successions. A large number of experiments defend the thesis in respect of such diverse topics as the composition of forces; action, reaction and reciprocities; principles of sufficient reason and inertia; concept of work; heat and light.

In the Genevan publication there is much confirmation of the views for the type of analysis expressed in this chapter by the present writer. Take, for example, the concept of work (Piaget 1975, pp. 94-9). It is argued that the concept can only be developed when it is recognised that there are two forces involved, one that is displaced (e.g. friction) and termed a passive force, and one that is used to displace it or the active force, and that these are equivalent. There is then the problem of the composition of a force and its displacement in terms of distance and often direction. This, for Piaget, involves a second-order relation or third-level abstraction and is equivalent to 'vector' in psychological complexity. Moreover, there is a composition between this relation—which is already a third-level abstraction—and the active force making possible the displacement of a passive one. Thus force is a third-level abstraction, but a higher-order concept than, say, a vector.

Nothing has been said in this chapter about the acceleration of conceptual development. There is now much evidence that training makes possible an improvement in performance on practically every type of logical or infralogical operation. But what is not certain is whether or not greater operativity is achieved by virtue of training when no vestige of the greater operativity existed before. One problem here is the measurement difficulty of operativity. Sustained good teaching and experience over the whole of the school years seems likely to show greater transfer effects than training does. We still do not know very much about the effect of training in respect of one concept on the growth of another which occurs near in time. Even less is known about the effects of relatively short training periods on long-term intellectual growth. These are matters for further research.

12. Mathematical thinking in children

Over the past decade it has become increasingly clear in most areas of the curriculum (Szeminska 1965; Furth 1970; Peel 1971; Collis 1972) that logical application of Piaget's theory to the curriculum tasks commonly set before children shows a vast discrepancy between expected outcomes and the child's ability to perform effective operative thinking. Nowhere is this more clear than in the area of mathematics teaching. It is the purpose of this chapter to take Piaget's developmental theory so far as it applies to school-age children and adolescents (7 to 17+ years) and examine it in the context of mathematics learning.

The years seven to seventeen-plus span the concrete-formal operational stages described by Piaget (Inhelder and Piaget 1958) and mark the period of development from the point where the child is capable of the kinds of conservation which enable him to deal effectively with various aspects of number to the point where he is able to handle quite complex problems involving abstract mathematical relationships. Moreover, Piaget has subdivided these two broad categories into four substages which form a developmental sequence. Each substage has its own characteristic developmental markers and can also be seen as a logical precursor to its successor. A series of studies by the writer and reported in various places (Collis 1971, 1972, 1973, 1974, 1975) has shown that these stages can be traced by means of elementary mathematical items. Let us examine these stages by taking their characteristics as set out by Piaget and looking at them in relation to items involving elementary mathematics.

Four stages

Piaget and Inhelder (1958) show that at the early concrete-operational stage (Stage IIA, about 7 to 9+ years) the child is confined in his reasoning to operations upon immediately observable physical phenomena. The physical elements may change, but the mental operation of knowing is directly related to the physical operation involved in making a particular change.

These notions, when investigated in the context of elementary mechanical arithmetic, mean that both the elements and operations of ordinary arithmetic must be related directly to physically available elements and operations, for example:

$$\to n(C) = n(A) + n(B) \to 7 = 3+4$$

(within the diagram: A xxx, B xxxx, C)

Closer examination of children's responses at this substage shows that unless the child actually closes the operation $(3+4 = 7$, say) he is likely to become uncertain about the uniqueness of the result and this, in fact, restricts his ability to work meaningfully with arithmetical operations to one operation on two elements. For example, in replacing an expression such as $2+3+4$ by the appropriate cardinal number (9 in this case), it is clear that a child can only close one operation at a time. Thus he may work along the following lines:

$2+3+4$	step 1
$= (2+3)+4$	step 2
$= 5+4$	step 3
$= (5+4)$	step 4
$= 9$	step 5.

In replacing $(2+3)$ by 5 and using 5 in combination with the '4' to obtain the result, he admits, tacitly perhaps, that the '$2+3$' combination is adequately represented by '5' *when it is combined in a further operation*. It is this latter that the child at this stage of development finds difficult to admit.

Moreover, his concepts of inverse and the logical necessity for consistency are in keeping with his limited cognitive capacity as described by Piaget. His notion of the inverse is physical, e.g. what is put down can be taken up as a meaning for subtraction. He does not seek a consistency in relationships with a system of elements selected two at a time and connected by an operation (Collis 1974) and, in fact, has no basis for so doing.

When the child moves to the next substage (Stage IIB, about 10 to 12+ years), Inhelder and Piaget (1958) see him as still reality bound and tending to work with qualitative correspondences, e.g. the closer, the bigger. The child's work also shows that he begins to feel for consistency between his qualitative correspondences and this leads him at times to consider quantitative compensations, but using additive procedures only—relationships are considered in terms of excess (e.g. two more than) rather than in terms of proportion (e.g. twice as big as).

In arithmetical items these children begin to show that they can work with the operations as such so long as uniqueness of result is guaranteed by their experience both with the operations and the elements operated upon. Thus they now become capable of working meaningfully with two or more operations closed in sequence if the numbers are small, or with one familiar operation using numbers beyond their verifiable range, e.g. they can cope with items involving the following types of combinations, $(3+7+4)$ and $(783+243)$.

As far as their developing notion of the inverse is concerned, it tends to be qualitative. The children, for example, regard subtraction as 'destroying' the effect of addition without specifically relating to the operations themselves or realising any necessary connection between them. For example, if they are asked to find the value of y in $y+4 = 7$, they regard y as a unique number to which 4 has been added; subtracting 4 *happens* to destroy the effect of the original addition. The term 'destroy' is used advisedly for, having obtained $y = 3$ by the process described, they are not content to reverse the operation last performed to obtain

$$y+4 = 3+4 = 7.$$

They would find it meaningful to start again with $y = 3$ and go forward by adding 4 to obtain $y+4 = 7$, but would regard the two procedures as completely independent entities.

Exercises designed to test for the development of a notion of consistency as a necessary condition for a system of operations (Neimark and Lewis 1967; Collis 1974) show that the children at this substage begin to recognise the need without being able to give a logical reason for their preference for consistency. The feel for the necessity of consistency fits well with their desire to have satisfactory dealings with their empirical reality. However, they do not appear at this stage to have internalised and rationalised this feeling so that it has become an integral part of their cognitive processing apparatus.

Piaget regards the next substage (Stage IIIA, about 13 to 15+ years) as marking the beginning of formal operations. His various tests show that the child often comes close to Piaget's criteria for formal operational thinking, but that, in general, the subjects concerned tend to fall short of the complete deduction which would make the full formal-operational use of a transformation rule available. The adolescent at this stage typically accepts the reliability of a rule on the evidence of a few specific positive instances. It does not occur to him to test with counter examples, look for negative instances or use limiting situations. The writer has elsewhere (Collis 1969, 1972, 1975) described the type of thinking involved here as a *concrete generalisation* because, although the child is still tied to empirical reality, he does, within the limitations imposed by this restriction, seek generalised solutions. His weakness lies in the way in which he forms the generalisation. Even when he is operating upon what the observer may see as variables, he seems to reason by using a series of closures of the operation involved to ensure that he has at each step a unique result.

These deductions from the Piaget protocols are readily reflected in items using elementary mathematics as the medium. For instance, the child often appears to have developed an ability to work with operations and abstractions as such, but it is usually a simple matter to show that the subject is soon lost unless the uniqueness of the operation(s) involved is guaranteed in some way. He may well be able to determine that $\dfrac{285 \times 694}{285}$ is equivalent to $\dfrac{491 \times 694}{491}$ but would not necessarily be able to understand and use meaningfully the generalisation, $\dfrac{an}{a} = \dfrac{bn}{b}$.

Evidence from a recent pilot study (Firth 1974) bears on this same phenomenon. Firth found that adolescents (age range 14·8 to 15·7) who had been classified as at the concrete-generalisation stage by using a test devised by the writer (Collis 1973) were able to deduce and work with a rule for solving equations of a certain form. The rule was such that it was valid only for equations in this particular form. In the criterion test the subjects were asked to solve a number of equations for which the rule worked, followed by a number of others for which the rule was invalid. As an essential step in each item the subject was asked to test his solution in the original statement. The results showed that, when these students came to the items for which the rule was invalid, they responded by either ceasing to check their results or by redefining the operation to force their result to satisfy the original statement of the rule. Although they were given the opportunity to amend the rule so that it would be valid for the later items, a negligible proportion succeeded in doing so. The lack of flexibility, the premature closure on a rule from a few positive instances followed by the inability to reopen the closure when it became necessary, the *apparent* ability to work with variables while in fact relying on closures at each stage—all are typical of this level of thinking.

The concept of an inverse process at this stage level tends to fit with a notion of 'undoing' an operation previously performed and, in general, appears to be successfully applied only with operations with which the child is thoroughly familiar. He would be able to solve for y in $y+4 = 7$. However, he would still regard y and $y+4$ as unique, but unknown, numbers—but adding 4 can be undone by subtracting 4. This notion of 'undoing' an operation is a significant advance on the stage IIB child's idea of 'destroying' the operation. What has been 'undone' can be 'done up', that is, it is reversible; in contrast 'destroying' is irreversible. Thus the Stage IIIA child having 'undone' $y+4 = 7$ to $y = 3$, can go back to his starting point by a reverse procedure while, as explained above, the IIB child cannot.

Another important advance which is made at this substage is the recognition of the necessity for consistency as an integral part of a system of operations. However, although the majority show a distinct preference for consistency, not all are able to express clearly a logical reason for this preference (Neimark and Lewis 1967; Collis 1974). A consistent system, judging by their responses, seems to be more satisfying to them on pure empirical or pragmatic grounds.

The final substage (Stage IIIB, 16+ years) which Piaget delineates, arrives when the child's cognitive development comes into full-bloom. Now, as Piaget points out, the adolescent is able to develop transformation rules which completely solve the problems presented to him. Moreover, he comes to a problem with a set of abstract hypotheses to test; he needs no longer to rely completely on reality for his ideas as he can envisage and manipulate abstract variables which may have a bearing on the solution. No longer is he satisfied that one or two specific demonstrations are sufficient basis upon which to generalise. Furthermore, he looks upon closure or uniqueness as being an abstract condition which makes certain things possible—the propositions and conditions themselves are the reality and these do not require that a link be established with the physical world prior to working on a problem where the system is defined. The Firth (1974) subjects who, at this stage of development, worked with the original rule until it broke down, were able to indicate why it was not valid in the new cases and then were successful

F

in devising a more general rule which was valid on all occasions for the operations involved.

A big leap forward is made with respect to the notion of inverse also. This process is now regarded as working directly with the operations themselves in such a way as to balance or compensate without necessarily affecting the existence of the earlier operation; for example, these students, unlike their comrades at earlier levels of development, can handle well items such as, if $(p \ o \ r) \ oq = (a \ o \ b) \ oq$ then $p \ o \ r = a \ o \ b$ (the elements p, r, q, etc., and the operation 'o' with its inverse, being suitably defined). In all such cases they require that a system of operations be consistent—they readily recognise inconsistencies and eschew them in their reasoning.

ALC and MIS and the four stages

Acceptance of Lack of Closure (ALC) and ability to handle Multiple Interacting Systems (MIS) may be seen as the two concepts whose development has been traced in the last section; the former performing an enabling function for the latter. The original exposition of the significance of 'closure' as both a descriptive and an explanatory concept in the context being considered here appeared in Collis (1972). However, as the two concepts have been fully explicated and related one to the other by Lunzer (1973), the reader is referred to this latter paper for a detailed account. The intention in this section will be to draw the reader's attention to the relevance of ALC and MIS to the four stages outlined in the previous section.

In the context of this chapter the level of *closure* at which the child is able to work with the operations of elementary arithmetic depends on his ability to regard the outcome of an operation (or series of operations) as unique and 'real' (in the sense that it is related to the individual's reality). At its lowest level (apparent by age 7+) this requires that two elements connected by the operation be *actually replaced* by a third element which the child recognises as belonging to the same set. In terms of numbers this means that at this level the four operations of elementary arithmetic *can* be meaningful when used singly with small numbers within the child's experience. However, both the numbers and operations must be relatable, by the child, to the physical world with which he is familiar. He would be able to decide that $3+2 = 5$ and would consider the statement meaningful.

The next level (beginning around age 10 years) involves the child in the ability to regard the outcome of performing an operation as necessarily unique; that is, the two elements connected by the operation are replaceable by a third from the same set, but it is not necessary to make the actual replacement to guarantee this. The child may now use numbers beyond his empirically verified range (e.g. $273 + 472$). He may also use expressions involving (say) two operations which can be closed sequentially $(6+4+5)$. Later (about 13 years) this ability to refrain from actual closure, so long as there is a guarantee that a unique familiar result is available at any time if required, becomes general and the child may be expected to move on to what has been termed above *concrete generalisations*. At this point he is capable of working with formulae such as $V = L \times B \times H$ provided he is able to consider that each letter stands for a unique number and each binary operation involved may be closed at any stage.

The final stage of development so far as this concept is concerned (beginning at about 16 years) enables the adolescent to consider 'closure' in a formal sense because he is able to work on the operations themselves and does not need to relate either the elements or the operations to a physical reality. He now becomes capable of dealing with the variables as such because he can hold back from drawing a final conclusion until he has considered various possibilities, an essential strategy for obtaining a relationship as distinct from obtaining a unique result. For instance, given $V = L \times B \times H$, he would not only be able to obtain unique results by appropriate substitutions in the formula, but would also be able to discuss meaningfully the effect of various transformations on the formula; for example, what would one predict for V if one increased L, decreased B and held H constant?

What has been said above about ALC may be seen as directly related to what Halford (1970) has pointed out with respect to the acquisition of concrete operations. Halford says that for the acquisition of concrete operations children need to combine judgments, be they numbers or other units, two at a time and select those combinations which give unique results. In other words, they reorganise their judgments until they achieve closure on a unique result. It is a useful extension of this theory to consider that to attain formal operations the child must also be able to combine two units but one of these units may itself be an operation.

At the concrete operational level two numbers may be combined to give a unique result, e.g. $4 + 2 = 6$, whereas at the formal operational level the adolescent can work with a combination such as $(p \ o \ r) \ oq = c$ (where 'o', p, r, q and c are suitably defined). In the latter case an operation $(p \ o \ r)$ is itself combined with another $(o \ q)$ to yield a unique result. The important element on all such occasions is that an operation must have some meaning as a unit even though the individual cannot 'close' it arithmetically.

Thus far in this section the development of higher levels of reasoning has been seen as closely related to the child's tolerance for unclosed operations. The closer to early concrete reasoning he is, the more the child depends on an immediate closure of the operation in order to make the situation meaningful. This phenomenon appears in various guises in all the diversity of tests used by the various researchers who have worked in the area of concrete operations (see, for example, Peel 1960, 1971). On the other hand, the nearer he comes to the top level of adolescent thinking, the more it becomes apparent that the subject can withhold closing while he considers the effect of the variables in the problem. This again is supported by other evidence (see Peel 1960, 1971).

Let us now turn to a brief consideration of the other concept which was mentioned at the beginning of this section, namely MIS. Although it is being argued that ALC has a crucial role to play in any consideration of the development of reasoning, it is clearly not the whole story. It was proposed earlier that ALC has an enabling role to play and that specifically the level of tolerance of lack of closure which the individual has available largely determines the complexity of the system within which he can work meaningfully. Lunzer (1973) distinguishes between simple and complex systems, the former available to concrete-operational reasoners and the latter to formal-operational reasoners. Simple systems are such that any solutions required can be effected by assimilation to one set of co-variations; complex systems are those where more than one system of co-variation is involved and any meaningful solution of a set problem depends upon working with the interaction of the two (or more) systems. The relevance of this concept (and, indeed, of ALC) to the many varieties of task used to distinguish formal reasoning, including those of Piaget and of Peel, is well brought out by Lunzer in his 1973 paper and need not be repeated here. However, it may be of value to take an illustration from school mathematics.

Consider the formula for the area of a rectangle, $A = L \times B$. It is suggested here and supported both by experimental evidence and classroom experience that the child in the late concrete-operational stage can work effectively with it at a certain level. He is able to recognise that, given *any rectangle* with specific units which measure L and B, he is able to find A. There is clearly a large number of possible rectangles and consequent As. But he is at home with the idea because it is, for him, essentially a single system of co-variation; for example, the area changes as the rectangle changes $L \times B$ changes as the rectangle changes. What he cannot do is relate changes in one or more of the variables A and L and B to changes in one (or more) of the others; for example, he would not be able to solve problems where A is to stay constant, B is to be changed in some way (doubling, taking a fraction of the original, etc.), and he is required to state what must be done to length L. This last type of problem involves the child in working with the inter-action between two systems. B is varied and L must be varied in a compensatory way in order to keep the product, $L \times B$, constant.

The relevance of MIS to the notion of negation is also readily discerned. Let us examine the problem which children, at various levels of ALC, have with solving a simple equation such as $y + 4 = 7$.

In terms of the theory set out so far, there are at least four levels at which children may be able to operate to find the value of y in the given equation. At the lowest level (up to age 8 to 9 years) the problem is regarded as a simple counting task: to find y he need only count from 4 until he reaches 7 and record the number of units used. This can be done by reciting the appropriate tables, e.g. $1 + 4 = 5$, $2 + 4 = 6$, or by the use of structural material, etc. At this stage the operation sign is only required as a stimulus to set the student responding in terms of counting, tables, etc., and does not imply any understanding of the mathematical implications of the operation of addition. Many children are quite capable of operating competently at this level in the Infant School classes.

At the second and third levels (substages IIB and IIIA, 10 to 15 years) one can see what appear to be operationally identical results obtained by different procedures. It is not proposed to repeat at this point what has been dealt with above with respect to the difference between 'destroying' and 'undoing' an operation, but to describe the fundamental operational basics which apply to either way of looking at the problem. The child necessarily regards both sides of the equation as representing a unique number, and considers the 7 as the specific and only possible representation for one side of the equation. However, he also 'closes' $y+4$. By this is meant that he now pays attention to the operation as indicating something performed on the two elements, but must regard the outcome as unique: y for him is a unique number, like 7, but for the time being unknown—if one does the operation of 'plussing 4' one still has, as a result, a unique number even though one does not yet know what it is. His problem in solving the equation $y+4 = 7$ reduces to: y is an unknown but unique number and so is $y+4$; the latter has been obtained by 'plussing' 4 to y and thus y can be found by subtracting 4 from $y+4$ which *happens* to be equal to 7, ergo, $y = 3$. This reasoning would best be recorded thus:

$$y+4 = 7$$
$$y \quad = 3$$

By the final stage (16+ years) the adolescent focuses on the operation and does not need to regard either side of the equation as unique and necessarily empirically constant. For example, 7 can be replaced by any one of a number of expressions without troubling him ($3+4$, $5+2$, $9-2$, etc.); y could be variable or constant. The problem for him is to find the operation which will act on the given operation in such a way as to negate it without upsetting the present state of the relationships and allowing for the possibility of returning to the original statement. In the present example subtraction is the negating operation and it is *convenient* to use the subtraction of 4 in order to isolate y; likewise he can work on the 7—replacing it by $3+4$ for convenience. His reasoning in this stage might be recorded thus:

$y+4 \quad = 7$	
$y+4-4 = 7-4$	negating the + operation, choosing a convenient number and maintaining the relationships
$y+(4-4) = 3+(4-4)$	replacing 7 by convenient expression and re-associating
$y+0 \quad = 3+0$	inverse axiom
$y \quad = 3$	identity axiom

Of course, he may very well set out his solution in the same way as his younger friends, but it would not take a mathematics teacher very long to find out that the older child has the ability to reason in this way while the younger child does not.

The examples given may be linked readily to Piaget's interpretation (Inhelder and Piaget 1958; Beth and Piaget 1966). Piaget clearly distinguishes between the two concepts of inverse and indicates also that they may vary in form at various levels of behaviour and, implicitly, in various contexts. Essentially he suggests that *negation* annuls the operation directly and that a *reciprocal strategy* leaves the operation untouched while neutralising its effect. In the beam balance experiment, for example, adding a weight to the left-hand pan is *negated* by removing it, but the same effect can be obtained by adding the same weight to the right-hand pan—a reciprocal strategy. The point is made that at the formal operational level the adolescent has both strategies available. It is suggested here that the method of isolating y, implicitly available to the fourth-level children, represents the *reciprocal* strategy and that the level II and III children are only able to operate with the *negation* strategy.

In mathematical material there are many occasions in even elementary formal mathematics where the reciprocal strategy is essential rather than optional and an attempt to use negation in such cases often gives rise to serious errors. Some of these occasions are due to the following: (*a*) the order in which operations are performed is important; (*b*) an operation often has to be performed on an expression as a whole and not on one of its constituent parts; and (*c*) an operation or a series of operations has to be performed while retaining the original expression in a particular form. For instance, to clear the fraction out of the equation $\frac{x}{2} + 3 = 7 - 2$, one must multiply throughout by 2, i.e. $x + 6 = 2(7 - 2)$, from which $x = 4$. However, a concrete-operational reasoner, using only the negation strategy, may apply the (to him) obvious procedure as follows: $\frac{x}{2} \times \frac{2}{1} + 3 = 7 - 2$—and so destroy the original relationship. He fails to distinguish between this case and the case where it is appropriate to operate on one term only, e.g. $\frac{1}{x-1} + \frac{1}{x+1}$ is equal to $\frac{1}{x-1} \times \frac{x+1}{x+1} + \frac{1}{x+1}$ because $\frac{x+1}{x+1}$ is simply a *replacement* for the identity element. The availability of the reciprocal transformation implies the ability to handle the total relationship whereas the negation strategy tends to apply to one element alone.

In brief, the lower-level use of the inverse may be seen as analogous to a simple system in that it operates immediately and directly upon the last operation performed without necessarily considering its effect on any other operation which may be interacting with it. By the same token, the reciprocal procedure may be said to involve a complex system as it takes into account interactions between the various variables involved. The reciprocal does not need to be applied immediately and directly to the latest operation, but may be applied to another part of the system (even other interacting variables) and may well involve compensatory action instead of direct action on the variable concerned.

Conclusion

The diagram opposite may be considered as a summary of the Piagetian stages from the point of view of a child's developing ability to handle mathematical items. It can be seen that his cognitive development in this respect traces a pattern of less and less need for the support offered by feedback from his empirical reality.

As the child emerges from the preoperational stage to the stage of concrete operations (7 to 9 years) he is able to operate as far as stage A. From age ten to fifteen years he gradually extends this ability to that represented by the highest level achievable in stage B, that is *concrete generalisations*. Stage C represents a movement to formal operations proper. As each stage in the hierarchy is achieved it subsumes its predecessors. As one moves up the sequence the stages become less reality bound and, as a consequence, more flexible and efficient. In addition, the process of subsumption is such that the individual can return to working at a lower level in the sequence should he feel that the occasion warrants it.

Stages A and B together (7 to 15 years) represent what are considered in this chapter to be the area of concrete operations and are seen as a necessary precursor

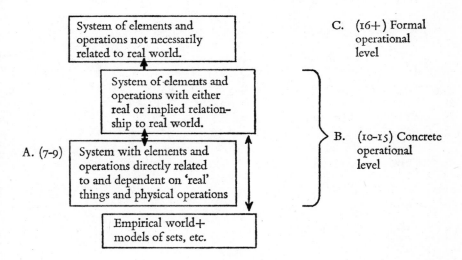

to the formal thinking represented by stage C. Stage A begins when the basic conservation and classification skills are established and ends at about age nine years when the child seems to be able to cope with one arithmetic operation on two positive integers so long as the integers remain within his empirically verifiable range. By the end of this stage he is able to map from a narrowly specified reality to a positive integral number field, perform the arithmetic operation corresponding to elementary set operations (e.g. addition related to union of disjoint sets) and map the result back into the real field again. He needs, literally, to be able 'to see' a unique result before the operations either on sets or numbers mean anything to him.

As the child develops through stage B he has the same basic skills to rely on as he had at the earlier stage. His major advance appears to be in the direction of less reliance on 'seeing' uniqueness in the results of his operations. He is still bound to empirical evidence, but he is more content both to infer beyond what can be demonstrated by model and to form a generalisation by example from a number of specific cases. For example, he can prove that $6 \times 64 = 3 \times 128$ by arguing from the partially completed model below:

64

```
     XXXXXXXXXXXXXXXXXXXXXXXXXXXXXXXXXXXXXXXXXXXXXXXXXXXXXXXXXXXXXXXXXXX
     XXXXXXXXXXXXXXXXXXXXXXXXXXXXXXXXXX...............................
     XXXXXXXXXXXXXXXXXXXXXXXXXXXXX.........................
6    XXXXXXXXXXXXXXXXXXXXXXXXX......................
     XXXXXXXXXXXXXXXXXXXXXXXXXXXXXXXXXXXXXXXXXX..............
     XXXXXXXXXXXXXXXXXXXX.....................
```

and, after a number of examples such as $\dfrac{2}{3} = \dfrac{2 \times 2}{2 \times 3} = \dfrac{3 \times 2}{3 \times 3} \ldots \dfrac{4}{5} = \dfrac{4 \times 5}{5 \times 5} \ldots$ he is willing to accept and use as a *concrete generalisation* the formula $\dfrac{a}{b} = \dfrac{m \times a}{m \times b}$. This ability to form generalisations from specific instances comes in the later half of the stage concerned and is undoubtedly a new and powerful tool for him. However, as was pointed out earlier, this tool has built into it a serious weakness, the tendency to generalise from a few specific positive instances. This weakness is, of course, an important way of distinguishing between the late concrete stage and the formal stage of reasoning.

In stage C, the adolescent moves away entirely from reliance on reality and is prepared to work with abstract elements using the operations themselves.

J. B. Biggs

13. Schooling and moral development

The impact of schools

'What is most distinctive about the schools as compared to other social institutions is their totality. No other institution . . . presumes to require unremunerated attendance and observance of its rituals by an entire age group for more than a decade, under penalty of either criminal or economic sanctions' (Friedenberg 1970, p. 17).

We have lived with the totality of the school for the best part of this century, yet it is only recently that we have begun to ask searching questions about its effects. With the catch-cry of 'accountability', the onus of proof is being thrown back to the school, particularly in the relatively easily measurable areas of basic literacy and numeracy. There has, however, been very little evaluation of the effects of schooling on affective functioning; that is, upon the student's feelings, values and attitudes to himself and to his relationships with others.

  Some educators, perhaps more so in the US than in the UK, argue that the schools should remain neutral on affective and value questions. Lohnes, for example, states that 'evaluating schooling is largely evaluating the enhancement of intelligence' (1973, p. 6). Several American writers have nevertheless shown that schools have a very strong, if covert, involvement in the transfer of particular values and attitudes (e.g. Kohlberg 1966; Dreeben 1968; Jackson 1968; Friedenberg 1970). As far as Britain is concerned, Lester Smith (1957) documents the official concern with 'character training', while the Plowden Report quite bluntly states: 'A school is not merely a teaching shop, it must transmit values and attitudes' (Central Advisory Council for Education 1967, para. 505). This concern is evidently shared by the general public: Wright (1971) quotes a 1969 National Opinion Poll finding that a good half of the population want and expect secondary schools to accord highest or second highest priority to 'moral training'.

  But whether the official stance is one of neutrality or not, 'morality is embedded in all formal education' (Sizer and Sizer 1970, p. 3) so that even the most cognitively oriented education has an affective impact: '. . . schooling is a much broader experience than being taught what is contained in textbooks. Students learn not only facts, skills and concepts but also rules of membership in a social institution. For well over a thousand hours a year, students are urged to follow routines and procedures, to get along with each other, and to respect adult authority. Every day, students' actions are praised and criticised, their movements are directed, and their values and beliefs are shaped. Often these experiences in institutional living may have greater impact on students' ultimate well-being than do those we commonly identify with the academic curriculum' (M. L. Silberman 1971, p. 1).

What is this greater impact? How do we assess it? What are the mechanisms involved? Can we mitigate the bad effects of the impact and maximise the good effects? Are different students affected differently? Important enough questions, surely, but questions on which the present state of research disallows an answer, for several reasons. First, much current research consists of anecdote and reportage which, for all its brilliance, often relies on little more than personal impressions (e.g. Jackson 1968; C. E. Silberman 1970; Henry 1972). Second, the area is large and conceptually loose, so that it has been difficult to construe the affective impact in terms of a general conceptual framework, which in turn makes it difficult to define and measure appropriate dependent variables. Finally, such research shares the methodological difficulties of cognitive accountability research, such as problems of long-term follow-up, the virtual non-existence of a control (no-schooling) group, and so on.

In this chapter we are mainly concerned with the problem of a conceptual framework, a problem to which Piaget and Kohlberg *inter alia* have much to offer. Consideration is then given to analysing the total school context in terms of what is known about moral development.

A theoretical framework

A major difficulty in this area is that of definition. Already we have been using terms such as 'affective', 'values', 'moral' and 'interpersonal' almost as if they were synonymous. A first step is therefore to attempt to introduce some terminological consistency.

Piaget (1962) reports a conversation between two bus conductors in which one said about a third person: 'He is a nice man; he is loyal; he is logical.' The conductor evidently didn't mean by this that his friend's thinking was a model of Aristotelean logic. He was referring to something quite different: that in his interactions with other people, his friend was dependable and coherent in his feelings and affective bonds. There is a 'logic of feeling' (op. cit) which has its own psycho-logical structure and dynamics, parallel to but different from the better understood 'logic of thought'. Just as cognitive development in the logic of thought increases effectance in handling the physical world in terms of increasingly general and complex schemata, so moral development in the logic of feeling facilitates effective interpersonal interaction.

Piaget further argues that the two basic operations in the development of the logic of thought, reversability and conservation, have their affective counterparts. *Morality* is the tendency to accept and follow a system of rules that regulate interpersonal behaviour on a reciprocal basis: 'it is the conservation of feelings and of affective values' (op. cit., p. 138). The feeling of gratitude, for instance, implies a conservation of feeling that impels reciprocity. A boy who is forced by his mother to offer his friend a sweet when the friend had already been kind to the boy is not behaving 'morally'; there is an open-loop system, as the necessity for the mother's intervention shows. In a closed-loop system, the feelings contingent upon the previous act of kindness would have been conserved and produced the reciprocal (moral) action.

It is also possible to trace other linkages between the logics of thought and feeling. One of the important discriminanda between preoperations, concrete operations and formal operations is the number of dimensions that can be handled simultaneously (Pascual-Leone 1972). Preoperational thought is unidimensional, in that only one organising attribute can be considered at a time; concrete operations are bidimensional, in that two such attributes can be handled simultaneously (as in logical multiplication); while formal operations are n-dimensional.

Likewise, at the egocentric stage in the logic of feeling, the self becomes the single dimension around which feelings and social interaction revolve. The second, sociocentric stage (Piaget and Weil 1951) corresponds to concrete operations, in that it is bidimensional: the individual can now handle himself as a dimension interacting with peer-group norms as the other dimension. The allocentric stage is multidimensional like formal operations: the individual can construe himself as a dimension in a matrix, including abstract principle and social norms as other dimensions. These stages are quite similar to the three levels outlined by Kohlberg (1963; see also Chapter 8 in this volume) of preconventional, conventional, and postconventional, each of which is subdivided into two stages, giving six stages in all.

Moral development proceeds more slowly than cognitive development. Children at age eleven typically operate (in our culture) at Stage 2 (egocentric/unidimensional), which is of course years after they would have moved into concrete operations; similarly, most people do not reach the postconventional level of moral judgment until their middle twenties, with a high proportion not even getting that far (Kohlberg 1973).

This disparity between cognitive and moral developments may be due to the excessively cognitive orientation of school, in turn reflecting the fact that our society is 'thing-oriented' rather than 'person-oriented'. Alternatively, there may be not two domains but one—cognitive—the stages in 'moral' development being nothing more than the application of cognitive schemata to rather ill-defined and vague tasks (the moral dilemma stories), hence the apparent 'retardation' in moral development.

The critical issue here concerns the relationship between moral judgment and action. The 'cognitive-only' hypothesis would leave the developing individual increasingly like Tolman's rat, 'lost in thought'. On the contrary, there appears to be a strong relationship between moral judgment and action, which increases with moral maturity. The locus of obligation is *internalised* with growth in moral maturity; clearly, one is far more committed to act in a 'moral' way (however that is defined) at Stage 6 than at Stage 1, where the commitment is to avoid punishment rather than stick by principles one has derived for oneself (see also Piaget 1962).

In the well-known obedience studies by Milgram (1963), it has been found that only a minority of subjects will refuse to administer electric shock, under instructions, up to the point where death is plausibly involved. However, Kohlberg and Turiel (1971) report that 75 per cent of Stage 6 subjects refused to follow instructions beyond mild levels of shock, compared to 13 per cent of all other subjects. In a study of the 1964 Berkeley sit-ins (Haan 1971), in which it was argued that there was a clear-cut issue between individual rights and conventional authority, 80 per cent of Stage 6 students sat-in, as opposed to 50 per cent for Stage 5, and 10 per cent for Stages 3 and 4.

It has also been found that a large majority of delinquents are preconventional, when similarly aged non-delinquents are typically conventional or even post-conventional (Freundlich and Kohlberg 1971; Fodor 1972; Ewanyk 1973). Fodor also reports that delinquents who yielded to pressure from the experimenter to change their judgments received *lower* scores on the Kohlberg scale than delinquents who resisted such influence. Even at this low level, we can see evidence of internalisation and commitment increasing with moral maturity.

Henshel (1971) found that (negative) correlations between 'honesty' scores (on a self-report questionnaire) and number of cheating incidents rose steeply and consistently from grades four through seven. Similarly, Schwartz, Feldman, Brown and Heingartner (1969) found that college students classified as 'high in level of moral thought' cheated significantly less than those classified as 'low', on Kohlberg's Moral Maturity Scale.

Finally, Broad (1973) found no relationship between susceptibility to change moral judgments (either upwards or downwards) and intelligence; it was not necessarily the bright children who moved upwards in moral development. In the Piagetian view, then, moral development is related to, but different from, cognitive development; in particular, it involves a commitment to action.

The nature of the relationship between judgment and action is critical. Kaufman (1970) has outlined a model that is particularly helpful in the present context. Kaufman (his model is modified slightly in the presentation here) proposes that the final behavioural outcome, in a moral decision-making situation, is an additive function of the following components:

1. V: values or attitudes specific to the situation.
2. i: the 'idealism' or commitment of the person, which expresses the probability of his reacting in terms of his values.
3. U: the utility of the choice, expressed as the algebraic sum of positive outcomes multiplied by their probabilities of occurrence, minus the negative outcomes multiplied by their probabilities.
4. H: habit, or response strength accountable to previous learning or modelling in similar situations.
Thus: *Behaviour Potential* $= f(iV + U + H)$

Note that the terms V, U and H are all situation-specific: i is the only factor that is more or less a personality constant. Further, i can be reinterpreted to correspond to stage level in Piaget's or Kohlberg's sense: as we have seen, individuals at higher stage levels are more committed to act in terms of their values than are those at lower stages.

When i is low, as at Stages 1 and 2, iV is diminished, leaving U and H to dominate moral choice behaviours. Thus, immature persons are easily swayed by pay-offs; in fact, U-type decisions are characteristic of Stage 2. Stage 6 is less likely to be bribed from his stance, but the model suggests that he too has his price (hostages may be coins in his currency).

Similarly, H may dominate the equation: despite years of involvement in psychology and education, I find that I react to children very much as my parents and teachers reacted to me. Due in this instance to modelling and to direct reinforcement, there is a very strong H term that overrides both iV and U: I 'know' that an aggressive punishing response to an irritating piece of behaviour has a low if not negative U. I also happen to disapprove of punishment on moral grounds. Yet a swift, cutting retort, designed to wound, remains in my repertoire with an unfortunately high probability. A visit to almost any classroom will indicate that H is probably the greatest obstacle to enlightened educational practice.

Kaufman focuses upon the i coefficient as the one likely to bring about *trans-situational*, and hence stable, changes in people's social behaviour. As is evident from the work on behaviour modification, it is relatively simple to bring about desirable change in a given context simply by manipulating either U (which implies individual choice) or H (which does not). However, as Kohlberg and Turiel (1971) point out, such short-term changes, desirable as they might be for immediate practical goals, do not really meet the educational desideratum of stable change over the long term. Kaufman's own suggestion for increasing the i coefficient is disappointing (op. cit., p. 133); i.e. providing a number of stimulus situations so that the notion that correspondence between attitudes and behaviours is generally desirable may be abstracted (he specifically uses Bruner, Goodnow and Austin as a paradigm). Other possibilities will be considered in due course.

To summarise, then, progression in the domain marked out by Piaget as the logic of feeling, and ordered into three two-stage levels by Kohlberg, implies an increasing tendency to act in terms of principle—principles at first backed up by an external, social, authority, and subsequently internalised with the authority of conscience. In addition, it seems reasonable to suggest that the link between moral judgment and behaviour in particular situations is moderated by the relevance of that situation to one's moral values, and by the utility and habit strength of alternative responses.

The logic of feeling structures our interpersonal environment; the logic of thought our physical environment. Both seem to be good targets for any comprehensive definition of schooling. Given the basic validity of the Kohlberg model, and a dash of faith in an emergent philosophy, then we have something that looks very like an aim for schooling. With all due respects to Piaget's (1970) reservations about 'The American Question' (i.e. intervening to hasten conservation), there is a great deal of intuitive force in maintaining that the role of a socialising agency such as the school should include helping the individual student to reach his maximal level of functioning in both cognitive and affective areas. As Kohlberg (1970) puts it, the fact that people *do* move towards Stage 6 is justification that people *should*.

Some conditions of upward stage change

Before considering the specific effects of the school on moral development, it is first necessary to examine the question of the docility of stage change. What are the conditions of stage change; is it possible to realise those conditions within the resources of the normal school? In view of the disappointing results with respect to a very similar problem in the logic of thought—the hastening of conservation under ordinary classroom conditions—the outlook may not seem promising.

Kohlberg's own view is that while the sequence of stages is invariant, and independent of cultural and subcultural influences, the *rate of progress* through the stages is culturally determined; further 'it is not our belief that the moral structures are inherited, but rather result from a self-constructive process of organism-environment interaction' (Rest, Turiel and Kohlberg 1969, p. 247).

The general mechanisms of change are held to be similar to those that apply in the parallel field of cognitive development: the environment presents information that throws the existing system into a state of disequilibrium, and through accommodation, a more adaptive, equilibrated, state develops that replaces the previous one. Such considerations have led Kohlberg and his colleagues to propose that one condition of upward change would be facilitated by their version of the 'optimal mismatch' hypothesis (Hunt 1961).

Accordingly, they proposed (Turiel 1966; Rest, Turiel and Kohlberg 1969) that subjects would judge statements that are *above* their own level as 'better', although more difficult to comprehend, and would be most likely to change upwards when the input statements are no more than one stage above their own (+ 1). They found some evidence to support their hypotheses. Statements at the subject's own level, or below, were rejected; + 1 statements led to upward change in some instances, while + 2 statements could not be comprehended and were instead reinterpreted in − 1 terms.

Whether or not change occurred under the + 1 condition depended further upon the amount of 'stage mixture' displayed by the subject (i.e. the variance of responses around the modal stage). Subjects showing a low variance (most responses classifiable as belonging to a given stage) showed little tendency to change; those with a high variance accepted the + 1 statements and accommodated to them. Stage mixture is thus taken as evidence of décalage and, functionally, of openness to change. Precisely what conditions promote the décalage itself, however, remain unclear. Support for the stage-mixture hypothesis comes from a study by Ewanyk (1973), who found that a stage-mixture score successfully predicted upward change.

Role-playing is another condition which theoretically is valuable in that it directly involves the subject in allocentrism, that is in taking the view of another

(Kohlberg 1969). The empirical support for role-playing is not very strong, however, even when the subject is required to enact a + 1 point of view (Ewanyk 1973). Taking a role, unless under exceptionally favourable circumstances, may not be as involving as a discussion and analysis of values one genuinely holds.

Kohlberg (1973) observes that none of his original sample of seventy-two boys had reached Stage 5 before the age of twenty-three years, and then the transition seemed to depend upon (*a*) an experience of sustained responsibility for the welfare of others, under conditions (*b*) where the basis of this responsibility could be questioned. The jump into postconventionality seems to require conditions of high involvement, where the individual is forced into autonomous decision-making because the conventional (Stage 4) constraints are seen to be inappropriate.

On the other hand, Beck, Sullivan and Taylor (1972) found that they were able to induce Stage 5 amongst senior high school students by the usual technique of group discussion and confrontation, but the effect was not measurable until one year after the treatment, when the percentage of Stage 5 responses jumped from 2 to 22 per cent in the experimental group, the control group remaining unchanged. This latency might be the function of this particular transition, or it might be general, in which case several apparently null studies might well have been fruitful had the follow-up been made.

Birnbaum (1972) reports that anxiety exerted different effects on Grade 7 students. Anxiety over parental rejection led to a regression in moral judgment, while anxiety over peer rejection led to greater flexibility in moral judgment: such a result is interpretable in terms of the nature of the preconventional/conventional transition.

Parental interaction seems to exert an effect on moral development. Holstein (1971) showed that *post*conventional mothers were more likely to have conventional children (at age twelve) than were conventional mothers themselves. Kohlberg, in attempting to salvage the + 1 hypothesis, interprets this as indicating that the postconventional mothers were capable of conventional messages, and 'integrated them in terms of the higher level, making them better moral educators even where the task is bringing the children to the conventional level' (Kohlberg 1970, p. 119). Haan, Smith and Block (1969) found that postconventional students and Peace Corps volunteers came from politically liberal homes, and that their moral maturity was associated with mother's (but not father's) education, but their relations with the mother were likely to be conflicted. This contrasted with conventional subjects, who tended to have a religious upbringing, with clear rules and rewards and punishments, and conflict-free relations with parents.

The results of Holstein, and of Haan *et al.*, appear to suit a modelling or social learning hypothesis rather than a + 1 optimal mismatch. Bandura and McDonald (1963) and Crane and Ballif (1973) also provide evidence for the effect modelling has upon moral judgment (see also the discussion in Maccoby 1968). For our purposes, which are practical rather than theoretical, it seems quite reasonable to suggest that upward stage change will be associated with modelling on appropriate parental, and possibly teacher, figures as well as with specifically structured environmental situations (see also Bull 1969).

In sum, the following conditions appear to be associated with stage change:

1.   A predisposition for change, characterised by 'stage mixture'. How far stage mixture may itself be facilitated, and how far it has to be regarded as a readiness factor, is not known at present.
2.   Presentation, in some involving format, of views incorporating a structure roughly one stage above that already existing in each subject.
3.   Home environment; postconventional parents tend to have postconventional children. It is not known how far this is explicable in terms of flexible parental control (e.g. using Stage 3 arguments to Stage 2 children despite the parents' own Stage 6 orientation), or of a principle additional to the +1 hypothesis, such as modelling.
4.   Different transitions have different conditions of optimal change, such conditions reflecting the inherent structure of the particular transition. Transitions to postconventionality require opportunities for the exercise of autonomy.
5.   In general, the change process is highly complex and appears to be triggered by different combinations of events in different individuals.

These conditions have some kind of empirical support; sufficient at least to look at school environments and ask whether they typically are likely to lead to upward change or not.

Aims and functions of schooling

We next need to conceptualise the involvement of schools in moral education. There are basically two kinds of role: a *maintenance* role, in which schools pass on the particular 'bag of virtues' (Kohlberg 1966) that are currently held to be important (cf. the NOP survey); and a *growth* role, in which schools help individuals to reach their own maximum potential in moral development. In the first role, the school would actively discourage children from moving beyond the conventional stage; and in the second, postconventionality would on the contrary be the major aim for as many students as possible.

We appear to have overcome the corresponding problem in the logic of thought. As Wilson (1973) points out, no longer do we assemble a bag of facts and tricks and say 'This is science: learn it, and you will know science.' Bruner's (1960) advocacy of the 'process' approach to the sciences is now fairly well accepted. What we now teach is the scientific method, the *process* of science. Correspondingly, Wilson claims we should teach the *process* of arriving at moral decisions.

'Process' in the cognitive domain has more recently come to refer to *psychological* rather than to discipline-centred processes. Biggs (1973, p. 25) defines process learning as 'learning experiences that affect the extent to which the learner copes *effectively* and *autonomously* with novel situations'. In this view, the focus is not upon Bruner's original concept of 'the structure of a discipline' (although that is initially one highly significant input), but upon the potentialities of the *learner*, in particular upon the development of a good self-concept, in which the learner acquires the belief that he is himself responsible for what happens to him (see also de Charms 1971). This implies as much delegation of decision-making to the learner as is realistic, and the conditions apply equally to the logic of feeling as to the logic of thought: internalisation and self-determination are involved in both.

Broadly, schooling can be oriented toward the transfer of particular *content* (the maintenance role) or the fostering of coping *processes* (the growth role). Given that the logic of feeling is as much the bailiwick of the school as is the logic of thought, we can discern four general categories of school function (see Table 1).

TABLE I   *The function of school—orientation × domain*

Orientation	Domain	
	Thought	Feeling
Content	(a) Instruction; reception learning of given facts and procedures.	(b) Transfer of particular values and attitudes; conformity to pre-established norms.
Process	(c) Discovery; development of problem solving strategies under minimal guidance	(d) Encouragement towards position of moral autonomy.

The transmission of content applies (a) to data and procedures affecting the physical world; and (b) to the values and norms chosen as 'right', with the corresponding pressures to conform to them. Likewise, the development of self-determination applies to (c) being able to handle novel situations and problems in the physical world; and (d) the encouragement as far as possible towards self-determination of values and principles of interpersonal conduct.

Categories (a) and (c) do not concern us any further. Category (b), despite disclaimers of 'neutrality', has been a major concern of schools; it is referred to here as the *conformity* model. Category (d) has been the explicit concern of few schools in the past—Summerhill being one outstanding example—but it is becoming increasingly popular today; it is referred to here as the *process* model.

Let us conceptualise this in terms of the Kaufman equation. All schools attempt to introduce consistency in students' behaviour. In the conformity model, the consistency is externally imposed. It derives from the inculcation of particular values (V), usually indirectly, backed up by sanctions and habit (U) and (H): rules, regulations and traditions would be emphasised, not only for their immediate utility but also as a means of transmitting values (e.g. it is a good thing to obey, whatever the rule).

In the process model, attention would be focused on maximising i, leaving it to the individual to derive his own specific values (V) for handling particular situations, and minimising the effects of U and H: we would expect to find maximum freedom for the individual student to come to his own moral decisions. There would be situations provided (for example, discussion groups, student government structures) for generating moral decisions and deriving values, with minimal use of rules, sanctions and tradition as a means of stabilising behaviour.

The critical difference between the two models, then, centres upon the *target* in our equation: to maximise V, U and H; or to play these down and maximise i. In practice, these two aims can be conceived as occupying opposing ends of a single dimension, described at one end by external controlling structures, and at the other by room for self-control. The external structures refer to virtually all areas of institutional life: Bidwell (1972) calls them the 'activity structures' of the school, which are set up to control interpersonal interaction and in which the student must perforce become actively involved.

It is inevitable that when numbers of people interact with a common purpose, as they do in any institution, there will be some expectations of conformity to given norms, and acceptance of the values they imply. It is important therefore to distinguish between norms that are functionally necessary, and which have little *excess meaning*; and the enforced adherence to norms, the utility of which is marginal compared to their salience. In this last case, the 'saturated' activity structures amount to what writers have variously called a hidden, unstudied or implicit curriculum of values (Dreeben 1968; Jackson 1968; Overley 1970; Illich 1971; M. L. Silberman 1971). The hidden curriculum, in Kohlberg's view, 'refers to the fact that teachers and schools are engaged in moral education without explicity and philosophically discussing or formulating its goals and methods' (1970, p. 29). In the process model of schooling, then, there will be little excess meaning in the activity structures of the school; in the conformity model, the structures will be accorded a meaning and importance far in excess of their functional utility, becoming thereby the vehicles for specific values and attitudes.

For example, Kohlberg (1970) quotes an incident from *Summerhill* in which Neill warns a recent arrival to the school against becoming pregnant, not because of any moral issue, but because it would harm the school. Kohlberg comments: 'Unquestioned loyalty to the school . . . seems to be the ultimate end of moral education at Summerhill' (op. cit., p. 29). This is unfair. Neill was clearly concerned about the continued existence of the school rather than about an implicit curriculum of loyalty: this little activity structure does not really carry excess meaning. King (1969), on the other hand, analyses the activity structures surrounding the prefect system in a British grammar school, such as the symbolism of 'passing authority' at the induction ceremony, privileges of dressing differently from the rest of the school, sitting apart, jumping dinner queues, administering punishments, and so on. The values that both privileged and not-yet-privileged learn from such activity structures are evident, while their functional utility is rather less so (e.g. punishment privileges are unnecessary for maintaining control).

Table 2 lists some of the characteristic differences between the conformity and process models.

The conformity and process models can be thought of as lying along a single dimension, determined by the extent to which the activity structures of the school carry excess meaning or not: any one school can, theoretically, be characterised as lying at a point nearer to either conformity or process ends. At the conformity end, the individual's room for determining his own goals and ways of achieving them will be restricted; the meaning of the structure may become transferred as a particular value. To the extent that the activity structures are purely functional, there is little excess meaning and the student can determine his own role in school. It would be expected that such successful self-determination would result in internalisation of values and in a greater commitment to them; that is, to an increase in *i*.

TABLE 2   *Some critical differences between conformity and process models of schooling*

CONFORMITY ←——————————————→ PROCESS

Activity structures (general)

Supra-functional (excess meaning; restricts room for individual self-determination of options)	Functional (room for self-determination)

Target variables

V, U, H	*i*

Aims

To produce *ideal* or *standard* pupil	To maximise individual potential and differentness

Methods

Content: syllabus bound	Process: content not important, often self-chosen
Expository	Discovery
Single track: homogeneity through moulding and selection	Multiple-track: diversity of goals and methods

Self-concept

Self-as-agent: belief in own role in so far as it is part of existing power structure	Self-as-originator: belief in own efficacy (and knowledge of own limitations)

Activity structures (particular)

Para-military ceremonial in assemblies	Informal assemblies
Punishment for deviance	Reward for acceptable behaviour
Emphasises 'tone', what people think (uniforms, public conduct)	Dress and public behaviour an individual responsibility
Teacher-pupil relations emphasise different status	Teacher-pupil distinctions not emphasised.
Streaming; ability grouping	Heterogeneous classes
Privileges for senior pupils	Equal rights for all pupils
Norm-referenced grading	Criterion-referenced grading

The aims, methods and self-concept of students are characteristically different between the two models. An illustrative list of activity structures and how they would materialise in the pure case of each model is included in Table 2.

Moral development and the school

The process-oriented school, committed to growth in the logic of feeling, would have a very different look from a school that is basically concerned with transferring particular values and habits. Schools would differ in two main ways: (*a*) in their total activity structures, which collectively comprise 'the moral atmosphere of the school' (Kohlberg 1966) and (*b*) in specific programmes within the school.

Let us take the second point first. Some writers consider that special provision needs to be made for certain experiences that would not normally be encountered. Such experiences would range from cognitively oriented 'values education' programmes, often included in social science (e.g. Newman and Oliver 1970; Metcalfe 1971), Wilson's (1973) suggestions for training in 'moralistic method', the various 'Kohlbergian' programmes (summarised in Rest 1974), to encounter-type experiences (e.g. Borton 1970; Grainger 1970).

The effective use of such specifically scheduled programmes has yet to be established. Rest (1974) has reviewed several Kohlbergian programmes and concludes that, although particular well-controlled laboratory studies have produced good results, they are not yet ready for general implementation in schools. He draws particular attention to the need for the equivalent of curriculum development: to help specify both the objectives of such programmes and associated measuring instruments, to clarify the critical conditions of upward change (the + 1 condition in his view is next to impracticable) and to analyse the teaching skills and teacher characteristics involved in satisfactory implementation. It would be fair to say evaluation of other specific programmes in moral education is even less advanced than this.

We turn, then, to the activity structures in the total school context and their effect on moral development. Many writers would expect the school, as a totality, to affect moral development more than any particular scheduled periods: moral education is not something which, as Wright (1971, p. 244) puts it, 'can be tacked on to the existing curriculum as an extra'. The first task is to systematise these structures; the next, to ask what evidence is there that those structures with excess meaning produce results consistent with the theory outlined here.

Four broad areas, where activity structures carry excess meaning and convey an implicit curriculum of values, may be distinguished:

1.   *Rules, routines and regulations* governing conduct within the school. Jackson (1968) refers to this complex of structures as 'the second set of 3 Rs'. They include a myriad of controls; as to dress, conventions of approaching and interacting with an authority figure, limitations on activities (as to going to the toilet, ordering lunch, addressing friends, etc.), meeting deadlines, procedures in school rituals and ceremonies, and the like. While some of these rules make for administrative convenience up to a point, others are evidently quite arbitrary: all are emphasised in many schools to a point far beyond functional utility (for example, the rigour with which many teachers punish deviations from the school uniform). Their function lies in their excess meaning, not their utility. As Farber (1970, pp. 19-20) says: 'The very point about such rules is their pointlessness . . . the real lesson is the method. . . . What it best teaches is . . . itself.' It teaches the child to *obey*; and to conventional parents, teachers and principals that is morally right (cf. the NOP sample's demand for 'moral training'). Some educators would claim that this set

of structures is functional; Dreeben (1968), for example, claims that the school must help the student to adjust to a world in which authority is important and in which he must obey regulations whose meanings are unclear to him.

2.   *Learning to withstand continuous evaluation of words and deeds*. The classroom is a place where judgments are passed publicly, before one's own friends, day after day. Most formal evaluation (grading) is norm-referenced; that is, the final grades are determined according to the relativities *within* the class, either by simple ranking, or in more sophisticated forms, for example by 'rationing' the top grades or by grading according to some *a priori* distribution. Bloom (1971) remarks that nowhere is one publicly evaluated so frequently and so relentlessly as in school. Again, then, we have evidence of excess meaning in a common school activity structure. A comment such as 'Johnny came top' tells us nothing very much about what it was that Johnny actually did, or how he did it; only that whatever it was, he did it better than anyone else, and that *that* is the important thing. If evaluation were simply a matter of providing informative feedback to student, parent and teacher, it would seem logical that schools would employ criterion-referenced evaluation techniques to a far greater extent than they do. The inference that common evaluation techniques are used for other purposes—for example, to inform students who is important and who is not, and to transfer a value of competition—seems inescapable.

3.   *Teacher-student interaction*, including teacher expectations about what children have to do to be 'good'. Examples here are legion. Friedenberg (1970) concentrates upon the way on which teachers set lower-middle-class standards of conduct ('Isn't Tommy good, boys and girls, his desk is so neat and tidy!'). Jules Henry, in an anthropological study of middle America, has many biting observations. The following comes from a chapter appropriately entitled 'Golden Rule Days: American Schoolrooms': 'Boris had trouble reducing "12/16" to the lowest terms, and could only get as far as "6/8". The teacher asked him quietly if that was as far as he could reduce it. She suggested he "think". Much heaving up and down and waving of hands by the other children, all frantic to correct him. Boris pretty unhappy, probably mentally paralysed. The teacher, quiet, patient, ignores the others and concentrates with look and voice on Boris. She says, "Is there a bigger number than two you can divide into the two parts of the fraction?" After a minute or two, she becomes more urgent, but there is no response from Boris. She then turns to the class and says, "Well, who can tell Boris what the number is?" A forest of hands appears, and the teacher calls Peggy. Peggy says that four may be divided into the numerator and the denominator' (Henry 1972, p. 243).

Henry observes: 'Boris's failure has made it possible for Peggy to succeed; his depression is the price of her exhilaration; his misery the occasion for her rejoicing. To a Zuni, Hopi or Dakota Indian, Peggy's performance would seem cruel beyond belief, for competition, the wringing of success from somebody's failure, is a form of torture foreign to those non-competitive redskins . . .' (op. cit., pp. 243-4). Here we see a contradiction between explicit and implicit curricula: if indeed the important aim for Boris is to 'learn arithmetic', the teacher's technique of handling the situation was grossly maladroit. But if the aim, albeit unconscious (such teaching behaviours have a high *H*), was to teach a lesson in survival values, then it is likely to have been quite successful.

4.   *Instructional*. There are many instructional devices that have the potential of transferring specific values *en passant*: biased textbooks, emphasising for example sex stereotyping (Bart 1974) or ethnocentricity in the social sciences (McDiarmid and Pratt 1971) or bogus 'consensus' presentations of the natural sciences (Apple 1971). Sugarman (in Wilson, Williams and Sugarman 1967, pp. 374-91) gives a useful analysis of many other activity structures (including size of school, co-educational or segregated, suborganisations within the school, group or individual methods of teaching, streaming, etc.) all of which plausibly have an effect on moral development.

We now turn to the final question: what evidence is there that the hidden curriculum of the school does effect the moral development of the students in the manner suggested? Bar-Yam and Kohlberg (1971) studied two groups of disadvantaged adolescents (matched for socioeconomic status, age and intelligence) one in a very free Kibbutz environment, the other in a conventional high school. They found that all the Kibbutz students were at least at the conventional stages, some having reached the postconventional stage; the controls ranged from preconventional to conventional, with none at the postconventional stages.

Minuchin, Biber, Shapiro and Zimiles (1968) conducted a comprehensive study of Grade 4 children in four schools in an upper-middle-class district of a large American city. Two schools were classified as 'traditional': they defined their task cognitively, as one of fostering intellectual growth. Pupils were evaluated in competitive terms: the teacher was seen as the fixed authority on questions of learning content and judgment of progress. The other two schools were classified as 'modern': they were more concerned that children were treated individually and developed emotionally as well as intellectually. The authority structures here were more relaxed and interpersonal cooperation was stressed, with much emphasis upon self-directed learning.

They found that the children from one of the 'modern' schools were markedly different from the others with respect to attitudes to authority, self-image, and moral judgments: they regarded something as 'wrong' in terms of principle, where the others saw 'wrong' in terms of infractions of specific school rules. The self-image of these 'modern' children involved feeling and fantasy, and integration and acceptance of the present. The other children looked ahead to future status, independence and, interestingly, conventional sex-typing. The writers conclude '... the codes they were formulating and the values underlying them reflected, to a degree, the mode of authority they had experienced in school' (p. 287).

There are a few studies on the activity structures of student-teacher interaction. Bradburn (1964) recorded the numbers of cooperative and uncooperative actions performed by primary children under (*a*) a teacher who praised and encouraged 'positive' moral attitudes, and (*b*) a teacher who criticised and punished infractions. The children taught by the nurturant teacher performed more cooperative actions.

Similarly, Kounin and Gump (1961) showed that aggression between children was significantly greater amongst those taught by punitive than by non-punitive teachers. Finally, Devereaux (1972) found that sixth-grade German children showed greater conformity to adult values and greater guilt about misdeeds when taking a test with teacher present rather than absent; the responses of the American children did not differ between the presence or absence of the teacher. He attributes these results to the greater authoritarianism of the German schools. Kay (1975), in a more sociologically oriented review of morality and schooling, comes to a similar conclusion: 'the ideal school is . . . a familial organisation which has eliminated all forms of elitism, and involves both teachers and pupils in policy and decision making' (p. 15).

These studies collectively suggest that both the activity structures of the school, and of the classroom teachers, do have some effect on moral development in the manner predicted. Excessively salient activity structures appear to be associated with conventional morality, whereas at least the foundations for postconventional morality appear to be laid in open environments, in which the individual is free to develop his own principles. It is regrettable, however, that the hard data on this matter is sparse, and that much of such research as exists is piecemeal, conceived within the individual framework of the workers concerned.

Summary and conclusions

This chapter began and ended above with a complaint about the state of research into the affective results of schooling. It would be desirable to close on a more constructive note.

The notion of interaction between a person and an environment, with consequent change in the person, is a classic case of Hunt's matching model (Hunt and Sullivan 1974), which *inter alia* draws attention to the need for conceptualising both the person variables and the environment, as well as their interaction. Accordingly, we have been concerned here with matters of definition, what to look for in the person (so we could decide whether he had changed and how), in the environment, and in their functional interaction.

On the person side, the affective domain is tied to Piaget's 'logic of feeling' (thus excluding, for example, aesthetic affect), growth in which becomes moral development. Moral development is seen as similar to but distinct in function from cognitive development: whereas the latter functions with respect to the physical world, the function of moral development is to order the social world. Moral development increasingly carries a *commitment to action* in terms of one's specific values. Where this commitment is low, as in egocentric or preconventional stages, the choice of behaviour in a moral dilemma is likely to be in terms of cost-benefits or of habits; at higher stages, behavioural choice is more likely to accord with one's moral values.

These relationships may be formalised as: $B = f(iV + U + H)$, where $B =$ behaviour potential, $i =$ strength of commitment, e.g. as expressed in Kohlberg stage; V = specifically relevant values; U = utility of particular alternatives; and H = habitual responses in similar situations. In this expression, i becomes the personological variable that controls behaviour transituationally; the others are situation-specific, and refer to characteristics that are as much environmental as personological. Values (V) are personally held, but an institution overtly and covertly transmits those values that would lead to 'acceptable' moral decisions; this is particularly so when activity structures within the school are accorded an emphasis that is disproportionate to their functional utility. The pay-offs of particular decisions (U) can also easily be manipulated in an institution: either by strong negative sanctions for disapproved behaviour (the traditional model), or by rewarding approved behaviours (as in behaviour modification). Similarly, H may be built up by strong routinised procedures, a heavy emphasis upon tradition, and use of modelling techniques: again, such characteristics may easily be discerned in the schools.

An environment that promotes moral development, then, would not be one in which moral behaviour is controlled by the factors extrinsic to iV, that is U and H. Ideally, then, rules and regulations should not exceed their functional utility; and routines and traditions should be minimised. In such an environment, it would become more possible for the individual to internalise his values and make his own moral decisions.

The operationalisation of growth in the logic of feeling has relied almost exclusively upon the Kohlberg Moral Maturity Scale, which is interpreted within Kohlberg's developmental stage concept of morality. Kurtines and Greif (1974) are critical of several aspects of Kohlberg's theory, and particularly about this reliance upon the MMS, which in their view, is psychometrically inadequate. These inadequacies would lead to substantive questions about the +1 hypothesis, the notion of stage mixture, cultural universality and invariance of stages. As has been noted, these are the very areas about which there is most doubt about Kohlberg's theory.

This does not mean that the Kohlbergian framework is useless. Such considerations lead to a reinterpretation of the phenomena of moral stages in terms of moral *styles* that may be learned or modelled, the simpler styles (at Stages 1 and 2) being acquired at earlier ages than the more complex ones. Thus, Minuchin *et al.* (1968) observed the (apparently postconventional) qualities of judging wrong in terms of inconsistency with internalised principles, instead of inconsistency with school rules, in Grade 4 children: this seems clearly to reflect a style of handling moral problems, rather than a developmental stage. Likewise, the fact that a ten-year-old and a forty-year-old can both be scored as Stage 3 on the MMS indicates a *similarity* in their way of handling moral dilemmas rather than equivalence.

Kohlberg himself (1970) appears to be sensing this kind of difficulty in his discussion of Holstein's findings: he suggests that conventional messages, filtered through postconventional schemata, lead more quickly to conventional morality than 'straight' conventional messages. In other words, there is a 'something-plus' about the message, which, it was noted earlier, seems to have something more to do with social learning or modelling than with a straight developmental sequence.

Kohlberg's work is most useful as a taxonomy of moral judgments, but there appears to be little justification for interpreting his work as evidence for an invariant developmental sequence, as he insists. Further, Kurtines and Greif's point is well taken: there needs to be much more work done on instrumentation.

Now we should turn to conceptualising the environment. The major factor here, stemming from the theory, is the + 1 hypothesis. While there is supporting evidence for it, it is at best only one, and non-necessary, condition of upward change: as Rest (1974) asks: 'Who was + 1 for Socrates?' Thus parental stage level, which is considerably in excess of + 1 for most transitions, was associated with moral development; by the same token, institutions stressing personal autonomy apparently produce students who are morally more advanced than those from more conventional institutions. At the very least, there needs to be ways other than the + 1 hypothesis to characterise the environment.

It was suggested here that the activity structures of the institution were critical in determining its moral atmosphere. Operationally, it would be necessary to assess institutions (i) on the number, kind, and particularly the importance placed upon, the structures that impinge upon students (for example teaching, evaluation, restrictions as to dress, speech, movement, expression, etc.); (ii) on the extent to which the utility of desired behaviours is manipulated within the school through sanctions or rewards; and (iii) on the emphasis given to tradition, routine and deliberate modelling. While some of these parameters would involve subjective judgment, others could be easily quantified.

The question asked at the beginning of this chapter—what is the affective impact of schools upon children—might better be rephrased: 'What *kinds of effects* on moral behaviour do *different kinds of schools* have?' We need to know more clearly what parameters are involved in characterising both the person and the school environment, and also their associated technologies of instrumentation. Kohlberg and Turiel (1971, p. 464) state that one important factor in moral growth is 'the creation of just schools, in which children participate fully'. That is a pretty fair assessment of our present state of knowledge; it would be hoped, however, that future assessments will be more analytic and more prescriptive.

E. A. Peel

14. The thinking and education of the adolescent

Introduction

In a publication four years ago, fresh evidence at the time was outlined on: concept formation from contextual settings; recognising superordinate classes; and the correlation between the adolescent's power to explain problems put in a textual setting and his capacity to utilise general ideas in his writing (Peel 1972). Since then the field of study has been widened and deepened. Research on the psychology of adolescent thinking has come to fruition and its results have been linked with secondary school intellectual activity. Therefore, for the present contribution, it is proposed to paint a broader canvas.

We may set out the extended field as follows. In situations where the pupil can respond rather more spontaneously than in a classroom (even in these days), evidence can be obtained of the existence of the following phenomena, apparently involved in the path to achieving mature thought:

Organisation, through the act of classifying, of the experience of perceiving phenomena in the environment, as a development from thematic groupings of a more private nature.

Identification of the groupings as concepts, in most cases through the medium of language, which, from this point on, plays an increasingly important role in intellectual growth.

Formation of concepts from terms and cues embedded in textual settings.

Recall of past experiences and organising generalisations as potential explanation of new problem material and situations leading to the emergence of the *possible* over and above the *actual*.

Formulation, selection and rejection of possible explanations, necessarily involving certain formal requirements and procedures in thought.

Explanation of the current here-and-now realities in terms of an optimal hypothesis.

Conversion of generalisations into abstract notions.

Emergence of mature forms of understanding, explaining and evaluating, involving in particular comprehension of the dynamics of stability and change in human, biological and physical situations.

In a very broad sense this list constitutes a sequence, but at any time in the adolescent's development of thought and language, several of the above trends may be operating together.

In what follows, it is proposed first to amplify some of these assertions and also to support them by fresh evidence before passing on to studies of secondary school pupils' comprehension and explanation of school material. Finally, we shall discuss consequences of these findings for teaching methods and curricula in secondary schools.

Basic characteristics of adolescent thinking

The intellectual progress of the adolescent is intimately interwoven with his receptive and productive powers of language, be it concerned with his vocabulary, his command of structure or his logical rigour. For this reason, language and other symbolic systems, as in mathematics and logic, are involved in higher-level thinking. We need, therefore, to research more into the adolescent's language proficiency in relation to the world he has to learn and act in. Also, estimates of his intellectual progress are probably best measured through the verbal medium. With this overall observation in mind, let us examine some of the above assertions.

By the end of childhood, the individual has acquired a vocabulary of lexical items denoting a wide range of objects and categories. We may use this vocabulary to test how far the thinker is able to organise the elements of his environment into classes of widening generality and abstraction. He has the labels to do this, but can he select appropriately from them? Using a test composed of items, some of which involved generalising, others abstracting, one investigator (Clarke 1974) followed up this question. A person is asked to complete the third term of a series of concepts of extending generality or abstraction (not told to the solver, who is, however, guided by a model line), as for example, in

Lager	beer	alcoholic drink (model)
Anthracite	coal	solid fuel (test)
		fire
		power station
		mining industry
		gas

where the required response is underlined. Clarke was able to obtain the following means and standard deviations from a large sample of nine- to sixteen-year-olds, 180 in each age group (see page 174). These figures provide confirmation of trends indicated earlier (Peel 1972), namely in the ability to recognise similar relations based on increasing generality and abstraction. They show that, in the medium of *language-directed* thought, the adolescent repeats to some extent the growth in classifying from arrays of *tangible objects* revealed in earlier childhood. Clarke might have obtained an even clearer picture had he restricted the basis of all his items to that of discovering the super-ordinate class, implying the widening generality, without admixing notions of abstraction as well.

Age group (mean in years)	Mean score (max. poss. 12)	S.D.
9·25	3·37	1·77
10·28	4·46	2·00
11·29	5·29	2·05
12·23	5·49	2·22
13·35	5·36	2·14
14·30	6·38	2·35
15·21	6·10	2·21
16·16	7·01	2·59

Much concept formation of adolescence is heavily dependent upon the context of the language and symbolic representation, and does not arise solely out of lists of instances. In the sciences there are statements giving the essentials of concepts, supported by examples. The humanities utilise textual material in which the concept plays a role, but educational test constructors do not overtly recognise that many of their vocabulary comprehension exercises, based on the text, are in fact assessing concept formation, as the following excerpts demonstrate:

I am too well acquainted with the generous catholicity of spirit which pervades the writing of our chief apostle of culture to identify him with these opinions; and yet one may cull from one and another of those epistles to the Philistines, which so much delight all who do not answer to that name, sentences which lend them some support.

What is the meaning of:
1. catholicity   narrowness   broadness   religiousness
2. pervades   is found throughout   escapes from   influences
3. cull   understand   gather   deduce
(extracted from a paper by T. H. Huxley entitled *Science and Culture*) (Diederich and Palmer 1964);

and

Alternatively, history can be conceived as a series of oscillations between worldliness and other-worldliness, or as a theatre of contest between greed and virtue, or between truth and error. Such points of view emphasise religion, morality, and contemplative habits eliciting generalisations of thought.

eliciting   *means*   giving r . . . . . . to

Comprehension itself becomes more complex (Peel 1975a) the more advanced and difficult the text. It goes far beyond recalling the simple referent or usage meaning of words, as the above instances illustrate. It calls for a range of cognitive activity, including inferential thought, reasoning from analogy, logical rigour, interpreting the language and ideas in the text and invoking knowledge outside that given in it.

It is therefore somewhat surprising that so little has been done on concept formation from textual material, with the object of determining the *psychological* factors entering into the process. Exceptions are the work on advanced textual organisers (Ausubel 1963) to facilitate new learning, the classical study on the meanings of words coded into sentences (Werner and Kaplan 1952) and the similar study of history passages (de Silva 1972). Almost all comprehension tests are educational in slant and concerned with subject-matter understanding. This has led to the limiting of responses to a multiple choice selection or a closed completion task, as illustrated above. One looks only for the correct response and rejects the others. What we require are analyses of open responses, for in the adolescent world of thought and language there may be few blacks and whites, but many shades of intermediate greys which can give us real psychological insights into what is going on.

In textual comprehension and analysis, the mature thinker feels his way to a solution by bringing his own ideas to the task, putting them up as possibilities and then back-checking against the textual structure and content. Such complex activity can only be revealed by allowing the testee to make open, elaborated responses (Peel 1971; de Silva 1972). Since the thinker often brings his own ideas to textual comprehension and criticism, we may conceive two kinds of concepts: those defined in the text by the fact that it is comprehensible, and those originating in the solver. The existence of these two types of concepts has severely restricted research on textual material to the study of retention and recall, or to filling in omitted words as in the Cloze technique (Taylor 1957) or detecting foreign bits of text as in the Chunking technique (Carver 1970). In all these measures, invocation of ideas from the thinker is minimised and the testing of understanding and explanation is lost. However, an analysis of the conceptual content of responses is currently being carried out (Peel 1975a) in terms of the connections between what are called in- and out-concepts. Counts are made of the number of the three types of connection—in-in, in-out, out-out—and indices defined which measure the amount of out-activity involved against in-activity. Connections are simply defined as subject-predicate links, but the method might permit a more sophisticated logico-linguistic analysis. What is important psychologically is that by this technique, we can ask questions on texts calling for responses at higher levels of intellectual activity.

The predisposition to shift from a generalisation to an abstraction, as implied in the change in thinking involved in the difference between a *democrat* and *democracy* or *sportsman* and *sport*, is an important tendency in higher-level thinking and discourse. Here is an example from such abstract thinking (Whitehead 1933): 'One of the most general philosophic notions to be used in the analysis of civilised activities is to consider the effect on social life due to the variations of emphasis between individual absoluteness and individual relativity. Here "absoluteness" means the notion of release from essential dependence on other members of the community in respect to modes of activity, while "relativity" means the converse fact of essential relatedness. In one of their particularisations these ideas appear in the antagonism between notions of freedom and of social organisation.' This distinction has not been widely recognised by psychologists and only then in connection with the thought of younger children (Braine 1962). It is interesting that language does not always provide the means of distinguishing between generalisations and abstractions as instanced above. In its stead we often have a single term, say, *poem*, which serves both purposes, often with the definite and indefinite article providing a clue. Thus a *poem* is a generalisation, the notion of *the poem* (as a literary form) is an abstraction. We may use this ambiguity to test the preference for either a generalisation or an abstraction (Peel 1975b). Test items were composed which presented four sentences to the testee, each containing the same key word used in a general, abstract, particular, or associative sense. He was asked to select the sentence having the most significance for him. The results, some of which follow in Table 1, indicate a clear rise in preference for abstraction, a less marked rise for generalising and a fall in tendency to particularise, across the age range of twelve to fifteen years.

TABLE I   *Mean tendencies to abstract and generalise*

	Age			
N	12+ 93	13+ 71	14+ 93	15+ 76
Tendency to:				
abstract	3·7	3·9	5·0	5·6
generalise	6·2	7·0	7·6	7·6
particularise	6·4	5·8	4·7	4·0
associate	4·7	4·3	3·7	3·8
Total number of items	21	21	21	21

Correlations between the quality of judgment in separate problem situations and the growing preference for abstraction are positive.

We may conclude this section on the psychology of adolescent thought by reproducing some definitive results on the growth of judgment and powers of explanation (Clarke 1974). They are set out in Table 2 in the form of the frequency of imaginative-explanatory judgments obtained by giving nine test items to ninety subjects in lower- and higher-ability age groups. There were also included ninety higher-ability adults with a mean age of thirty-five years. The results follow on the opposite page.

Four points about these figures merit particular comment:

1. the spurt between twelve and thirteen for the lower-ability groups;
2. that between eleven and twelve for the higher-ability groups;
3. the ceiling that is reached by the end of adolescence, with apparently little change thereafter; and
4. that even in maturity not all judgments are high-level (734 out of 810).

TABLE 2 *Incidence of imaginative-explanatory judgments*

Age		Lower ability	Higher ability
	Total no. of possible responses for each group	810	810
9:0		42	136
10:0		61	137
11:0		135	195
12:0		189	366
13:0		368	472
14:0		396	565
15:0		457	573
16:0		531	620
17:0		—	727
18:0		—	698
35:0		—	734

With this conclusion of the brief pinpointing of certain features of the development of adolescent thought, we may now consider evidence of this development in the setting of secondary school material.

Understanding school material

Research on understanding and explaining school material serves the purposes of providing further evidence on the maturation of judgment, already revealed by using non-specialist material, and also some knowledge of the pupil's insights into his subject-matter and readiness for further progress, particularly in more sophisticated material and modes of learning. With these objectives in mind, several investigations have been carried out of thinking in secondary school specialist subjects.

Two perceptive studies of thinking in geography (Rhys 1972) and history (de Silva 1972) have already received discussion, which need not be extended here, although the educational implications will be followed up briefly in the last section. More recent investigations have been carried out on thinking in other subjects. Of these we begin by referring to two concerned with English: one on poetry (Mason 1974) and the other on crisis situations portrayed in prose fiction (Ellis 1975). Then briefly we consider two on science thinking, in physical science (Wells 1972) and biology (Pitt 1974).

Mason (1974) tested seven year-groups of twenty comprehensive school pupils, ranging in age from eleven to seventeen-plus, the latter being a GCE 'A' level group, with four groups of four poems. The sixteen poems were short, complete and taken from school anthologies and represented a range including Haikai and, among others, poems by S. Smith, G. M. Hopkins, T. S. Eliot and E. Dickinson. The poems were presented with the question: 'What do these ns mean to you?' This evokes a wide range of responses which it was found ssible to categorise into six groups, showing:

1. lack of comprehension
2. repetition of poem content with little else
3. affective reaction, usually unfused, but sometimes with tenuous literary reference
4. cognitive awareness of a single referential element
5. coordinated generalisation, uniting cognitive and affective elements
6. explanation in terms of hypotheses linking the poem to wider human parallels.

Mason (op. cit., pp. 135-6) gives instances of these categories of responses to two poems. Marker reliability is high ($r = 0.94$).

The frequency distribution of responses in these categories according to age group is revealing (Table 3), where categories 1 and 2, 3 and 4, and 5 and 6 have been combined, since there is no real poetic distinction between 3 and 4 (a poem is a fusion of the affective and the cognitive) and there is little psychological distinction between 1 and 2, which are at a low intellectual level, and between 5 and 6, both of which are responses at a mature level.

TABLE 3   *Frequencies of responses by categories and age*

Age	Response Category			No. of responses
	1 and 2	3 and 4	5 and 6	
11+	68	11	1	80
12+	25	51	4	80
13+	28	45	7	80
14+	27	44	9	80
15+	5	39	36	80
16+	9	44	27	80
17+	8	15	57	80

Two features of these results are of particular note. First, the sharp change between domination by inadequate responses and later recognition of the affective and cognitive content of the poetry, occurring between eleven and twelve-plus. This may be compared with the similar ages of Table 2, where the results are drawn from simple comprehension material. Second, the substantial appearance of high-level answers (5 and 6) at the age of fifteen-plus, clearly happening much later than similar changes shown in Table 2.

Similar changes, perhaps not so clearly marked, characterise the appearance of materials in judging human situations portrayed in literature (Ellis 1975). The theme of sudden change in human affairs and its consequences constantly recurs in literature, and its understanding is an important element of literary comprehension and appreciation. Ellis took excerpts from several novels which embody sudden and sometime traumatic changes in the lives of characters in them and, after presenting the excerpts to his pupils, asked several questions tapping various aspects of the test situation.

One of his passages was taken from Somerset Maughan's *Of Human Bondage*, where Philip is told of his mother's death by Mr Carey. Six questions were asked in relation to the text, including the following:

Do you think Mr Carey could have done more to help Philip? Why do you think so?
What did Philip do and why at Blackstable the next day, do you think?
What was Philip doing and why a few weeks after this, do you think?

The frequencies of responses to these questions by four age groups of forty pupils in each are set out in Table 4 alongside the description of the category used.

TABLE 4   *Frequency of responses in different categories*

	Age			
Response category	12+	13+	14+	15+
1 Circular, irrelevant, no response	12	19	18	9
2 Invocation of no more than two facts from the passage	193	148	111	60
3 Use of facts and possibilities but no explicit explanation	35	62	68	104
4 Explicit discussion of the dynamics of the crisis situation and possible consequences	0	11	43	67

Here we may note that mature judgments first appear markedly at the age of fourteen-plus, somewhat lower than in the judgment of the poems but higher than in the case of simple comprehension material.

The main purpose in the following brief reference to studies of thinking by adolescents in physical and biological sciences (Wells 1972; Pitt 1974) is to demonstrate that even when the problem situations are not encased in language, the same trends are shown, from partial, restricted thinking to mere description and finally on to imaginative explanation. This latter is characterised by verbalised concepts, covering laws and deductive activity.

Wells worked with secondary modern school boys and found comparatively few clear-cut cases of imaginative explanations, and these were associated with chronological ages of fourteen years and over. For example, the responses to his ammonia-fountain experiment, demonstrated before the pupils, were distributed as shown in Table 5 (op. cit., p. 216).

We may note in passing that development in thinking is shown in this research to be more positively associated with mental age.

Pitt devised eight biological problems, including the hawk-tit-greenfly food-chain problem and various biological control experiments. He tested comprehensive school pupils, age range eleven to sixteen-plus, and obtained the results shown in Table 6.

G

TABLE 5   *Frequency of response by category and age (ammonia-fountain experiment)*

Category	Frequency	Mean CA	Mean MA
restricted	15	12:9	12:8
simple description	40	13:2	13:1
extended description	79	13:10	14:8
partial explanation	28	13:11	15:6
full explanation	11	14:6	16:11

TABLE 6   *Frequency of response by category and age (biological problems)*

Level	N	Mean CA	Mean MA
no response	55	13:2	12:3
restricted	442	13:4	13:3
simple description	517	14:0	14:11
extended description	152	15:2	17:6
true explanation	31	16:2	18:11

Again we confirm the transition to mature thinking at higher ages, this time at sixteen years of chronological age and eighteen years mental age. The sharp difference between these results and those obtained in the physical science tests is partly attributable to the sophistication and methodological bias of the biological problems.

Overall, however, all these investigations into the secondary school pupil's thinking across a wide range of subject matter confirm the trends discovered in general comprehension, with delays of up to three years in reaching mature levels of explanation and judgment.

Consequences for secondary education

The least that could come out of these studies is their power to heighten the teacher's sensitivity as to what may be going on, or not going on, in the mind of the individual pupil, beneath the regimentation of organised instruction. Then, accepting the aphorism that learning should not considerably out-pace thinking, material in all subjects should be graded accordingly, keeping in mind particularly the period of maximum growth from descriptive-repetition to imaginative-explanation.

The earlier build-up of experience and its organisation by generalisation are indispensable, not to be pursued as ends in themselves, but accepted as appropriate to their particular age levels. The ultimate aim must be imaginative thought and, for this end, experience must be made articulate through language and abstraction. The application of established ideas to new situations should be linked with this process.

Turning to specific subject areas, in English one would go a long way with Mason (1974, p. 135): 'Usefulness of the diorisms to teachers in any case can only be in terms of a starting point and guides, not as goals. An individual response to poetry, will remain a personal and, ultimately, unique matter.' We need teacher sensitivity, not instructional rigidity.

The understanding of history and geography ultimately requires competence in grasping the multiplicity of human affairs and principles of ecology. The researches encompassed in this chapter provide insights into the growth of such competence. Teaching based on them would accept partial and single explanations as a necessary lead-in to comprehensive understanding.

The lesson for science teaching and curricula may well be seen in the need 'to enlarge the pupils' store of possible explanations, i.e. to build up new concepts and to enrich and extend existing ones. There is also a need to provide experience of processing evidence and observation using both induction and deduction and to give experience of constructing and testing hypotheses' (Wells 1972, p. 223).

Finally the changing *quality* of intelligence over the secondary school years would seem to support the notion of a spiral curriculum, where it would be possible to return to topic areas with a greater conceptual repertoire and more mature form of intellectual enquiry.

Maurice Chazan and Theo Cox

15. Language programmes for disadvantaged children

Of the many possible effects of cultural deprivation upon the development of young children, the most crucial from the educational point of view is retardation in the growth of language skills. Language is of central importance as a mediator of thought and action, and although the relationship between language and thinking is highly complex and as yet poorly understood, there seems little doubt that many aspects of cognitive functioning are greatly facilitated by adequate language skills. Indeed, possession of such skills may be considered a prerequisite for efficient performance at the higher reasoning levels at least. Moreover, language, in its oral or written forms, is the main medium of teaching in schools, and if the child is to derive maximum benefit from formal education, command of certain language skills is essential. Thus, although Piaget (1954) has stressed that the development of logical thinking is not to be equated with the development of language, it seems reasonable to claim, with Vernon (1969), that the child's cognitive growth is highly dependent upon a sufficient degree of linguistic stimulation in his environment.

Over the past fifteen years or so, language development in early childhood, hitherto a relatively neglected field, has been given increased attention. In particular, the linguistic deficiencies of culturally deprived children have been the subject of much discussion amongst psychologists and sociologists. The interest in language development has not remained purely at a theoretical level, but has resulted in the construction of a variety of language programmes for disadvantaged children. All early childhood programmes for culturally deprived children have put language development high on the list of goals, and all have stressed the importance of the child's language environment (Stendler-Lavatelli 1968).

The first part of this contribution outlines research on the language skills and deficits of disadvantaged children, and the second part reviews the language programmes developed for these children in the United States and Britain. It will be possible only to attempt an overview and general appraisal of a selection of these programmes. In the space available, little detail can be given about the content of the programmes or the design of the studies undertaken to evaluate them, and the reader will need to consult the references given for a fuller understanding of the issues discussed. The review will be confined to early childhood (that is, up to about eight years of age), and, as far as Britain is concerned, will not deal with language schemes designed specifically for immigrant children, such as *Scope*

(Schools Council 1969) and *Concept 7-9* (Schools Council 1972). It will focus on those programmes (a term used here in a very wide sense) intended for use with children educationally at risk because of a background offering little stimulation for cognitive learning. In the context of this volume it will also be appropriate to comment on the contribution of Piagetian theory to the development of language programmes for disadvantaged children.

Part I
Recent research on the language of disadvantaged children

Language and social class

The earlier research into the environmental correlates of children's language development stressed the importance of social class. McCarthy (1954), summarising the relevant literature then available, emphasised the marked relationship between the social class status of the family and the child's linguistic development. Perceptively, she highlighted the evidence indicating that habits of family life and parental attitudes towards their children were the really important factors in language development, both factors being related to social class. More recent research has confirmed the importance of social class, or rather its associated variables, in determining the level and quality of children's language growth. For example, Deutsch (1965) in the USA carried out a 'verbal survey' of large samples of negro and white first- and fifth-grade children of varying social class membership in which a wide range of cognitive and language tests was used. Social class differences on some of the measures were found at both grades, but these were more pronounced at the fifth grade, especially on the more abstract tasks. In Britain, the national study carried out by Pringle *et al.* (1966) revealed marked social class differences in the oral language skills of seven-year-old children as rated by their teachers.

However, social class membership is a rather crude index of the quality or level of cultural provision in the home background, and in recent years studies have been carried out on the language development of children defined as disadvantaged on the basis of more sensitive social and psychological measures of such provision. For example, Tough (1971, 1973a) carried out a longitudinal study of selected groups of children from age three to age seven and a half years. One group was rated as having a favourable home background with respect to the fostering of linguistic skills, and the other group a less favourable environment. The 'advantaged' group came from 'middle-class' homes and the 'disadvantaged' group from 'working-class' backgrounds, but the selection of the samples was not based upon indices of social class but on an assessment of the quality of the language environment in the home. This assessment was made through a structured interview with the mother which explored parental attitudes toward the use of language in the home and the opportunities afforded to the child for developing and practising language skills.

A major finding of this study was that there were considerable differences between the two groups of children in the *purposes* for which they used language. Whereas all of the children used language in order to satisfy their own personal needs, to initiate and maintain relationships with others, to regulate their own actions and those of others, and to report on present experience, children from the 'advantaged' backgrounds appeared to have developed the following uses of language much more strongly than their counterparts from less advantageous homes:

to report on past experiences
to extend the imaginative situation
to offer explanations and justifications
to predict and plan
to consider alternative possibilities
to recognise, and work for the solution of, problems.

Associated with these differences in language use were significant differences between the two groups in favour of the 'advantaged' children on various indices of linguistic complexity, although there were some situations where the complexity of the language produced by the 'disadvantaged' children was markedly higher than that in most of the situations sampled and more comparable with that of the 'advantaged' group. Tough hypothesised that the 'disadvantaged' children were predisposed to use language for purposes which do not demand a high degree of linguistic complexity, and that, in situations where more complex language is appropriate, they may not produce it because of their relative unfamiliarity with such language uses.

Intra-class differences

Studies involving comparisons of groups of children drawn from *within* social classes have revealed significant differences between such groups, reflecting differences in the quality of the language-fostering environment of the home. Brandis and Henderson (1970) found significant differences in language performance among groups of children within both 'middle-class' and 'working-class' backgrounds. Two other recent British investigations which have been concerned with differences within 'working-class' areas are of relevance here.

The first is the enquiry by Phillips *et al.* (1972), in which samples were studied of six- to seven-year-old and ten- to eleven-year-old boys from highly socially handicapped families (Focus Groups), with control groups of families showing only moderate or low degrees of social handicap, according to a specially devised index. Both Focus and Control samples were drawn from predominantly working-class' families living in 'twilight' inner-ring areas of Birmingham, and attending the same schools. It was found that the Focus Group boys scored significantly lower than their controls on several psychological tests of verbal and non-verbal abilities. Moreover, on some of the measures, including one of vocabulary development, a clear relationship between degree of social handicap and level of development was found (low handicap being associated with higher scores) at both age levels, but particularly in the younger age group.

The second study to be cited, which was carried out as part of the work of the Schools Council Research and Development Project in Compensatory Education based at Swansea between 1967 and 1972 (Chazan *et al.*, in press), consisted of an enquiry in depth into the effects of cultural deprivation upon infant school children's development. The study sample comprised fifty-two pairs of children, matched for age, sex, school and non-verbal intelligence but differing in that one member of each pair came from a relatively deprived home background in the cultural and material sense (Deprived Group) and the other from a more advantaged background (Control Group). The assessment of home background was made on the basis of a specially devised parental interview questionnaire. All the children were drawn from schools serving catchment areas considered 'deprived' in the judgment of the local education authorities concerned. The study concentrated on oral language skills, but within a comprehensive assessment programme.

Both structural and functional aspects of language were assessed, the former through tests of speech, vocabulary, grammar and syntax as well as sentence formation, and the latter through tasks involving classification, description, comprehension and narration. These measures were supplemented by teachers' ratings of various aspects of children's oral language skills. It was found that the Control Group children achieved significantly higher scores on most of the language tests. In structural aspects the superiority of these children covered the range from simpler skills such as speech articulation to more complex skills such as grasp of sentence structure and defining word meanings. In functional aspects the two groups were significantly differentiated in the use of language for describing and classifying, and in following oral instructions, but the between-group differences in the measures related to the story-telling task fell well below significance. The teachers' ratings of the children's language skills fully supported the general pattern of test findings, and although differences in favour of the Control Group were found also on a wide range of school-related measures, the most consistent and pronounced differences emerged in the area of oral language skills.

Criticisms of the 'deficit' approach

Taken as a whole, research into environmental influences upon children's language development, illustrated above, shows very clearly that children from culturally unstimulating home backgrounds tend to perform at a poorer level than their more favoured contemporaries on a wide range of language measures, but particularly those concerned with the use of language as a tool for organising, abstracting from and interrelating experience. As Bruner (1975) puts it, whereas advantaged children use language as an instrument of analysis-and-synthesis in problem-solving, and without dependence upon shared percepts or actions, 'lower-class language, in contrast, is more affective and metaphoric than formal or analytic in its use, more given to narrative than to causal or generic form. It is more tied to place and affiliation, serving the interests of concrete familiarity rather than generality, more tied to finding than to seeking.' If this is accepted, the question arises as to the extent of these apparent language disabilities. Are they genuine 'across the board' deficits or are they confined to the more formal language assessment situations commonly found in research studies? Bernstein (1969) and Labov (1970) have argued that the language deficits of disadvantaged children are more apparent than real, and that, potentially at least, such children *can* use more elaborated language forms and handle logical and abstract concepts, even though they may not do so in the school setting or in the formal test situation. In support of this view there is some evidence, for example, in the study by Tough cited earlier, that, in certain situations, disadvantaged children may produce more elaborated language structures than they normally do and thus compare more favourably with their advantaged peers in indices of language performance. Francis (1974) reported that, while the speech of a group of socially disadvantaged infant-school children in a story recall task was less well-developed than that of an advantaged group, the difference lay in the *frequency* of use of various complex forms and not in their presence or absence. In addition, Severson and Guest (1970) have summarised the motivational and other factors which can depress the language performance of disadvantaged children in the formal test situation. Furthermore, linguists of the 'generative grammar' school such as Chomsky (1965) and McNeill (1970) postulate that the child's ability to master the grammatical structures of his language are largely innately determined and require only minimal exposure to samples of the child's native language.

Thus there is an apparent conflict between the findings of the research described above and the claims of some linguists that culturally disadvantaged children do not have any real language deficits. A possible resolution of this conflict lies in the distinction between *structure* and *function* in language, a distinction emphasised by Piaget (1952). McAffrey *et al.* (1970) suggest that whilst the child's mastery of the *structural* processes in language (i.e. grammar) may be innately determined to some degree, the child has to learn the *functions* of language through a process of social interaction: this aspect of linguistic development is, therefore, relatively more subject to environmental influence. This is a useful hypothesis, though the view that the child's acquisition of grammar is innately determined has not gone unchallenged (Herriot 1970). Halliday (1969) has proposed seven models of language function which are typically apprehended by children at the age of school entry, and argues that the child limited to the 'restricted code' (see below) lacks two of these models, namely the 'personal' and the 'heuristic', as a result of insufficient experience. These models relate respectively to the functions of language in expressing one's individuality and as a means of finding out about the external world; a grasp of both of these functions is, in Halliday's view, crucial to the child's success in school.

The contention that children from certain home backgrounds lack familiarity

with uses of language crucially important in the educational setting is well supported by the theoretical work of Bernstein (1971a). Following his earlier distinction between the 'restricted' and 'elaborated' codes (the latter reflecting the use of
language as a tool of logical thinking and as a means of ordering and communicating
experience), and their association with 'working-class' and 'middle-class' groups
respectively, Bernstein has subsequently refined his theory. The crude notion of
social class as a governor of the type of language used in the family is replaced by
the concept of 'family role system'. Such systems are represented by what he terms
'positional families' (where social control of the child tends to be realised through
less elaborated language, orientated not so much toward the individual child as
toward his formal social status) and 'person-centred families' (where the individuality of family members is stressed and, consequently, meanings have to be
made verbally explicit, through more elaborated language). These family role
systems, which can be found within any social class grouping, are associated with
different types and uses of language, the 'positional family' with the 'restricted'
code and the 'person-centred family' with the 'elaborated' code. The concept of
linguistic code has itself been refined, and Bernstein (1971b) asserts that even a
'restricted' code speaker can and may in some specific contexts use 'elaborated
speech variants'. Nevertheless, Bernstein suggests that the child brought up in a
'positional family' will tend to be orientated toward the use of the 'restricted' code.
Bernstein's theory is supported by a fairly substantial body of observational
research into the patterns of mother-child interaction and their influence on the
growth of children's language skills (Hess and Shipman 1965; Bee *et al.* 1969;
McAffrey *et al.* 1970).

In discussing the 'language deficit' controversy outlined above, the Bullock
Report (Department of Education and Science 1975) states, on the evidence of
research studies, that there is an indisputable gap between the language experiences
that some families provide and the linguistic demands of school education. The
report expresses the view that a child should not suffer limited opportunities
because he does not have the range of language that society demands. Whilst
accepting the sincerity of the viewpoint of critics of the 'deficit hypothesis', the
authors of the report consider that it is not a condemnation of a language form to
point out that there are some functions which it does not adequately serve.

Implications for language programmes

From the point of view of equipping disadvantaged children to cope with the
demands of formal education, the research discussed above suggests that a primary
aim of any compensatory programme should be to develop the ability and motivation of these children to use language as a means of classifying and ordering their
experience and as a medium of logical thought. Although by reason of his grasp
of the basic grammatical structures of his language, a child may be *potentially* able
to develop such uses, he needs the guidance and encouragement of appropriately
orientated adults in order to develop such a capacity; he also needs a basis of

suitable concrete experience upon which fundamental concepts can be built. As the Bullock Report points out, it is necessary for educationists to create the conditions and contexts in which the ability of children to use 'higher-order' language (for example, to explore, recall, predict, plan, explain and analyse) can be developed. However, it may also be necessary in some cases to help disadvantaged children to achieve a firmer grasp of the structures of standard English dialect, and a subsidiary aim of compensatory language programmes might well concern the development of children's vocabularies, grasp of grammatical structures and quality of speech articulation in this dialect. Finally, it is important that the application of special programmes should be informed by an awareness on the part of teachers not only of the wide range of individual differences amongst disadvantaged children, but also of the patterns of language forms and functions which characterise the subcultures or family role systems of these children.

Part II
A survey of language programmes for disadvantaged children

Approaches in the USA

The programmes designed for disadvantaged children in the USA have been so heterogeneous in content and so wide in scope that it is difficult to classify their approaches in any precise way. In general, programmes have been analysed along the following main dimensions (see Bartlett 1972):

1.   *goals:* emphases on particular language structures and functions;
2.   *interactional patterns:* the type of teacher-child or child-child interaction encouraged;
3.   *amount of preorganisation:* the extent to which the programme is structured or follows a planned sequence of activities.

A variety of categories has been used to indicate differences in emphasis along these dimensions. The Stanford Research Institute has distinguished between 'preacademic', 'cognitive discovery' and 'discovery' approaches in compensatory programmes (Bissell 1973), while Weikart (1967) differentiates between 'traditional', 'structured' and 'task-oriented' programmes. Bartlett (1972) categorises language schemes in terms of those which emphasise 'pattern repetition', 'instructional dialogue' or 'improvised interaction', and Hammill and Larsen (1974) refer to approaches which stress 'psycholinguistic' training. On the basis of these analyses, the main approaches characterising language programmes in the USA will, for convenience, be categorised here as follows:

1.   traditional (informal) enrichment
2.   cognitive discovery
3.   preacademic

4.   psycholinguistic training
5.   instructional dialogue.

These categories will be used only to indicate differences in emphasis between programmes. However great the differences between language programmes appear to be, they often have much in common, and, as Bissell (1973) states, the classifying of educational approaches requires detailed analyses of programme content if it is to be meaningful. Further, the orientation claimed by a programme is not always borne out in practice, and some of the more successful projects in the USA, for example, those carried out by the Institute for Developmental Studies in New York (Deutsch *et al.* 1967) and by Gray and Klaus (1970) in Nashville, Tennessee, have adopted a broad framework for their activities which does not fit neatly into any one of the categories listed above.

1. *Traditional (informal) enrichment*

This approach, characteristic, for example, of the Bank Street College programmes (Wolotsky 1967) and those of the Education Development Center in Newton, Massachusetts (see Little and Smith 1971), is one modelled on the 'traditional' philosophy and practices of the British infant school, where informal help and encouragement from adults is seen as providing the best opportunity for children to increase their linguistic skills (Parry and Archer 1974). The emphasis is on a flexibility of approach, free play and self-expression, incidental language learning in an appropriate environment rather than on specific language lessons, with highly structured materials or situations, and on unobtrusive guidance rather than direction by the teacher. Language learning is important, but equally important is the development of the child 'as a whole', especially his personal adjustment. So many approaches are subsumed under this heading that it is particularly difficult to evaluate the effects of 'informal' or 'traditional' programmes, but in general these have been found to be less effective with disadvantaged children than the more structured approaches described below (Weikart 1972; Karnes 1973). However, most educationists would agree that, for some part at least of their school day, informal approaches and free activity are desirable for young children.

2. *Cognitive discovery*

The 'cognitive discovery' approach, which is particularly influenced by the theories of Piaget, aims at promoting 'the growth of cognitive processes, such as categorising, differentiating, abstracting, and inferring, by providing continuous verbal accompaniment to children's sequenced exploration' (Bissell 1973, p. 69). This approach will be illustrated by reference to Weikart's cognitive programmes and the Florida parent-educator model.

Weikart's cognitive programmes.   The Perry Preschool project was started in 1962 for three- and four-year-old disadvantaged Negro children at Ypsilanti, Michigan

(Sonquist and Kamii 1967). Inspired by Piagetian theory, the project used techniques of 'verbal bombardment', in which the child was involved in a series of questions designed to help him to move gradually from the sensorimotor stage to the preconceptual stage, from contact with an actual object to verbal symbolisation of it (Laing 1968).

Following the Perry Project, the Ypsilanti Early Education Programme was put into operation from 1967 to 1970. This programme aimed to develop a preschool curriculum, based on Piaget's theories, for disadvantaged four-year-old children (Kamii and Radin 1970; Kamii 1973). In the early stages of the programme, the tendency was to simplify certain Piagetian tasks and to try to help children to go from one stage to the next as quickly as possible; but, as the project proceeded, it was felt that it was important to help the child to develop his total cognitive framework rather than emphasise particular tasks such as seriation or conservation. The general procedure was for the teacher to set up a situation or propose an activity, and to see how the children reacted before deciding what to pick upon in order to extend the child's thinking: 'The teacher does not shape a response, nor transmit or program the input of knowledge (the empiricist approach). She does not go to the other extreme either of passively watching children play while waiting for "readiness" to unfold (a maturationist approach). She structures the environment for children to activate and apply their schemes (i.e. the cognitive structures through which external stimuli are understood). She then intervenes unobtrusively by applying Piaget's exploratory method so that the children will test out their ideas against objects and other people, and build new schemes by differentiation and integration of previously constructed schemes. A curriculum based on this interactionism can, therefore, never be presented in a cookbook fashion' (Kamii 1973, p. 227). In this programme, language is considered important as a tool for precise communication and as a stimulator of cognitive development, but language is not seen as the source or cause of logical thinking.

A controlled enquiry, comparing the 'cognitive discovery' approach with other models, showed that this approach produced good results, though these were no better than those found in the case of other programmes involving careful planning, expert teaching, and well-defined objectives (Weikart 1972).

Florida Parent-Educator Programme.   One of the main aims of this project was to educate mothers of very young infants, in their own homes, in specific techniques of cognitive and verbal stimulation accompanying a warm interpersonal relationship (Gordon 1968). The design of the programme was influenced firstly by the Piagetian view of the importance of the sensorimotor period in the intellectual development of the child, and secondly by Bernstein's linguistic theory: the mother was helped to provide a model of a more elaborate language code than she might have used without the guidance given. Specially trained 'home tutors', themselves from disadvantaged backgrounds, used role-playing and demonstration techniques to train the mothers. They taught the mothers to make play materials, and encouraged them to verbalise in a variety of ways in interacting with their infants.

The evaluation carried out gave encouraging results, and this home-focused approach is strongly supported by Bronfenbrenner (1974), who, on the basis of a review of early intervention programmes in the USA over the past decade, concluded that programmes actively involving parents, especially those working in the home with parent and child simultaneously, were more effective than approaches where parents were not active participants.

3. *Preacademic*

The emphasis in the academically-oriented early childhood programme, which has its basis in behaviour modification theory, is on promoting language development through direct teaching of specific skills, using a demanding rather than a persuasive approach, and requiring imitative and structured, rather than individual and intuitive, responses from the children. This approach was strongly advocated by Bereiter and Engelmann (1966) and has since been further developed by Engelmann and his associates (Engelmann *et al.* 1970). It stresses that disadvantaged children are particularly weak in language skills, and that this aspect of development is of paramount importance. The teacher takes on a highly directive role, making use of pattern repetition and extrinsic reinforcement as much as possible, and the child's success is judged in terms of how accurately he imitates the teacher's language model.

The 'preacademic' approach has been much criticised, particularly on the grounds of its lack of flexibility, its reliance on direct teaching and rote repetition, its ignoring of individual differences and its emphasis on teaching materials rather than cognitive processes (Blank 1973a). However, in spite of the criticisms, the results of evaluation studies of this approach have supported its effectiveness, not only in the USA (Bereiter 1972; Karnes 1973), but in other cultures, such as Australia (Nurcombe *et al.* 1973).

4. *Psycholinguistic training*

A number of language programmes have been developed on the basis of Osgood's (1957) linguistic theory and the Illinois Test of Psycholinguistic Abilities (ITPA: Kirk *et al.* 1968) associated with his formulation. While there are many different psycholinguistic theories, Hammill and Larsen (1974), in a review of the effectiveness of what they call 'psycholinguistic training', use this term to refer to those programmes which have been inspired by the Osgood model. Psycholinguistic programmes of this kind, which are based upon the assumption that discrete elements of language behaviour are identifiable, measurable and, if defective, remediable, will be exemplified here by reference to a language handbook prepared by Merle Karnes and colleagues in 1968, and to the Peabody Language Development Kit (Dunn and Smith 1964).

Activities for Developing Psycholinguistic Skills (*Karnes* et al. *1968*).   This is the title of a manual containing varied suggestions for activities for improving the skills of communication and information-processing of four-year-old culturally disadvantaged children. Largely following the ITPA model, the manual suggests activities to help these children in auditory and visual decoding (understanding), auditory vocal and visual motor association, vocal and motor encoding (expression), grammatical and visual closure (integration) and auditory vocal and visual motor memory. It is stressed that the manual is intended as a guide, not a curriculum, and that a number of different communication processes will often be involved simultaneously in the activities listed in the handbook.

Peabody Language Development Kit (PLDK).   The PLDK is designed, through a series of 180 carefully sequenced daily lessons, to stimulate the receptive, associative and expressive components of oral language development. It provides a variety of teaching aids, including pictorial material, puppets, life-sized plastic fruits and vegetables, magnetic shapes and strips, and recordings of different sounds. The Teacher's Manual is very detailed and gives explicit instructions for using the kit.

According to the devisers of the programme, which is influenced not only by Osgood but also by Skinner (1957), Torrance (1962) and Guilford (1967), the PLDK stresses overall oral language and verbal intelligence training rather than specific training in selected psycholinguistic processes. It aims to encourage divergent as well as convergent and associative thinking. The kit is broad in coverage, offering varied types of activities and embracing general vocabulary enrichment, the teaching of key sentence patterns and the use of language to serve many functions, ranging from logical and mathematical to social and emotional.

Evaluation of psycholinguistic training.   Hammill and Larsen (1974) have reviewed thirty-nine studies between 1964 and 1974, including work with retarded children, which have attempted to evaluate psycholinguistic approaches. Although some studies reported success with disadvantaged children, most of the skills identified in the ITPA (particularly visual and grammatic closure, and visual and auditory reception skills) were not responsive to intervention. However, the review suggested that at least one of the skills tapped by the ITPA (i.e. verbal expression) could be improved by direct training. Hammill and Larsen concluded that the idea that psycholinguistic constructs, as measured by the ITPA, can be trained by existing techniques remains invalidated. Although better results may be obtained with improved techniques, they consider that without further research caution is needed in making claims for the trainability of psycholinguistic processes.

5. Instructional dialogue

In this approach, the emphasis is on discussion between the teacher and the individual child. The task of the child is not to imitate the teacher, but rather to use language to convey and organise information accurately. The teacher provides structured learning situations and guides the child's thinking by asking leading questions and making suggestions, but the child has greater freedom of action and response than, for example, in the 'preacademic' approach. The 'instructional dialogue' approach will be illustrated here by reference to the work of Blank and Solomon (1968, 1969; see also Blank 1973b).

A tutorial language programme.   Blank and Solomon (1968) have developed an approach which is based on dialogue between teacher and child for about fifteen to twenty minutes each day. They emphasise that the most effective teaching is carried out through individual tutoring. The child should not be allowed to leave a task unfinished: if necessary, the task can be simplified, but the child should still be required to meet the demands set by the teacher. The main aim of the programme is to help the child to progress towards abstract thinking. During the teaching session, the teacher uses no gestures, but helps the child to use language to complete the task set. The child is encouraged to extend his thinking beyond the concrete situation, for example, by discussing alternative courses of action or attempting explanations of events. Errors made by the child in his verbal responses are used by the teacher as a basis for developing the child's thinking skills. Common and inexpensive objects readily available in the child's environment (e.g. paper, crayons, blocks, toys, simple books) are all that is needed for the programme.

A small-scale evaluation of this approach showed a marked gain in IQ for three- and four-year-old children who received the specialised tutoring for four months, and no significant gains in the case of children not receiving any special programme, or given individual attention without the specialised training.

While it is more satisfactory to use measures of specific aspects of language development rather than intelligence tests to assess the effectiveness of language programmes, the results of this evaluation are encouraging.

Language programmes in Britain

As compared with the USA, very few language programmes have been developed in Britain. Consequently, with insufficient resources to embark on the construction of their own programmes, some projects for disadvantaged children in Britain have been forced to use American-based materials in at least a part of their work. In particular, the Peabody Language Development Kit has been found useful, perhaps mainly because its explicitness, while not arousing as much hostility as the Bereiter and Engelmann approach, makes evaluation somewhat less difficult than is the case with other programmes. However, several language programmes or handbooks have been, or are being, specifically devised for use in nursery or infant schools in Britain, for example those by Gahagan and Gahagan (1970), Shiach (1972), Downes (to be published) and Tough (1973b). These approaches will be described below, after a discussion of the language programmes forming part of, firstly, the Educational Priority Area (EPA) projects and, secondly, the action research undertaken by the National Foundation for Education Research (NFER). Little work has been carried out in Britain along the lines of the Florida Parent-Educator Programme described above, but mention will be made of a small-scale mother-child interaction project in Scotland (Donachy 1973).

The EPA projects

Projects in England.   In the national EPA action-research project which began in 1968, the Peabody Language Development Kit (Level P) was selected as one of the instruments for intervention experiments in a number of nursery schools, there being 'no British pre-school language programme available' (Halsey 1972). Although nearly all the children involved enjoyed the programme, the teachers and assistants using the kit reacted in a wide variety of ways (Quigley 1971). Some were very hostile, some were highly enthusiastic, while others had mixed feelings about the kit. Most of the criticisms arose because the materials, although robust and attractive, had been designed for use with American children. In general, although the structure of the course was not considered altogether unsuitable, it was clear that many teachers in Britain were not happy with the idea of having a specific and regular session of language activities.

Controlled comparisons were made between the groups of children using the PLDK and children not receiving any special programme. Most of the experimental groups did show an improvement in language development over a period of a year, but very few of the differences between the experimental and control groups were statistically significant.

In addition to the use of the Peabody Kit, project teams in different parts of England also developed language programmes of their own. In Liverpool, twenty-four stories were written, each accompanied by a large wall picture and a puppet presenter (a popular feature in the PLDK). In London, the emphasis was put on directing the attention of nursery school staff to 'language-producing situations' and on helping them to increase the quality of their own verbal interactions with the children, by a greater concentration on one-to-one contact. The West Riding project developed an individual language programme based on Marion Blank's tutorial method described above. These small-scale experiments indicated that it would be worthwhile developing a variety of language programmes that would be of direct help to disadvantaged children and yet would be acceptable to British teaching traditions.

Dundee Project.   As part of an EPA research project in Dundee, Scotland, an experimental study of educational compensation was carried out, initially involving over five hundred children from nine pre-school establishments (Harvey and Lee 1974). In this project, there was no specific language programme, but language growth was encouraged in the framework of an integrated scheme designed to enhance general cognitive development. 'Themes' were planned, usually lasting for a full week and maintaining continuity of emphasis on a single cognitive concept. Each theme was introduced by an activity or experience, and then the selected concept was dealt with from different points of view, i.e. through different senses, using varied play material, differently contrived situations and a wide range of songs, nursery rhymes and stories. As in the English EPA project, the analysis of the results of the experiment showed that, while there was evidence of the value of the programme, many of the comparisons between experimental and control groups being in the expected direction, few of the differences between the groups were statistically significant.

NFER Pre-School Project

This action-research project, which began in 1968, aimed to introduce and evaluate a compensatory programme of language, perceptual and general cognitive training for disadvantaged children attending nursery schools (H. L. Williams 1973). The Peabody Language Development Kit, radically revised to suit the needs of the children participating in the project, was used as one of the main procedures to enhance language development. In addition, verbal exchange between adult and child in the classroom was encouraged in a variety of other ways, including the use of a graded series of games. The results of the evaluation of the programme are not yet available.

'Talk Reform' (Gahagan-Bernstein)

The main aim of this programme, developed for infant school children by Gahagan and Gahagan (1970) and inspired largely by the work of Bernstein, was to elaborate and broaden the spoken language of children who live in an environment where language is seen as serving rather limited functions. Based on situations occurring continually during the normal infant school day, the programme sets up tasks in which a 'restricted' mode of speech would not be adequate: it combines 'intensive, formal training' with an enriching environment, and encourages the child to give greater attention to oral language and to use language more explicitly. A variety of activities and techniques, including some advocated by Bereiter and Engelmann, are suggested for daily twenty-minute lessons over the three infant school years. The materials, which are not elaborate or expensive, are frequently changed and the level of difficulty is increased gradually.

An evaluation of the programme showed improvement in the children's ability to generate sentences, to make and code finer discriminations among objects presented visually or tactually, and to master the more difficult problems on a verbal concept sorting test. Cazden (1972) comments that, with such an imaginative programme and such initially promising results, the Gahagan-Bernstein programme provides an important base for further curriculum work. As a visitor from the United States, she was surprised to find that compensatory education programmes in Britain were operating largely independently of this work and depending instead on less interesting ideas imported from the USA.

'Teach Them to Speak' (Shiach)

Shiach (1972) presents a language development programme in 200 lessons. Influenced by Luria, Vygotsky and Bernstein, he aims to help teachers of children within the age range four to seven years to develop the oral language skills of all their pupils. No special kit is provided, and the materials recommended can be easily collected or bought by the class teacher, e.g. picture cards, posters, colour cubes, hand puppets and various objects. The lessons, one for each day, last for about half an hour, and are designed to give a feeling of success through graded steps. There is constant revision, drill and repetition, with the emphasis on descriptions and explanations in well-structured, grammatically complete and correct sentences.

No evaluation study or even details of pilot work are mentioned in Shiach's book. Cox (1973) considers that the programme is potentially useful, especially for inexperienced teachers, in its emphasis on structured language activities. However, there is no clear grading in the level of difficulty of the lessons, and the emphasis is on class teaching rather than on teaching individuals or small groups. Some of the activities, too, are rather stereotyped and could be dull for young children. Further, great stress is laid on 'expansion' by the teacher; that is, modifying and extending the child's oral responses to achieve a desired sentence form. This approach is less stimulating, and likely to be less successful, than 'modelling' as suggested by Cazden (1965), in which the adult responds to the child's utterance not by expanding it but by making a fresh statement logically related to it, or the 'dialogue' approach evolved by Blank and Solomon (1968).

Communication Skills in Early Childhood Project

Following a Pre-School Language Project lasting eighteen months, the Communication Skills in Early Childhood Project is currently being developed at Leeds under the direction of Joan Tough (1973c). In these projects, the emphasis has been put on formulating ideas about what might be the best way of discovering what children can do with their language, and how the teacher can stimulate the child to use language for his own purposes and for extending his thinking. In the Communication Skills project, the main objective is to develop a guide to the fostering of language skills in the nursery and infant classroom that will be useful for teachers.

This project is concerned with language in early childhood in general rather than specifically with disadvantaged children, but has clear implications for work with children from a restricted linguistic environment. Tough (1973b) emphasises that such children need skills in using language as a means of examining the detail, the relationships and the structure of the world around them: the development of these skills in school is dependent upon a particular kind of relationship between the teacher and the child, one which encourages flexible ways of thinking. A different kind of learning environment for disadvantaged children is not called for, but the content of the dialogue between teacher and child will differ in the case of the disadvantaged, because of the need to stimulate his interest. The teacher will use the child's response as a starting point from which talk might lead into deeper and more complex thinking. For the disadvantaged child, the teacher may be the only person who can provide the development of new uses of language and who can help him to see that communicating his ideas is worth while.

With the aid of teachers' groups, the Communication Skills project is developing along lines of its own, but its 'instructional dialogue' approach has much in common with that of Marion Blank mentioned above.

Schools Council Project in Compensatory Education

The Programme Development Unit (PDU) of the Schools Council Project in Compensatory Education has produced a handbook of suggestions for teachers of disadvantaged children in their first year in the infant school (Downes, to be published). The PDU adopts a rationale similar to that of Blank and Solomon in that it focuses upon the vocabulary and language structures associated with logical thinking and reasoning. The main aim is to help disadvantaged children to develop more elaborated speech—accurate descriptions and explanations, and the use of questions to elicit information. The handbook contains a set of guidelines and suggested activities from which the teacher can select and adapt as required, rather than a detailed, pre-sequenced 'package' of language activities. The normal resources of the infant classroom can be used to provide the enrichment which the deprived child needs: for example, some of the teachers' groups operating in the project analysed the familiar activity corners of the infant classroom in order to see how these could be used to enhance language development. Language games, too, are suggested as a useful way of helping the child to acquire appropriate concepts and structures. Audio-visual materials have also much potential in the infant school (see Chazan and Downes 1971), but the PDU puts the emphasis on the teacher using her own ingenuity to produce these materials rather than relying on a set of materials being widely available (P. Williams 1973).

The activities suggested in the handbook have been tried out by a number of infant school teachers in various parts of the country, and the results of a preliminary controlled evaluation study of the 'programme', involving eighty-eight children (mean age 4 years 10 months) from five schools have been encouraging (Downes 1975).

Home-based programmes

As previously mentioned, experiments in the United States suggest that home-based programmes are of value, and should be tried out on a wide scale. This view is supported by a small-scale enquiry carried out in Renfrewshire, Scotland (Donachy 1973), in which an experimental group of nine pre-school culturally deprived children was exposed to six months of weekly home sessions during which health visitors used toys and books to stimulate verbal interaction between mother and child. The experimental group made significantly greater gains in IQ, though not in language, than either of two control groups, one of which received weekly visits and non-educational gifts from health visitors, the other receiving no intervention between pre- and post-tests. Following this pilot study, a project focusing on mother-child interaction has been organised through schools in deprived areas, with encouraging results, including the incidental benefits of the better motivation of the parents and teachers, a diffusion effect on siblings, and improved parent-teacher relations.

The influence of Piaget

Ever since his book on *The Language and Thought of the Child* (1923, revised 1959), a pioneering contribution to the understanding of language development, Piaget has illuminated the relationship between language and thinking in many of his works. However, it cannot be said that his theoretical formulation has had a substantial influence on the development of language programmes for disadvantaged children in Britain, although Piaget's general theory of cognitive growth has widely influenced other aspects of the school curriculum, particularly mathematics and science. As shown above, some programmes in the USA have been inspired by Piagetian theory, but there is little evidence of Piaget's influence in other programmes. Since the work of Piaget is widely disseminated in courses in education and psychology at all levels, it is of interest to speculate why it has, apparently at least, had so little impact on those concerned with the construction of language programmes.

Several possible reasons may be suggested for this ostensible lack of influence. Firstly, while language is important to Piaget, and is seen by him as the vehicle by which thought is socialised, he does not consider it to be the original basis of, or the whole of, logical thinking (Phillips 1969). For Piaget, the ability to use language to express logic is an outcome of activity, and attempts to improve the child's logic solely through instructing him in the use of language are not likely to be very successful (Almy 1966).

Secondly, Piaget has not explicitly put forward a theory of *language* acquisition, although Sinclair-de-Zwart (1969) has speculated on the general form that such a theory might take. The latter writer points out that in the relatively few works that he has written on language, Piaget has been concerned with language as a factor in the child's cognitive development and not with the content and structure of the child's language as such. Piaget's writings, therefore, provide little guidance as to how children's linguistic skills might be enhanced.

Thirdly, Piaget's writings, which are not always easy to understand, have not been addressed to educators. It is not surprising, therefore, if work on the educational applications of his theories is not far advanced.

Finally, Piaget has not been enthusiastic about the acceleration of mental development, even if he admits the possibility of such acceleration (Phillips 1969).

However, it is probable that Piaget has had a much wider influence on approaches to language learning than would superficially appear to be the case. As Beard (1969) observes, Piaget's work provides support for the varied and stimulating environment provided by British nursery and infant schools, but also stresses that attention from adults, especially in answering questions and in conversation, is immensely important to development in early childhood. It also implies the need for increasingly structured activities for children as they grow older, so that they can move from complete dependence on concrete materials to partial dependence on these, and then gradually to dispensing with concrete aids altogether. Piaget has also emphasised the need to understand how the child sees things, and to realise that the limitations of the child's thinking are sometimes masked by language. For example, as Almy (1966) points out, in the case of socially disadvantaged children, no adequate comparison of quantities can be made by a child who does not understand the terms 'more' and 'less' or 'most' and 'least', but comprehension of these terms may not be developed through words alone or even associations of word and picture, but rather through a combination of manipulation and verbalisation. Further, Piaget's work indicates that a wide range of activities in teaching any concept is particularly valuable, and that, where children are introduced too soon to any kind of activity, they are likely to become confused and develop a distaste for learning (Beard 1969). Even at the nursery or infant school stage, the teacher will be dealing with several 'levels' of cognitive development and must, therefore, adopt a predominantly individual approach.

Kamii (1971) has described in what ways a pre-school based on Piagetian principles differs from other pre-schools. She asserts that Piaget's theory gives a unique developmental perspective to early childhood education, encompassing all the activities that have been developed by the traditional nursery school as well as adding a great deal of depth to these activities. Piaget's work, in her view, helps the teacher to delineate and teach the broad basic abilities that are necessary for all the subjects that the child has to cope with in later school life. In the Ypsilanti projects described above, Kamii, who feels that the teaching of broad basic abilities is more fruitful than sequencing teaching goals by subject matter, has demonstrated how the Piagetian perspective can be translated into an educational programme. However, teachers are likely to need much expert guidance if they are to put such a programme into operation.

Conclusion

In general, controlled comparisons of different experimental approaches in early childhood intervention programmes (including those concerned with language) in the USA have not shown any one approach to be markedly superior to others. However, children involved in programmes that were carefully planned and expertly directed have recorded somewhat greater gains in cognitive performance and academic achievement than children exposed to less well-designed programmes or those following the normal curriculum. In Britain, no large-scale evaluation of language programmes for disadvantaged children has been undertaken: the more recent programmes have not been evaluated, and those evaluation studies which have been carried out (see above) have been on a very limited scale, involving small samples of children over relatively short periods.

Thus, from the work completed to date, it is not feasible to suggest clear guidelines for the future development of language programmes. However, the American experience indicates that particular attention should be paid to increasing the awareness on the part of teachers of the language problems of disadvantaged children, and to cultivating the skills of teachers in dealing with these problems. Further, while the teacher will find it helpful to have varied resources to meet a wide range of individual needs—and all the programmes so far developed have something to offer—it is important that she should have reasonably well-defined objectives if her methods are to be effective. It is likely that, in the British context, a judicious combination of structured activities in small groups and the individual 'instructional dialogue' approach will help disadvantaged children to improve their language skills, but much further experimental work is needed before clearer indications can be given about the best direction in which to go. Certainly the evidence so far available, while disappointing in some respects, suggests that the language of disadvantaged children does need special attention within the nursery and infant school, and that such attention should be sustained over a substantial period, supplemented as much as possible by work in the home.

References

An appreciation of Piaget's work

BRYANT, P. E. and TRABASSO, T. (1971) 'Transitive inferences and memory in young children.' *Nature*, **232**, 456.

DE BOYSSON-BARDIÈS, B. and O'REGAN, K. (1973) 'What children do in spite of adults' hypotheses.' *Nature*, **246**, 531-4.

DONALDSON, M. and LLOYD, P. (1976) 'Sentences and situations: children's judgements of match and mismatch.' In BRESSON, F. (ed.) *Current Problems in Psycholinguistics*. Paris: Centre National de la Recherche Scientifique.

GAGNÉ, R. M. (1966) *The Conditions of Learning*. New York: Holt, Rinehart and Winston.

INHELDER, B. and PIAGET, J. (1958) *The Growth of Logical Thinking*. London: Routledge.

INHELDER, B., SINCLAIR, H. and BOVET, M. (1974) *Learning and the Development of Cognition*. London: Routledge.

LAWRENSON, W. and BRYANT, P. E. (1972) 'Absolute and relative codes in young children.' *J. child Psychol. Psychiat.*, **13**, 25-35.

LUNZER, E. A. (1970) *On Children's Thinking*. Slough: NFER.

LUNZER, E. A. (1976a) 'Formal reasoning: a reappraisal.' In PRESSEISEN, B. F. and GOLDSTEIN, D. (eds.) *Topics in Cognitive Psychology: Language and the Development of Thought*. New York: Plenum.

LUNZER, E. A. (1976b) 'The development of advanced reasoning abilities.' *Italian J. Psychol.*, **2**, 369-90.

LUNZER, E. A. (1976c) 'Operativity, language and memory in children aged five to seven years.' In GEBER, B. A. (ed.) *Structure and Development in Social Psychology: The Contribution of Piaget's Theory*. London: Routledge.

MCGARRIGLE, J. and DONALDSON, M. (1976) 'Conservation accidents.' *Cognition*, in press.

MODGIL, S. (1974) *Piagetian Research*. Slough: NFER.

PIAGET, J. (1970) 'Piaget's theory.' In MUSSEN, P. H. (ed.) *Carmichael's Manual of Child Psychology*. New York: Wiley.

PIAGET, J. (1971) *Science of Education and the Psychology of the Child*. London: Longman.

PIAGET, J. and INHELDER, B. (1956) *The Child's Conception of Space*. London: Routledge.

PIAGET, J. and INHELDER, B. (1971) *Mental Imagery in the Child*. London: Routledge.

WHITE, S. A. (1965) 'Evidence for a hierarchical arrangement of learning processes.' In LIPSITT, L. P. and SPIKER, C. C. (eds.) *Advances in Child Development and Behaviour*, Vol. II. New York: Academic Press, 187-220.

The course of cognitive growth

ACHENBACH, T. M. (1969) '"Conservation" below age three: fact or artefact?' *Proceedings of the 77th Annual Convention of the American Psychol. Assoc.*, **4**, 275-6.

BAER, D. M. and SHERMAN, J. A. (1964) 'Reinforcement control of generalized imitation in young children.' *J. exper. child Psychol.*, **1**, 37-49.

BANDURA, A. (1969) *Principles of Behaviour Modification.* New York: Holt, Rinehart and Winston.

BANDURA, A. (1971) *Social Learning Theory.* Morristown: General Learning Press.

BAYLOR, G. W. and GASCON, J. (1974) 'An information processing theory of aspects of the development of weight seriation in children.' *Cognitive Psychol.*, **6**, 1-40.

BEILIN, H. (1968) 'Cognitive capacities of young children: a replication.' *Science*, **162**, 920-1.

BERTALANFFY, L. von (1960) 'Comments on Professor Piaget's paper.' In TANNER, J. M. and INHELDER, B. (eds.) *Discussions on Child Development, IV.* London: Tavistock.

BLAKEMORE, C. (1973) 'Environmental constraints on development in the visual system.' In HINDE, R. A. and STEVENSON-HINDE, J. (eds.) *Constraints on Learning.* New York: Academic Press, 51-74.

BLOOM, L. (1970) *Language Development: Form and Function in Emerging Grammars.* Cambridge, Mass.: M.I.T. Press.

BORNSTEIN, M. H. (1975) 'Hue is an absolute code for young children.' *Nature*, **256**, 309-10.

BOWER, T. G. R. (1974) *Development in Infancy.* San Francisco: W. H. Freeman & Co.

BOWERMAN, M. (1973) 'Structural relationships in children's utterances: Syntactic or semantic?' In MOORE, T. E. (ed.) *Cognitive Development and the Acquisition of Language.* New York: Academic Press.

BRACHT, G. H. (1970) 'Experimental factors related to aptitude-treatment interactions.' *Rev. educ. Res.*, **40**, 627-45.

BRAINERD, C. J. (1974) 'Neo-Piagetian training experiments revisited: is there any support for the cognitive-developmental stage hypothesis?' *Cognition*, **2**, 349-70.

BROADBENT, D. E. (1975) 'Cognitive psychology and education.' *Br. J. educ. Psychol.*, **45**, 162-76.

BRYANT, P. (1974) *Perception and Understanding in Young Children.* London: Methuen.

BUNDERSON, V. C. (1965) 'Transfer of Mental Abilities at Different Stages of Practice in the Solution of Concept Problems.' Ph.D. Dissertation, Princeton University, Princeton, N.J.

CALHOUN, L. G. (1971) 'Number conservation in very young children: the effect of age and mode of responding.' *Child Dev.*, **42**, 561-72.

CARNAP, R. (1958) *Meaning and Necessity.* Chicago: University of Chicago Press.

CELLÉRIER, G. (1972) 'Information processing tendencies in recent experiments in cognitive learning—theoretical implications.' In FARNHAM-DIGGORY, S. (ed.) *Information Processing in Children.* New York: Academic Press, 115-23.

CHOMSKY, N. (1967) 'The general properties of language.' In MILLIKAN, C. H. and DARLEY, F. L. (eds.) *Brain Mechanisms Underlying Speech and Language.* New York: Grune and Stratton.

CRONBACH, L. J. (1957) 'The two disciplines of scientific psychology.' *Am. Psychol.*, **12**, 671-84.

CRONBACH, L. J. (1975) 'Beyond the two disciplines of scientific psychology.' *Am. Psychol.*, **30**, 116-27.

CRONBACH, L. J. and SNOW, R. E. (1975) *Aptitudes and Instructional Methods.* New York: Irvington.

DAGENAIS, Y. (1973) 'Analyse de la cohérence opératoire entre les groupements d'addition des classes, de multiplication des classes et d'addition des relations asymétriques.' Unpublished doctoral dissertation, Université de Montréal.

DUNHAM, J. L. and BUNDERSON, V. C. (1969) 'Effect of decision-rule instruction upon the relationship of cognitive abilities to performance in multiple-category concept problems.' *J. educ. Psychol.*, **60**, 121–5.

EYSENCK, H. J. (1967) 'Intelligence assessment: a theoretical and experimental approach.' *Br. J. educ. Psychol.*, **37**, 81–98.

FILLMORE, C. J. (1968) 'The case for case.' In BACH, E. and HARMS, R. T. (eds.) *Universals in Linguistic Theory*. New York: Holt, Rinehart and Winston, 1–90.

FLAVELL, J. H. (1971) 'Stage-related properties of cognitive development.' *Cognitive Psychol.*, **2**, 421–53.

FLAVELL, J. H. (1972) 'An analysis of cognitive-developmental sequences.' *Genet. Psychol. Monogr.*, **86**, 279–350.

FLAVELL, J. H. and WOHLWILL, J. F. (1969) 'Formal and functional aspects of cognitive development.' In ELKIND, D. and FLAVELL, J. H. (eds.) *Studies in Cognitive Development*. New York: Oxford University Press.

GENTNER, D. (1975) 'Evidence for the psychological reality of semantic components: the verbs of possession.' In NORMAN, D. A. and RUMELHART, D. E. (eds.) *Explorations in Cognition*. San Francisco: W. H. Freeman.

GELMAN, R. (1972) 'Logical capacity of very young children: number invariance rules.' *Child Dev.*, **43**, 75–90(a).

GEWIRTZ, J. L. and STINGLE, K. G. (1968) 'Learning of generalized imitation as the basis for identification.' *Psychol. Rev.*, **75**, 374–97.

GLASER, R. and RESNICK, L. B. (1972) 'Instructional Psychology.' *Ann. Rev. Psychol.*, 207–76.

GREENO, J. G. (1975) 'Theory of instructional objectives: knowledge for solving problems and answering questions.' In KLAHR, D. (ed.) *Cognition and Instruction*. New York: Lawrence Erlbaum Associates.

GUILFORD, J. P. (1967) *The Nature of Human Intelligence*. New York: McGraw-Hill.

HEARNSHAW, L. S. (1972) 'The concepts of aptitude and capacity.' In WALL, W. D. and VARMA, V. P. (eds.) *Advances in Educational Psychology 1*. London: University of London Press, 21–31.

HUTT, S. J. (1973) 'Constraints upon learning: some developmental considerations.' In HINDE, R. A. and STEVENSON-HINDE, J. (eds.) *Constraints on Learning*. New York: Academic Press, 457–67.

INHELDER, B. (1972) 'Information processing tendencies in recent experiments in cognitive learning—empirical studies.' In FARNHAM-DIGGORY, S. (ed.) *Information Processing in Children*. New York: Academic Press.

KAGAN, J. and KOGAN, N. (1970) 'Individual variation in cognitive processes.' In MUSSEN, P. (ed.) *Carmichael's Manual of Child Psychology, Vol. 1*, 3rd edn. New York: Wiley, 1273–365.

KESSEN, W. (1962) 'Stage and structure in the study of children.' In KESSEN, W. and KUHLMAN, C. (eds.) 'Thought in the Young Child.' *Monogr. Soc. Res. Child Dev.*, **27**, 2, 65–86.

KLAHR, D. and WALLACE, J. G. (1970) 'An information processing analysis of some Piagetian experimental tasks.' *Cognitive Psychology*, **1**, 350–87.

KLAHR, D. and WALLACE, J. G. (1972) 'Class inclusion processes.' In FARNHAM-DIGGORY, S. (ed.) *Information Processing in Children*. New York: Academic Press.

KLAHR, D. and WALLACE, J. G. (1973) 'The role of quantification operators in the development of conservation of quantity.' *Cognitive Psychol.*, **4**, 301–27.

KLAHR, D. and WALLACE, J. G. (1975) *Cognitive Development: An Information Processing View*. New York: Lawrence Erlbaum Associates.

LEMERISE, T. and PINARD, A. (1971) 'Synchronisme ou asynchronisme génétique dans la solution d'un ensemble de tâches numériques élémentaires.' *Enfance*, **1-2**, 17-30.

MCCAWLEY, J. D. (1968) 'The role of semantics in a grammar.' In BACH, E. and HARMS, R. T. (eds.) *Universals in Linguistic Theory.* New York: Holt, Rinehart and Winston.

MACNAMARA, J. (1972) 'Cognitive basis of language learning in infants.' *Psychol. Rev.*, **79**, 1-13.

MCNEILL, D. (1970) *The Acquisition of Language.* New York: Harper and Row.

MEHLER, J. and BEVER, T. G. (1967) 'Cognitive capacity of very young children.' *Science*, **158**, 141-2.

MELTON, A. W. (1967) 'Individual differences and theoretical process variables: General comments on the conference.' In GAGNÉ, R. M. (ed.) *Learning and Individual Differences.* Columbus, Ohio: Merrill.

MITTLER, P. J. (1973) 'Purposes and principles of assessment.' In MITTLER, P. J. (ed.) *Assessment for Learning in the Mentally Handicapped.* Edinburgh: Churchill Livingstone, 1-21.

MORTON, J. (1971) (ed.) *Biological, Social and Linguistic Factors in Psychology.* Logos Press.

NEWELL, A. and SIMON, H. A. (1972) *Human Problem Solving.* New York: Prentice-Hall.

NORMAN, D. A., GENTNER, D. R. and STEVENS, A. L. (1975) 'Comments on learning: schemata and memory representation.' In KLAHR, D. (ed.) *Cognition and Instruction.* New York: Lawrence Erlbaum Associates.

OSHERSON, D. N. (1974) *Logical Abilities in Children, II.* Potomac, Maryland: Lawrence Erlbaum Associates.

PASCUAL-LEONE, J. (1975) 'Constructive cognition and substance conservation: towards adequate structural models of the human subject.' Toronto: York University, pre-publication draft.

PIAGET, J. (1941) 'Le mécanisme du développement mental et les lois du groupement des opérations.' *Arch. Psychol., Genève*, **28**, 215-85.

PIAGET, J. (1956) 'Les stades du développement intellectuel de l'enfant et de l'adolescent.' In OSTERRIETH, P. *et al.* (eds.) *Le problème des stades en psychologie de l'enfant.* Paris: Presses Univer. France, 33-41.

PIAGET, J. (1957) 'Logique et équilibre dans les comportements du sujet.' In APOSTEL, L., MANDELBROT, B. and PIAGET, J. 'Logique et Équilibre.' *Etudes d'Epistémologie Génétique*, **2**, 27-113.

PIAGET, J. (1959) 'Apprentissage et connaissance: II.' In GOUSTARD, K., GRÉCO, P., MATALON, B. and PIAGET, J. 'La Logique des Apprentissages.' *Etudes d'Epistémologie Génétique*, **10**, 159-88.

PIAGET, J. (1960) In TANNER, J. M. and INHELDER, B. (eds.) *Discussions on Child Development*, **IV**. London: Tavistock, 3-27, 77-83.

PIAGET, J. (1968) 'Quantification, conservation and nativism.' *Science*, **162**, 796-9.

PIAGET, J. (1974) *La Prise de Conscience.* Paris: Presses Universitaires de France.

PINARD, A. and LAURENDEAU, M. (1969) '"Stage" in Piaget's cognitive-developmental theory.' In ELKIND, D. and FLAVELL, J. H. (eds.) *Studies in Cognitive Development.* New York: Oxford University Press, 121-70.

QUILLIAN, M. R. (1968) 'Semantic memory.' In MINSKY, M. (ed.) *Semantic Information Processing.* Cambridge, Mass.: M.I.T. Press.

RISLEY, T. R. and BAER, D. M. (1973) 'Operant behaviour modification: the deliberate development of behaviour.' In CALDWELL, B. M. and RICCIUTI, H. N. (eds.) *Review of Child Development Research*, **3**. Chicago: University of Chicago Press, 283-329.

ROHWER, W. D. Jr. (1971) 'Learning, race and school success.' *Rev. educ. Res.*, **41**, 191-210.

ROTHENBERG, B. and COURTNEY, R. (1968) 'Conservation of number in very young children: a replication of and a comparison with Mehler and Bever's study.' *J. Psychol.*, **70**, 205-12.

RUSSELL, J. (1974) 'Review of P. Bryant "Perception and Understanding in Young Children".' *B.P.S. Bulletin*, **27**, 505.

SCHANK, R. C. (1973a) 'Development of Conceptual Structures in Children.' Stanford University: Artificial Intelligence Memorandum 203.

SCHANK, R. C. (1973b) 'Identification of Conceptualizations Underlying Natural Language.' In SCHANK, R. C. and COLBY, K. M. (eds.) *Computer Models of Thought and Language*. San Francisco: W. H. Freeman.

SINCLAIR, H. (1973) 'Some remarks on the Genevan point of view on learning with special reference to language learning.' In HINDE, R. A. and STEVENSON-HINDE, J. (eds.) *Constraints on Learning*. New York: Academic Press, 397-415.

SLOBIN, D. I. (1973) 'Cognitive prerequisites for the development of grammar.' In FERGUSON, C. A. and SLOBIN, D. I. (eds.) *Studies of Child Language Development*. New York: Holt, Rinehart & Winston.

SMEDSLUND, J. (1961) 'The acquisition of conservation of substance and weight in children: I. Introduction.' *Scand. J. Psychol.*, **2**, 11-20.

SMEDSLUND, J. (1964) 'Concrete reasoning: a study of intellectual development.' *Child Dev. Monogr.*, **29**, 2.

SMEDSLUND, J. (1966a) 'Microanalysis of concrete reasoning I. The difficulty of some combinations of addition and subtraction of one unit.' *Scand. J. Psychol.*, **7**, 145-56.

SMEDSLUND, J. (1966b) 'Microanalysis of concrete reasoning II. The effect of number transformations and non-redundant elements, and some variations in procedure.' *Scand. J. Psychol.*, **7**, 157-63.

SMEDSLUND, J. (1966c) 'Microanalysis of concrete reasoning III. Theoretical overview.' *Scand. J. Psychol.*, **7**, 164-7.

UNDERWOOD, B. J. (1975) 'Individual differences as a crucible in theory construction.' *Am. Psychol.*, **30**, 128-34.

WALLACE, J. G. (1972) *Stages and Transition in Conceptual Development: An Experimental Study*. Slough: NFER.

WHITE, B. L. and HELD, R. (1966) 'Plasticity of sensori-motor development in the human infant.' In ROSENBLITH, J. F. and ALLINSMITH, W. (eds.) *Causes of Behavior*, **2**. Boston: Allyn and Bacon.

WISEMAN, S. (1972) 'Environmental Handicap and the Teacher.' In WALL, W. D. and VARMA, V. P. (eds.) *Advances in Educational Psychology I*. London: University of London Press, 53-74.

WOHLWILL, J. F. (1966) 'Piaget's theory of the development of intelligence in the concrete operations period.' *Amer. J. ment. Def., Monogr. Suppl.* **70**, 57-83.

WOHLWILL, J. F. (1973) *The Study of Behavioral Development*. New York: Academic Press.

YOUNG, R. M. (1973) 'Children's seriation behaviour: A production system analysis.' Unpublished doctoral dissertation, Carnegie-Mellon University.

Environment and intelligence

AEBLI, H. (1951) *Didactique Psychologie*. Neuchâtel: Delachaux et Niestlé.

BERRY, J. W. and DASEN, P. R. (1972) (eds.) *Culture and Cognition: Readings in Cross-Cultural Psychology*. London: Methuen.

BLOOM, B. S. (1964) *Stability and Change in Human Characteristics*. New York: John Wiley.

BRISLIN, R. W., LONNER, W. J. and THORNDIKE, R. L. (1973) *Cross-Cultural Research Methods*. New York: John Wiley.

BRUNER, J. S., OLVER, R. and GREENFIELD, P. M. (1966) *Studies in Cognitive Growth*. New York: John Wiley.

BURKS, B. S. (1928) 'The relative influence of nature upon mental development.' *Yrbk. Nat. Soc. Stud. Educ.*, **27**, 1, 219–316.

BURT, C. L. (1966) 'The genetic determination of differences in intelligence: a study of monozygotic twins reared apart.' *Br. J. Psychol.*, **57**, 137–53.

CLARKE, A. D. B. and CLARKE, A. (1974) *Mental Deficiency: A Changing Concept* (3rd edn). London: Methuen.

DASEN, P. R. (1972) 'The development of conservation in aboriginal children: a replication study.' *Int. J. Psychol.*, **7**, 75–85.

DE LEMOS, M. M. (1969) 'The development of conservation in aboriginal children.' *Int. J. Psychol.*, **4**, 255–69.

DENNIS, W. and NARJARIAN, P. (1957) 'Infant development under environmental handicap.' *Psychol. Monogr.*, **71**, No. 436.

DUCKWORTH, E. (1964) *Piaget Rediscovered*. Cornell University: School of Education.

FRASER, E. (1959) *Home Environment and the School*. London: University of London Press.

FREEMAN, F. N., HOLZINGER, K. J. and MITCHELL, B. C. (1928) 'The influence of environment on the intelligence, school achievement, and conduct of foster children.' *Yrbk. Nat. Soc. Stud. Educ.*, **27**, 1, 103–217.

GOLDFARB, W. (1955) 'Emotional and intellectual consequences of psychologic deprivation in infancy: a re-evaluation.' In HOCH, P. H. and ZUBIN, J. (eds.) *Psychopathology of Childhood*. New York: Grune & Stratton.

GOTTFRIED, A. W. (1973) 'Intellectual consequences of perinatal anoxia.' *Psychol. Bull.*, **80**, 231–42.

HEBB, D. O. (1949) *The Organization of Behaviour*. New York: John Wiley.

HERRNSTEIN, R. J. (Sept. 1971) 'IQ'. *Atlantic Monthly*, 43–64.

HUNT, J. MCV. (1961) *Intelligence and Experience*. New York: Ronald Press.

HUSÉN, T. (1951) 'The influence of schooling upon IQ.' *Theoria*, **17**, 61–88.

INHELDER, B. (1968) *The Diagnosis of Reasoning in the Mentally Retarded*. New York: John Day.

JENSEN, A. R. (1969) 'How much can we boost IQ and scholastic achievement?' *Harvard Educ. Rev.*, **39**, 1–123.

JENSEN, A. R. (1973a) *Educability and Group Differences*. New York: Harper & Row.

JENSEN, A. R. (1973b) 'Genetic and behavioral effects of nonrandom mating.' Duplicated paper. Berkeley, Calif.: University of California.

KLINEBERG, O. (1935) *Negro Intelligence and Selective Migration*. New York: Columbia University Press.

KOLUCHOVA, J. (1972) 'Severe deprivation in twins: a case study.' *J. child Psychol. Psychiat.*, **13**, 107–14.

LAWRENCE, E. M. (1931) 'An investigation into the relation between intelligence and inheritance.' *Br. J. Psychol. Monogr. Suppl.*, No. 16.

LEAHY, A. M. (1935) 'Nature-nurture and intelligence.' *Genet. Psychol. Monogr.*, **17**, 235–308.

LEE, E. S. (1951) 'Negro intelligence and selective migration: a Philadelphia test of the Klineberg hypothesis.' *Am. sociol. Rev.*, **16**, 227–33.

LEVINE, S. (1960) 'Stimulation in infancy.' *Scient. Am.*, **202**, 80–6.

LORGE, I. (1945) 'Schooling makes a difference.' *Teach. Coll. Rec.*, **46**, 483–92.

MODGIL, S. (1974) *Piagetian Research: A Handbook of Recent Studies*. London: NFER.

NEWMAN, H. H., FREEMAN, F. N. and HOLZINGER, K. J. (1937) *Twins: A Study of Heredity and Environment.* Chicago: University of Chicago Press.

PIAGET, J. (1950) *The Nature of Intelligence.* London: Routledge & Kegan Paul.

ROSENTHAL, R. and JACOBSON, L. (1968) *Pygmalion in the Classroom.* New York: Holt, Rinehart & Winston.

SATTLER, J. (1970) 'Racial "Experimenter Effects" in experimentation, testing, interviewing and psychotherapy.' *Psychol. Bull.*, **73**, 137-60.

SCHAFFER, H. R. (1974) 'Early social behaviour and the study of reciprocity.' *Bull. Br. Psychol. Soc.*, **27**, 209-16.

SCHULL, W. J. and NEEL, J. V. (1965) *The Effects of Inbreeding on Japanese Children.* New York: Harper & Row.

SHUEY, A. (1966) *The Testing of Negro Intelligence* (2nd edn). New York: Social Science Press.

SKEELS, H. M. (1966) 'Adult status of children with contrasting early life experiences: a follow-up study.' *Monogr. Soc. Res. Child Dev.*, **31**, No. 105.

SKODAK, M. and SKEELS, H. M. (1949) 'A final follow-up study of one hundred adopted children.' *J. genet. Psychol.*, **75**, 85-125.

SPITZ, R. A. (1945-46) 'Hospitalism.' In *The Psychoanalytic Study of the Child*, Vols. I and II. New York: International Universities Press.

URBACH, P. (1974) 'Progress and degeneration in the IQ debate.' *Br. J. Phil. Sci.*,

VERNON, P. E. (1955a) 'The psychology of intelligence and G.' *Quart. Bull. Br. Psychol. Soc.*, **26**, 1-14.

VERNON, P. E. (1955b) 'The assessment of children.' *Univ. Lon. Inst. Educ. Stud. in Educ.*, **7**, 189-215. London: Evans.

VERNON, P. E. (1957) 'Intelligence and intellectual stimulation during adolescence.' *Indian Psychol. Bull.*, **2**, 1-6.

VERNON, P. E. (1969) *Intelligence and Cultural Environment.* London: Methuen.

Emotions and intelligence

ANTHONY, E. J. (1957) 'The system makers: Freud and Piaget.' *Br. J. med. Psychol.*, **30**, 3, 255-69.

ANTHONY, E. J. (in press) 'The Growth of Knowledge from the Developmental and Dynamic Points of View.' In BASCH, M. (ed.) *Annals of Psychoanalysis.* Chicago: Quadrangle.

CARMICHAEL, L. (1946) (ed.) *Manual of Child Psychology* (first edition). New York: John Wiley.

CARMICHAEL, L. (1954) (ed.) *Manual of Child Psychology* (second edition). New York: John Wiley.

DÉCARIE, T. G. (1966) *Intelligence and Affectivity in Early Childhood: An Experimental Study of Jean Piaget's Object Concept and Object Relations* (trans. BRANDT, E. P. and BRANDT, L. W.). New York: International Universities Press.

FREUD, S. (1915) *The Unconscious.* In *The Standard Edition of the Complete Psychological Works of Sigmund Freud, Vol. 14.* London: Hogarth Press, 1957.

LEWIN, K. (1940) 'Formalization and progress in psychology.' *University of Iowa Studies in Child Welfare*, **16**, no. 3.

MUSSEN, P. H. (1970) (ed.) Preface. In *Carmichael's Manual of Child Psychology.* New York: John Wiley.

PIAGET, J. (1951) *Play, Dreams and Imitation in Childhood.* New York: Norton.

PIAGET, J. (1932) *The Moral Judgment of the Child*. London: Kegan, Paul.

PIAGET, J. (1953-54) 'Les relations entre l'affectivité et l'intelligence dans le développement mental de l'enfant.' *Bull. de Psychol.*, **7**.

PIAGET, J. (1973) 'The affective unconscious and the cognitive unconscious.' *J. Am. Psychoanalyt. Assoc.*, **21**, 2, 249-61.

SCHACHTEL, E. G. (1959) *Metamorphosis*. New York: Basic Books.

TANNER, J. S. and INHELDER, B. (1960) (eds.) *Discussions in Child Development, Vol. 4*. New York: International Universities Press.

The measurement of development

ANDERSEN, E. B. (1973) 'A goodness of fit test for the Rasch model.' *Psychometrika*, **38**, 123-40.

ANDERSON, J., KEARNEY, G. E. and EVERETT, A. B. (1968) 'An evaluation of Rasch's structural model for test items.' *Br. J. math. statist. Psychol.*, **21**, 231-8.

BENTLER, P. M. (1971) 'An implicit metric for ordinal scales: implications for assessment of cognitive growth.' In GREEN, D. R., FORD, M. P. and FLAMER, G. B. (eds.) *Measurement and Piaget*. New York: McGraw-Hill.

BENTLER, P. M. (1973) 'Assessment of developmental factor change at the individual and group level.' In NESSELROADE, J. R. and REESE, H. W. (eds.) *Life-span Developmental Psychology*. New York: Academic Press.

BIRNBAUM, A. (1968) 'Some latent trait models and their use in inferring an examinee's ability.' In LORD, F. M. and NOVICK, M. R. (eds.) *Statistical Theories of Mental Test Scores*. Reading, Mass.: Addison-Wesley.

BRINK, N. E. (1972) 'Rasch's logistic model vs. the Guttman model.' *Educ. psychol. Measur.*, **32**, 921-7.

BRUNER, J. S. (1966) *Toward a Theory of Instruction*. Cambridge, Mass.: Harvard University Press.

BURT, C. (1951) 'Test-construction and the scaling of items.' *Br. J. Psychol., Statistical Section*, **4**, 95-129.

DOCKRELL, W. B. (1970) (ed.) *On Intelligence*. London: Methuen.

ELLIOTT, C. D. (1974) 'The British Intelligence Scale Project: Phase 2.' *J. Assoc. Educ. Psychol.*, **3**, 6, 9-13.

ELLIOTT, C. D. (1975a) 'The British Intelligence Scale: final report before standardisation, 1975-76.' Paper presented to the Annual Conference of the British Psychological Society, Nottingham.

ELLIOTT, C. D. (1975b) 'Innovation and decision-making in psychological assessment: a further reply to Gillham.' Paper presented at the Annual Conference of the British Psychological Society, Nottingham.

EYSENCK, H. J. (1973) *The Measurement of Intelligence*. Lancaster: Medical and Technical Publishing.

GOLDSCHMID, M. L. and BENTLER, P. M. (1968) *Concept Assessment Kit—Conservation*. San Diego: Educational and Industrial Testing Service.

GREEN, D. R., FORD, M. P. and FLAMER, G. B. (1971) (eds.) *Measurement and Piaget*. New York: McGraw-Hill.

GUTTMAN, L. (1955) 'A generalised simplex for factor analysis and a facetted definition of intelligence.' *Psychometrika*, **20**, 173-92.

HAMBLETON, R. K. and TRAUB, R. E. (1973) 'Analysis of empirical data using two logistic latent trait models.' *Br. J. math. statist. Psychol.*, **26**, 195-211.

HUNT, J. MC V. (1974) 'Discussion: developmental gains in reasoning.' *Am. J. ment. Defic.*, **79**, 127-33.

JENSEN, A. R. (1970) 'Hierarchical theories of mental ability.' In DOCKRELL, W. B. (ed.) *On Intelligence*. London: Methuen.

KOHLBERG, L. (1969) 'Stage and sequence: the cognitive developmental approach to sociali-sation.' In GOSLIN, D. A. (ed.) *Handbook of Socialisation Theory and Research*. Chicago: Rand McNally.

KOHLBERG, L. (1971) 'Stages of moral development as a basis for moral education.' In BECK, C. M., CRITTENDEN, B. S. and SULLIVAN, E. V. (eds.) *Moral Education: Inter-disciplinary Approaches*. Toronto: University Press.

KOHLBERG, L. (1974) 'Discussion: developmental gains in moral judgment.' *Am. J. ment. Defic.*, **79**, 142-6.

LAZARSFELD, P. F. and HENRY, N. W. (1968) *Latent Structure Analysis*. Boston: Houghton Mifflin.

LEVY, P. (1973) 'On the relation between test theory and psychology.' In KLINE, P. (ed.) *New Approaches in Psychological Measurement*. London: Wiley.

MODGIL, S. (1974) *Piagetian Research: a Handbook of Recent Studies*. Windsor: NFER.

MURRAY, D. (1975) 'Rasch item analysis and scaling.' Paper presented to the Annual Conference of the British Psychological Society, Nottingham.

PEARSON, L. (1975) 'Developmental Scales in the British Intelligence Scale.' Paper presented to the Annual Conference of the British Psychological Society, Nottingham.

PIAGET, J. (1971) 'The theory of stages in cognitive development.' In GREEN, D. R., FORD, M. P. and FLAMER, G. B. (eds.) *Measurement and Piaget*. New York: McGraw-Hill.

PIAGET, J. and INHELDER, B. (1969) *The Psychology of the Child*. London: Routledge and Kegan Paul.

RASCH, G. (1960) *Probabilistic Models for some Intelligence and Attainment Tests*. Copenhagen: Danish Institute for Educational Research.

RASCH, G. (1966a) 'An item analysis which takes individual differences into account.' *Br. J. math. statist. Psychol.*, **19**, 49-57.

RASCH, G. (1966b) 'An individualistic approach to item analysis.' In LAZARSFELD, P. F. and HENRY, N. W. (eds.) *Readings in Mathematical Social Science*. Chicago: Science Research Associates.

STEPHENS, B. (1974) 'Symposium: developmental gains in the reasoning, moral judgement, and moral conduct of retarded and nonretarded persons.' *Am. J. ment. Defic.*, **79**, 113-15.

THURSTONE, L. L. (1925) 'A method of scaling psychological and educational tests.' *J. educ. Psychol.*, **16**, 433-51.

THURSTONE, L. L. (1927) 'The unit of measurement in educational scales.' *J. educ. Psychol.*, **18**, 505-24.

THURSTONE, L. L. (1928) 'The absolute zero in intelligence measurement.' *Psychol. Rev.*, **35**, 175-97.

TINSLEY, H. E. A. and DAWIS, R. V. (1975) 'An investigation of the Rasch simple logistic model: sample free item and test calibration.' *Educ. psychol. Measur.*, **35**, 325-39.

TUDDENHAM, R. D. (1970) 'A "Piagetian" test of cognitive development.' In DOCKRELL, W. B. (ed.) *On Intelligence*. London: Methuen.

TUDDENHAM, R. D. (1971) 'Theoretical regularities and individual idiosyncrasies.' In GREEN, D. R., FORD, M. P. and FLAMER, G. B. (eds.) *Measurement and Piaget*. New York: McGraw-Hill.

WARD, J. (1972) 'The saga of Butch and Slim.' *Br. J. educ. Psychol.*, **42**, 267-89.

WARD, J. and PEARSON, L. S. (1973) 'A comparison of two methods of testing logical thinking.' *Can. J. behav. Sci.*, 5, 385-98.

WILLMOTT, A. S. and FOWLES, D. (1974) *The Objective Interpretation of Performance: the Rasch Model Applied*. Windsor: NFER.

WILMUT, J. (1975) 'Objective test analysis: some criteria for item selection.' *Research in Education*, No. 13.

WOODCOCK, R. W. (1973) *Woodcock Reading Mastery Tests*. Circle Pines: American Guidance Service.

WRIGHT, B. D. (1968) 'Sample-free test calibration and person measurement.' *Proceedings of the 1967 Invitational Conference on Testing Problems*. Princeton: Educational Testing Service, 85-101.

WRIGHT, B. D. and DOUGLAS, G. A. (1974) 'Best test design.' Unpublished manuscript.

WRIGHT, B. D. and PANCHAPAKESAN, N. (1969) 'A procedure for sample-free item analysis.' *Educ. psychol. Measur.*, 29, 23-48.

Perception and cognition: where do we stand in the mid-seventies?

BALL, W. A. (1973) *The perception of causality in the infant*. Report 27, Developmental Programme, Department of Psychology, University of Michigan.

BOND, E. K. (1972) 'Perception of form by the human infant.' *Psychol. Bull.*, 77, 225-45.

BOWER, T. G. R. (1966) 'The visual world of infants.' *Scient. Am.*, 215, 80-92.

BOWER, T. G. R. (1967) 'The development of object permanence: some studies of existence constancy.' *Percept. Psychophys.*, 2, 9, 411-18.

BOWER, T. G. R. (1971) 'The object in the world of the infant.' *Scient. Am.*, 225, 4, 31-8.

BOWER, T. G. R. (1972) 'Object perception in infants.' *Perception*, 1, 15-30.

BOWER, T. G. R. (1974) *Development in Infancy*. San Francisco: W. H. Freeman.

BOWER, T. G. R. and PATERSON, J. G. (1972) 'Stages in the development of the object concept.' *Cognition*, 1, 1, 47-55.

BRUNER, J. S. (1957) 'On perceptual readiness.' *Psychol. Rev.*, 64, 123-52.

BRUNER, J. S. and KOSLAWSKI, B. (1972) 'Visually preadapted constituents of manipulatory action.' *Perception*, 1, 1, 1-14.

BRYANT, P. E. (1974) *Perception and Understanding in Young Children*. London: Methuen.

BUTTERWORTH, G. E. (1974) 'The development of the object concept in human infants.' Unpublished D.Phil. thesis, University of Oxford.

BUTTERWORTH, G. E. (1975) 'Mapping the self on to the world in infancy.' Paper presented to the International Society for the Study of Behavioural Development, University of Surrey, July 1975.

CHARLESWORTH, W. R. (1968) 'Cognition in infancy: where do we stand in the mid-sixties?' *Merrill-Palmer Q.*, 14, 25-46.

DAY, R. H. and MCKENZIE, B. E. (1973) 'Perceptual shape constancy in early infancy.' *Perception*, 3, 315-26.

EVANS, W. F. and GRATCH, G. (1972) 'The stage IV error in Piaget's theory of object concept development, difficulties in object conceptualisation or spatial localisation?' *Child Dev.*, 43, 682-8.

GARDNER, J. K. G. (1971) 'The development of object identity in the first six months of life.' Paper presented at the meeting of the Society for Research in Child Development, Minneapolis, Minnesota, April 1971.

GIBSON, J. J. (1968) *The Senses Considered as Perceptual Systems*. London: George Allen & Unwin.

GRATCH, G., APPEL, K. J., EVANS, W. F., LECOMPTE, G. K. and WRIGHT, N. A. (1974) 'Piaget's stage IV object concept error: evidence of forgetting or object conception?' *Child Dev.*, **45**, 1, 71-7.

GRATCH, G. and LANDERS, W. F. (1971) 'Stage IV of Piaget's theory of infants' object concepts: a longitudinal study.' *Child Dev.*, **42**, 359-72.

HARRIS, P. L. (1973) 'Perseverative errors in search by young children.' *Child Dev.*, **44**, 28-33.

HARRIS, P. L. (1974) 'Perseverative search at a visibly empty place by young infants.' *J. exp. child Psychol.*, **18**, 535-42.

HARRIS, P. L., CASSEL, T. L. and BAMBOROUGH, P. (1974) 'Tracking by young infants.' *Br. J. Psychol.*, **65**, 345-9.

HEIN, A. (1974) 'Prerequisites for development of visually guided reaching in the kitten.' *Brain Res.*, **71**, 259-63.

HELD, R. and BAUER, J. A. (Jr.) (1967) 'Visually guided reaching in infant monkeys after restricted rearing.' *Science*, **155**, 718-20.

HOFFMAN, W. C. (1966) 'The LIE algebra of visual perception.' *J. math. Psychol.*, **3**, 65-98.

LEE, R. N. and ARONSON, E. (1974) 'Visual-proprioceptive control of standing in human infants.' *Percept. Psychophys.*, **15**, 3, 529-32.

MARATOS, O. (1973) 'Origins of imitation in early childhood.' Unpublished Ph.D. thesis, University of Geneva.

MCDOUGALL, W. (1928) *An Outline of Psychology* (4th edn). London: Methuen.

MCKENZIE, B. E. and DAY, R. H. (1972) 'Object distance as a determinant of visual fixation in early infancy.' *Science*, **178**, 1108-10.

MICHOTTE, A. (1950) 'A propos de la permanence phénoménale, faits et théories.' *Acta psychol.*, **7**, 298-322. Reprinted in MICHOTTE, A. (ed.) *Causalité, Permanence et Réalité Phénoménales*. Publications Universitaires, 2 Place Cardinal Mercier, Louvain, 246-371.

MOORE, M. K. and MELTZOFF, A. N. (1975) 'Neonate imitation: a test of existence and mechanism.' Paper presented to the Society for Research in Child Development, Denver, Colorado, April 1975.

MUNDY-CASTLE, A. C. and ANGLIN, J. M. (1969) 'Looking strategies in infants.' Paper presented at the meeting of the Society for Research in Child Development, Santa Monica, March 1969. Reprinted in STONE, W., SMITH, H. T. and MURPHY, L. B. (eds.) *The Competent Infant*. London: Tavistock, 713-17.

NELSON, K. E. (1971) 'Accommodation of visual tracking patterns in human infants to object movement patterns.' *J. exp. child Psychol.*, **12**, 182-96.

NELSON, K. E. (1974) 'Infants' short term progress toward one component of object permanence.' *Merrill-Palmer Q.*, **20**, 1, 3-8.

PAILLARD, J. (1974) 'Le Traitement des informations spatiales.' In *De l'espace corporel à l'espace écologique*. Paris: Presses Universitaires de France, 7-54.

PIAGET, J. (1953) *The Origins of Intelligence in the Child*. New York: International Universities Press.

PIAGET, J. (1954) *The Construction of Reality in the Child*. New York: Basic Books.

PIAGET, J. (1969) *The Mechanisms of Perception*. London: Routledge and Kegan Paul.

QUINTON, A. (1973) *The Nature of Things*. London: Routledge and Kegan Paul.

SALAPATEK, P. and KESSEN, W. (1966) 'Visual scanning of triangles by the human newborn.' *J. exp. child Psychol.*, **3**, 155-67.

SCAIFE, M. and BRUNER, J. S. (1975) 'The capacity for joint visual attention in the infant.' *Nature*, **253**, 265.

H

STONE, L. J., SMITH, H. T. and MURPHY, L. B. (1974) *The Competent Infant*. London: Tavistock.

WOHLWILL, J. F. (1962) 'From perception to inference, a dimension of cognitive development.' In KESSEN, W. and KUHLMAN, C. (eds.) 'Thought in the young child.' *Monogr. Soc. Res. Child Dev.*, **27**, 87-112.

On the social origins of symbolic functioning

BOWER, T. G. R. (1974) *Development in Infancy*. San Francisco: W. H. Freeman.

BRUNER, J. S. (1968) *Processes of Cognitive Growth in Infancy, Vol. III*. Clark Univ. Press. See also KALNINS, I. and BRUNER, J. S. (1973) 'The co-ordination of visual observation and instrumental behaviour in early infancy', *Perception*, **2**, 307-14.

CONDON, W. S. and SANDER, L. W. (1974) 'Neonate movement is synchronised with adult speech.' *Science*, **183**, 99.

LANGER, J. (1970) 'Werner's Theory of Development.' In MUSSEN, P. H. (ed.) *Carmichael's Manual of Child Psychology*, 3rd edn. New York: Wiley.

NEWSON, J. and PAWLBY, S. (1975) 'On Imitation.' Paper presented to an inter-university colloquium at Nottingham University, 18 January.

NEWSON, J. and SHOTTER, J. D. S. (1974) 'How babies communicate.' *New Society*, 8 August.

O'NEILL, J. (1973) 'Embodiment in child development: a phenomenological approach.' In DREITZEL, H. P. (ed.) *Childhood and Socialisation* (Recent Sociology No. 5). New York: Collier Macmillan.

PIAGET, J. and INHELDER, B. (1969) *The Psychology of the Child*. London: Routledge and Kegan Paul.

PIAGET, J. (1970) 'Piaget's Theory.' In MUSSEN, P. H. (ed.) *Carmichael's Manual of Child Psychology*, 3rd edn. New York: Wiley.

SCHAFFER, H. R. (1971) *The Growth of Sociability*. Harmondsworth: Penguin Books.

SCHAFFER, H. R. (1974) 'Behavioural synchrony in infancy.' *New Scientist* (Developmental Psychology Forum), 14 April.

SHOTTER, J. S. S. (1973) 'Prolegomena to an understanding of play.' *J. Theory soc. Behav.*, **3**, 47-89.

SHOTTER, J. D. S. and GREGORY, S. (in press) 'Oh Clever Girl . . . (pause) . . . AREN'T YOU CLEVER.' In HARRE, R. (ed.) *Life Sentences*. New York: Wiley.

TREVARTHEN, C., HUBLEY, P. and SHEERAN, J. (1975) 'Psychological actions in early infancy.' *La Recherche*.

VYGOTSKY, L. S. (1966) 'Development of Higher Mental Functions.' In *Psychological Research in the USSR*. Moscow: Progress Publishers.

Moral development: the cognitive-developmental approach

ARONFREED, J. (1968) *Conduct and Conscience*. New York and London: Academic Press.

ALSTON, W. P. (1971) 'Comments on Kohlberg's "From is to ought".' In MISCHEL, T. (ed.) *Cognitive Development and Epistemology*. New York and London: Academic Press, 269-84.

ARMSBY, R. E. (1971) 'A re-examination of the development of moral judgments in children.' *Child Dev.*, **42**, 4, 1241-8.

BANDURA, A. (1969) 'Social learning of moral judgments.' *J. Person. soc. Psychol.*, **11**, 3, 275-9.

BANDURA, A. and MCDONALD, F. J. (1963) 'The influence of social reinforcement and the behaviour of models in shaping children's moral judgments.' *J. abnorm. soc. Psychol.*, **67**, 274-81.

CHANDLER, M. J., GREENSPAN, S. and BARENBOIM, C. (1973) 'Judgments of intentionality in response to videotaped and verbally presented moral dilemmas: the medium and the message.' *Child Dev.*, **44**, 315-20.

COSTANZO, P. R., COIE, J. D., GRUMET, J. F. and FARNILL, D. (1973) 'A re-examination of the effects of intent and consequences on children's moral judgments.' *Child Dev.*, **44**, 154-61.

COWAN, P. A., LANGER, J., HEAVENRICH, J. and NATHANSON, M. (1969) 'Social learning theory and Piaget's cognitive theory of moral development.' *J. Person. soc. Psychol.*, **11**, 3, 261-74.

DURKIN, D. (1959a) 'Children's concepts of justice: a comparison with the Piaget data.' *Child Dev.*, **30**, 59-67.

DURKIN, D. (1959b) 'Children's acceptance of reciprocity as a justice principle.' *Child Dev.*, **30**, 289-96.

DURKIN, D. (1959c) 'Children's concepts of justice: a further comparison with the Piaget data.' *J. educ. Res.*, **5**, 252-7.

FISHKIN, J., KENISTON, K. and MACKINNON, C. (1973) 'Moral reasoning and political ideology.' *J. Person. soc. Psychol.*, **27**, 1, 109-19.

FONTANA, A. F. and NOEL, B. (1973) 'Moral reasoning in the university.' *J. Person. soc. Psychol.*, **27**, 3, 419-29.

GLASSCO, J. A., MILGRAM, N. A., and YOUNISS, J. (1970) 'Stability of training effects in intentionality in moral judgment in children.' *J. Person. soc. Psychol.*, **14**, 360-5.

GRAHAM, D. (1972) *Moral Learning and Development*. London: Batsford.

GRIM, P. F., KOHLBERG, L. and WHITE, S. H. (1968) 'Some relationships between conscience and attentional processes.' *J. Person. soc. Psychol.*, **8**, 239-53.

GUTKIN, D. C. (1972) 'The effects of systematic story changes on intentionality in children's moral judgments.' *Child Dev.*, **43**, 1, 187-95.

HOFFMAN, M. L. (1963) 'Parent discipline and the child's consideration for others.' *Child Dev.*, **34**, 573-88.

JENSEN, L. C. and HAFEN, G. E. (1973) 'The effect of training children to consider intentions when making moral judgments.' *J. genet. Psychol.*, **122**, 223-33.

JENSEN, L. C. and LARM, C. (1970) 'Effects of two training procedures on intentionality in moral judgments among children.' *Dev. Psychol.*, **2**, 2, 310.

KING, M. (1971) 'The development of some intention concepts in young children.' *Child Dev.*, **42**, 1145-52.

KOENIG, F., SULZER, J., NEWLAND, V. and STURGEON, L. (1973) 'Cognitive complexity and moral judgment in middle and lower class children.' *Child Study Journal*, **3**, 1, 43-52.

KOHLBERG, L. (1963) 'The development of children's orientations toward a moral order. 1. Sequence in the development of moral thought.' *Vita hum.*, **6**, 11-33.

KOHLBERG, L. (1966) 'Moral education in the schools: a developmental view.' *School Rev.*, **74**, 1-30.

KOHLBERG, L. (1969) 'Stage and sequence: the cognitive-developmental approach to socialization.' In GOSLIN, D. A. (ed.) *Handbook of Socialization Theory and Research*. Chicago: Rand-McNally, 347-480.

KOHLBERG, L. (1971) 'From is to ought.' In MISCHEL, T. (ed.) *Cognitive Development and Epistemology*. New York and London: Academic Press, 151-235.

KUGELMASS, S. and BREZNITZ, S. (1968) 'Intentionality in moral judgment: adolescent development.' *Child Dev.*, **39**, 249-56.

LEE, L. C. (1971) 'The concomitant development of cognitive and moral modes of thought: a test of selected deductions from Piaget's theory.' *Genet. Psychol. Monogr.*, **83**, 93-146.

LUNZER, E. A. and MORRIS, J. F. (1968) 'Problems of motivation.' In LUNZER, E. A. *The Regulation of Behaviour.* London: Staples Press, 304-61.

MCGEORGE, C. (1974) 'Situational variation in level of moral judgment.' *Br. J. educ. Psychol.*, **44**, 2, 116-22.

PETERS, R. S. (1971) 'Moral development: a plea for pluralism.' In MISCHEL, T. (ed.) *Cognitive Development and Epistemology.* New York and London: Academic Press, 237-67.

PIAGET, J. (1932) *The Moral Judgment of the Child.* London: Routledge and Kegan Paul.

REST, J., TURIEL, E. and KOHLBERG, L. (1969) 'Level of moral development as a determinant of preference and comprehension of moral judgments made by others.' *J. Pers.*, **37**, 225-52.

RUBIN, K. H. and SCHNEIDER, F. W. (1973) 'The relationship between moral judgment, egocentrism and altruistic behaviour.' *Child Dev.*, **44**, 661-5.

SCHLEIFER, M. and DOUGLAS, V. J. (1973) 'Effects of training on the moral judgment of young children.' *J. Person. soc. Psychol.*, **28**, 1, 62-8.

SELMAN, R. L. (1971) 'The relation of role-taking to the development of moral judgment in children.' *Child Dev.*, **42**, 79-91.

STUART, R. B. (1967) 'Decentration in the development of children's concepts of moral and causal judgment.' *J. genet. Psychol.*, **111**, 59-68.

TURIEL, E. (1969) 'Developmental processes in the child's moral thinking.' In MUSSEN, P. H. et al. (eds.) *Trends and Issues in Developmental Psychology.* New York: Holt, Rinehart and Winston, 92-133.

TURIEL, E. and ROTHMAN, G. R. (1972) 'The influence of reasoning on behavioural choices at different stages of moral development.' *Child Dev.*, **43**, 741-56.

TURNER, G. N. H. (1966) 'A re-examination of certain of Piaget's inquiries on children's moral judgments in the light of his later theory.' Unpublished thesis, University of Manchester.

Memory: theory and application

ALTEMEYER, R. A., FULTON, D. and BERNEY, K. M. (1969) 'Long-term memory improvement: confirmation of a finding by Piaget.' *Child Dev.*, **40**, 845-57.

APPEL, L. F., COOPER, R. G., MCCARRELL, N., SIMS-KNIGHT, J., YUSSEN, S. R. and FLAVELL, J. H. (1972) 'The development of the distinction between perceiving and memorizing.' *Child Dev.*, **43**, 1365-81.

BALLARD, P. B. (1913) *Obliviscence and Reminiscence. Br. J. Psychol. Monogr. Suppl.*, No. 2.

BARTLETT, F. C. (1932) *Remembering.* Cambridge: Cambridge University Press.

BOWER, G. H. (1972) 'Mental imagery and associative learning'. In GREGG, L. W. (ed.) *Cognition in Learning and Memory.* New York: Wiley, 51-88.

BUTTERFIELD, E. C., WAMBOLD, C. and BELMONT, J. M. (1973) 'On the theory and practice of improving short-term memory.' *Am. J. ment. Defic.*, **77**, 654-69.

FLAVELL, J. H. (1970) 'Developmental studies of mediated memory.' In REESE, H. W. and LIPSETT, L. P. (eds.) *Advances in Child Development and Behavior, Vol. 5.* New York: Academic Press, 181-211.

FLAVELL, J. H. et al. (1971) 'Symposium: What is memory development the development of?' *Human Dev.*, **14**, 225-86.

FURTH, H. G., ROSS, B. M. and YOUNISS, J. (1974) 'Operative understanding in reproductions of drawings.' *Child Dev.*, **45**, 63-70.

HERRIOT, P., GREEN, J. M. and MCCONKEY, R. (1973) *Organisation and Memory: A Project in Subnormality*. London: Methuen.

HUNT, E. and LOVE, T. (1972) 'How good can memory be?' In MELTON, A. W. and MARTIN, E. (eds.) *Coding Processes in Human Memory*. New York: Wiley, 237-60.

HUNTER, I. M. L. (1964) *Memory*. Harmondsworth: Penguin.

INHELDER, B. (1969) 'Memory and intelligence in the child.' In ELKIND, D. and FLAVELL, J. H. (eds.) *Studies in Cognitive Growth*. New York: Oxford University Press, 337-64.

KOBASIGAWA, A. (1974) 'Utilization of retrieval cues by children in recall.' *Child Dev.*, **45**, 127-34.

LURIA, A. R. (1969) *The Mind of a Mnemonist*. London: Cape.

MANDLER, G. (1970) 'Words, lists, and categories: an experimental view of organized memory.' In COWAN, J. L. (ed.) *Studies in Thought and Language*. Tucson: University of Arizona Press, 99-131.

MEACHAM, J. A. (1972) 'The development of memory abilities in the individual and society.' *Human Dev.*, **15**, 205-28.

MILLER, G. A., GALANTER, E. and PRIBRAM, K. H. (1960) *Plans and the Structure of Behavior*. New York: Holt, Rinehart and Winston.

MOELY, B. E. and JEFFREY, W. E. (1974) 'The effect of organization training on children's free recall of category items.' *Child Dev.*, **45**, 135-43.

MOYNAHAN, E. D. (1973) 'The development of knowledge concerning the effect of categorization upon free recall.' *Child Dev.*, **44**, 238-46.

PIAGET, J. and INHELDER, B. (1973) *Memory and Intelligence*. London: Routledge and Kegan Paul.

SMIRNOV, A. A. (1973) *Problems of the Psychology of Memory*. New York: Plenum Press.

Programmes for cognitive growth

AYRES, A. J. (1965) 'Patterns of perceptual-motor dysfunction in children: a factor analytic study.' *Percep. mot. Skills*, **20**, 335-68.

BEREITER, C., and ENGELMANN, S. (1966) *Teaching Disadvantaged Children in the Pre-School*. Englewood Cliffs, N.J.: Prentice Hall.

BRYANT, P. (1974) *Perception and Understanding in Young Children*. London: Methuen.

CRATTY, B. J. (1970) *Perceptual and Motor Development in Infants and Children*. New York: Collier-Macmillan.

CRATTY, B. J. (1972) *Physical Expressions of Intelligence*. Englewood Cliffs, N.J.: Prentice Hall.

CRUICKSHANK, W. M. et al. (1961) *A teaching method for brain-injured and hyperactive children* (Syracuse University Special Education and Rehabilitation Monograph Series, 6). New York: Syracuse University Press.

CRUICKSHANK, W. M. and HALLAHAN, D. P. (1973) *Psychoeducational Foundations of Learning Disabilities*. Englewood Cliffs, N.J.: Prentice Hall.

DELACATO, C. H. (1963) *The Diagnosis and Treatment of Speech and Reading Problems*. Springfield, Ill.: C. C. Thomas.

DELACATO, C. H. et al. (1966) *Neurological Organisation and Reading*. Springfield, Ill.: C. C. Thomas.

FROSTIG, M. and HORNE, D. (1964) *Frostig Program for the Development of Visual Perception—Teachers' Guide*. New York: Follett Publishing Co.

GULLIFORD, R. (1975) 'Enrichment methods.' In WEDELL, K. (ed.) *Orientations in Special Education*. New York: Wiley.

INHELDER, B. (1968) *The Diagnosis of Reasoning in the Mentally Retarded*. New York: John Day.

KEPHART, N. C. (1971) *The Slow Learner in the Classroom*. New York: Merrill.

KERSCHNER, J. R. (1968) 'Doman Delacato's theory of neurological organization applied with retarded children.' *Exceptional Children*, **34**, 441-52.

MODGIL, S. (1974) *Piagetian Research; a handbook of recent studies*. Slough: NFER.

MYERS, P. I., and HAMMILL, D. D. (1969) *Methods for Learning Disorders*. New York:Wiley.

PIAGET, J. and INHELDER, B. (1969) *The Psychology of the Child*. London: Routledge and Kegan Paul.

ROBBINS, M. P. (1966) 'The Delacato interpretation of neurological organisation.' *Reading Research Quarterly*, **1**, 57-78.

WARD, J. (1975) 'Behaviour modification in special education.' In WEDELL, K. (ed.) *Orientations in Special Education*. New York: Wiley.

WEDELL, K. *et al.* (1972) 'An exploratory study of the relationship between size, constancy and experience of mobility in cerebral palsied children.' *Dev. Med. Child Neurol.*, **14**, 615-20.

WEDELL, K. (1973) *Learning and Perceptuo-motor Disabilities in Children*. New York: Wiley.

WEDELL, K. (1975) 'Specific learning disabilities.' In WEDELL, K. (ed.) *Orientations in Special Education*. New York: Wiley.

WOODWARD, W. M. (1970) 'The assessment of cognitive processes.' In MITTLER, P. (ed.) *The Psychological Assessment of Mental and Physical Handicaps*. London: Methuen.

Understanding scientific concepts

ALLEN, L. R. (1968) 'An examination of the visual classificatory ability of children who have been exposed to one of the 'new' elementary science programmes.' *Science Education*, **52**, 432-39.

ANNETT, M. (1959) 'The classification of four common class concepts by children and adults.' *Br. J. educ. Psychol.*, **29**, 223-36.

ARCHENHOLD, W. F. (1975) 'A study of the understanding of the concept of potential in sixth form students.' M.Phil. thesis, University of Leeds.

BRAINE, M. D. S. (1962) 'Piaget on reasoning: A methodological critique and alternative proposals.' In 'Thought in the Young Child', *Monogr. Soc. Res. Child Dev.*, **27**.

BRAINERD, C. J. (1971) 'The development of the proportionality scheme in children and adolescents.' *Dev. Psychol.*, **5**, 469-76.

BRAINERD, C. J. and ALLEN, T. W. (1971) 'Training and generalization of density conservation: effects of feedback and consecutive similar stimuli.' *Child Dev.*, **42**, 693-704.

HAZLITT, V. (1930) 'Children's thinking.' *Br. J. Psychol.*, **20**, 354-61.

INHELDER, B. (1968) Foreword to *Logical Thinking in Children* (eds. SIGEL, I. E. and HOOPER, F. H.). New York: Holt, Rinehart and Winston.

INHELDER, B. and PIAGET, J. (1958) *The Growth of Logical Thinking*. London: Routledge and Kegan Paul.

INHELDER, B. and PIAGET, J. (1964) *The Early Growth of Logic in the Child*. London: Routledge and Kegan Paul.

KARPLUS, R. (1973) 'Opportunities for concrete and formal thinking on science tasks.' Paper given at the Third Annual Meeting of the Jean Piaget Society, Philadelphia, 22nd May.

LOVELL, K. (1974) 'Intellectual growth and understanding science.' *Studies in Science Education*, **1**, 1-19.

LOVELL, K., KELLETT, V. and MOORHOUSE, E. (1962) 'The growth of the concept of speed: a comparative study.' *J. child Psychol. Psychiat.*, **3**, 101-10.

LOVELL, K. and SLATER, A. (1960) 'The growth of the concept of time: a comparative study.' *J. child Psychol. Psychiat.*, **1**, 179-90.

LUNZER, E. A. (1968) 'Formal reasoning.' In LUNZER, E. A. and MORRIS, J. F. (eds.) *Development in Learning 2*. London: Staples.

LUNZER, E. A. (1973) 'Formal reasoning: a reappraisal.' Paper given at the Third Annual Meeting of the Jean Piaget Society, Philadelphia, 22nd May.

MATALON, B. (1962) 'Étude génétique de l'implication.' In *Implication, formalisation et logique naturelle*. Paris: Presses Universitaire de France.

OSHERTON, D. N. (1974) *Logical Abilities in Children*, Vol. 2. New York: Wiley.

PIAGET, J. (1969) *The Child's Conception of Movement and Speed*. London: Routledge and Kegan Paul.

PIAGET, J. (1969) *The Child's Conception of Time*. London: Routledge and Kegan Paul.

PIAGET, J. (1970) *Genetic Epistemology*. New York: Columbia University Press.

PIAGET, J. (1975) *Understanding Causality*. New York: Norton.

PIAGET, J. and INHELDER, B. (1956) *The Child's Conception of Space*. London: Routledge and Kegan Paul.

PIAGET, J. and INHELDER, B. (1960) *The Child's Conception of Geometry*. London: Routledge and Kegan Paul.

PINARD, A. and LAURENDEAU, M. (1969) 'Stage in Piaget's cognitive developmental theory: exegesis of a concept.' In ELKIND, D. and FLAVELL, J. H. (eds.) *Studies in Cognitive Development*. New York: Oxford University Press.

SHAPIRO, B. J. and O'BRIEN, T. C. (1970) 'Logical thinking in children ages six through thirteen.' *Child Dev.*, **41**, 823-29.

SHAYER, M. (1972) 'Some aspects of the strengths and limitations of the application of Piaget's developmental psychology to the planning of secondary school science courses.' M. Ed. thesis, University of Leicester.

SHAYER, M. (1974) 'Conceptual demands in the Nuffield 'O' level biology course.' *School Science Review*, **56**, 381-8.

THOMPSON, J. (1944) 'The ability of children of different grade levels to generalise in sorting tests.' *J. Psychol.*, **11**, 119-26.

TYLER, R. W. (1967) 'Resources, models and theory in the improvement of research in science education.' *J. Res. in Sci. Teaching*, **5**, 43-51.

Mathematical thinking in children

BETH, E. W. and PIAGET, J. (1966) *Mathematical Epistemology and Psychology*. Dordrecht: Reidel.

COLLIS, K. F. (1969) 'Concrete operational thinking and formal operational thinking in mathematics.' *The Australian Mathematics Teacher*, **25**, 77-84.

COLLIS, K. F. (1971) 'A study of concrete and formal reasoning in school mathematics.' *Aust. J. Psychol.*, **23**, 289-96.

COLLIS, K. F. (1972) 'A study of concrete and formal operations in school mathematics.' Ph.D. thesis, University of Newcastle, N.S.W.

COLLIS, K. F. (1973) 'A study of children's ability to work with elementary mathematical systems.' *Aust. J. Psychol.*, **25**, 121-30.

COLLIS, K. F. (1974) 'The development of a preference for logical consistency in school mathematics.' *Child Dev.*, **45**, 978–83.

COLLIS, K. F. (1975) *A Study of Concrete and Formal Operations in School Mathematics: A Piagetian Viewpoint*. Melbourne: Australian Council for Educational Research.

FIRTH, D. E. (1974) 'Rule-bound behaviour: An investigation of the tendency to adhere to an invalid rule.' Paper delivered to Seminar on Current Research Projects in Mathematics Education, University of Nottingham.

FURTH, H. G. (1970) *Piaget for Teachers*. Englewood Cliffs: Prentice-Hall.

HALFORD, G. S. (1970) 'A theory of the acquisition of conservation.' *Psychol. Rev.*, **77**, 302–16.

INHELDER, B. and PIAGET, J. (1958) *The Growth of Logical Thinking from Childhood to Adolescence*. London: Routledge and Kegan Paul.

LUNZER, E. A. (1973) 'Formal Reasoning: A Reappraisal'. Keynote paper (now in press). Symposium, Jean Piaget Society, Philadelphia, Spring, 1973.

NEIMARK, E. D. and LEWIS, N. (1967) 'The development of logical problem-solving strategies.' *Child Dev.*, **38**, 107–17.

PEEL, E. A. (1960) *The Pupil's Thinking*. London: Oldbourne.

PEEL, E. A. (1971) *The Nature of Adolescent Judgement*. London: Staples.

SZEMINSKA, A. (1965) 'The Evolution of Thought: Some Applications of Research Findings to Educational Practice.' In MUSSEN, P. H. (ed.) 'European Research in Cognitive Development', *Monogr. Soc. Res. Child Dev.*, **30**, 47–57.

Schooling and moral development

APPLE, M. W. (1971) 'The hidden curriculum and the nature of conflict.' *Interchange*, **2**, 4, 27–40.

BANDURA, A. and MCDONALD, F. (1963) 'Influence of social reinforcement and behaviour of models in shaping moral judgement.' *J. abnorm. soc. Psychol.*, **67**, 274–281.

BART, P. D. (1974) 'Why women see the future differently from men.' In TOFFLER, A. (ed.) *Learning for Tomorrow*. New York: Random House.

BAR-YAM, M. and KOHLBERG, L. (1971) 'Development of moral judgement in the Kibbutz.' In KOHLBERG, L. and TURIEL, E. (eds.) *Recent Research in Moral Development*. New York: Holt, Rinehart and Winston.

BECK, C., SULLIVAN, E. and TAYLOR, N. (1972) 'Stimulating transition to postconventional morality: The Pickering High School study.' *Interchange*, **3**, 4, 28–37.

BIDWELL, C. E. (1972) 'Schooling and socialization for moral commitment.' *Interchange*, **3**, 4, 1–27.

BIGGS, J. B. (1973) 'Content to process.' *Aust. J. Educ.*, **17**, 225–38.

BIRNBAUM, M. (1972) 'Anxiety and moral judgement in early adolescence.' *J. genet. Psychol.*, **120**, 13–26.

BLOOM, B. S. (1971) 'Affective consequences.' In BLOCK, J. (ed.) *Mastery Learning*. New York: Holt, Rinehart and Winston.

BORTON, T. (1970) *Reach, Touch, and Teach: Student Concerns and Process Education*. New York: McGraw-Hill.

BRADBURN, E. (1964) 'The Teacher's Role in the Moral Development of Children in Primary Schools.' Unpublished Ph.D. thesis, University of Liverpool. Cited in GRAHAM, D. 'Children's moral development', in BUTCHER, H. J. (ed.) *Educational Research in Britain 1*. London: University of London Press, 1968.

BROAD, R. D. (1973) 'Experimental modification of the moral judgement of intellectually gifted and average male students.' *Dissert. abstr. inter.* **33**, 7–13.

BRUNER, J. S. (1960) *The Process of Education*. Cambridge, Mass.: Harvard University Press.

BULL, N. J. (1969) *Moral Education*. London: Routledge and Kegan Paul.

CENTRAL ADVISORY COUNCIL FOR EDUCATION (ENGLAND) (1967) *Children and their Primary Schools*. London: HMSO (The Plowden Report).

CRANE, V. and BALLIF, B. (1973) 'Effects of adult modeling and rule structure on responses to moral situation of children in 5th grade classrooms.' *J. exp. Educ.*, **41**, 3, 49-52.

DECHARMS, R. (1971) 'From Pawns to Origins.' In LESSER, G. S. (ed.) *Psychology and Educational Practice*. Glenview, Ill.: Scott, Foresman.

DEVEREAUX, E. C. (1972) 'Authority and moral development among German and American children: A cross-national pilot experiment.' *J. comp. fam. Stud.*, **3**, 99-124.

DREEBEN, R. (1968) *On What is Learned in School*. Reading, Mass.: Addison Wesley.

EWANYK, D. (1973) 'Disequilibrium as a Source of Inducing Higher Moral Reasoning in Delinquent Boys.' Unpublished M.Ed. thesis, University of Alberta.

FARBER, J. (1970) *The Student as Nigger*. New York: Pocket Books.

FODOR, E. M. (1972) 'Delinquency and susceptibility to social influence among adolescents as a function level of moral development.' *J. soc. Psychol.*, **86**, 251-60.

FREUNDLICH, D. and KOHLBERG, L. (1971) 'Moral judgement in delinquents.' In KOHLBERG, L. and TURIEL, E. (eds.) *Recent Research in Moral Development*. New York: Holt, Rinehart and Winston.

FRIEDENBERG, E. Z. (1970) 'Curriculum as educational process: The middle class against itself.' In OVERLEY, N. V. (ed.) *The Unstudied Curriculum: Its Impact on Children*. Washington, D.C.: Assoc. for Super. and Curriculum Dev.

GRAINGER, A. J. (1970) *The Bullring: A Classroom Experiment in Moral Education*. London: Pergamon.

HAAN, N. (1971) 'Activism and moral judgement.' In KOHLBERG, L. and TURIEL, E. (eds.) *Recent Research in Moral Development*. New York: Holt, Rinehart and Winston.

HAAN, N., SMITH, M. B. and BLOCK, J. (1969) 'Moral reasoning of young adults: Political-social behaviour, family background and personality correlation.' *J. Person. soc. Psychol.*, **10**, 183-201.

HENRY, J. (1972) *Culture Against Man*. Harmondsworth: Penguin Books. (First published, New York: Random House, 1963.)

HENSHEL, A. M. (1971) 'The relationship between values and behaviour: A developmental hypothesis.' *Child Dev.*, **42**, 6, 1997-2007.

HOLSTEIN, C. (1971) 'Parental determinants of the development of moral judgement.' In KOHLBERG, L. and TURIEL, E. (eds.) *Recent Research in Moral Development*. New York: Holt.

HUNT, D. E. and SULLIVAN, E. V. (1974) *Between Psychology and Education*. Hinsdale, Ill.: Dryden Press.

HUNT, J. MC V. (1961) *Intelligence and Experience*. New York: Ronald Press.

ILLICH, I. (1971) 'The alternative to schooling.' *Sat. Rev.*, June, 19.

JACKSON, P. W. (1968) *Life in Classrooms*. New York: Holt, Rinehart and Winston.

KAUFMAN, H. (1970) *Aggression and Altruism*. New York: Holt, Rinehart and Winston.

KAY, W. (1975) *Moral Education*. London: Allen and Unwin.

KING, R. (1969) *Values and Involvement in a Grammar School*. London: Routledge and Kegan Paul.

KOHLBERG, L. (1963) 'The development of children's orientations toward a moral order: 1. Sequence in the development of moral thought.' *Vita hum.*, **6**, 11-33.

KOHLBERG, L. (1966) 'Moral education in the schools: A developmental view.' *School Rev.*, **74**, 1-30.

KOHLBERG, L. (1969) 'Stage and sequence: The cognitive-developmental approach to socialization.' In GOSLIN, D. (ed.) *Handbook of Socialization Theory and Research.* Chicago: Rand McNally.

KOHLBERG, L. (1970) 'Stages of moral development as a basis for moral education.' In BECK, C. and SULLIVAN, E. (eds.) *Moral Education.* Toronto: University of Toronto Press.

KOHLBERG, L. (1973) 'Stages and aging in moral development: some speculations.' *Gerontologist*, **13**, 497-502.

KOHLBERG, L. and TURIEL, E. (1971) 'Moral development and moral education.' In LESSER, G. S. (ed.) *Psychology and Educational Practice.* Glenview: Scott Foresman.

KOUNIN, J. S. and GUMP, P. V. (1961) 'The comparative influence of punitive and nonpunitive teachers upon children's concepts of school misconduct.' *J. educ. Psychol.*, **52**, 44-9.

KURTINES, W. and GREIF, E. B. (1974) 'The development of moral thought: review and evaluation of Kohlberg's approach.' *Psychol. Bull.*, **81**, 453-70.

LEDERMAN, J. (1969) *Anger and the Rocking Chair.* New York: McGraw-Hill.

LESTER SMITH, W. O. (1957) *Education.* Harmondsworth: Penguin Books.

LOHNES, P. R. (1973) 'Evaluating the schooling of intelligence.' *Educational Researcher*, **2**, 2, 6-13.

MACCOBY, E. (1968) 'Development of moral values and behaviour.' In CLAUSEN, J. (ed.) *Socialization and Society.* Boston: Little, Brown.

MCDIARMID, G. and PRATT, D. (1971) *Teaching Prejudice.* Toronto: Ontario Institute for Studies in Education, Curriculum Series No. 12.

METCALFE, L. (1971) *Values Education: Rationale, Strategies and Procedures.* Washington: National Council for the Social Studies, Forty-first Yearbook.

MILGRAM, S. (1963) 'Some conditions of obedience and disobedience to authority.' *Hum. Relat.*, **18**, 57-75.

MINUCHIN, P., BIBER, B., SHAPIRO, E. and ZIMILES, H. (1968) *The Psychological Impact of School Experience.* New York: Basic Books.

NEWMAN, F. and OLIVER, D. W. (1970) *Classifying Public Controversy: An Approach to Teaching Social Studies.* Boston: Little, Brown.

OVERLEY, N. V. (1970) (ed.) *The Unstudied Curriculum: Its Impact on Children.* Washington: Association for Supervision and Curriculum Development, National Educational Association.

PASCUAL-LEONE, J. (1972) *Cognitive Development and Cognitive Style.* Boston: Heath (Lexington Books).

PIAGET, J. (1962) 'Will and action.' *Bull. Menninger Clinic*, **26**, 138-45.

PIAGET, J. (1970) 'A conversation with Jean Piaget.' *Psychology Today*, **3**, 25-32.

PIAGET, J. and WEIL, A. M. (1951) 'The development in children of the idea of the homeland and of relations with other countries.' *Int. Soc. Sch. Bull.*, **3**, 561.

REST, J. (1974) 'Developmental psychology as a guide to value education: a review of "Kohlbergian" programs.' *Rev. educ. Res.*, **44**, 241-9.

REST, J., TURIEL, E. and KOHLBERG, L. (1969) 'Relations between level of moral judgement and preference and comprehension of the moral judgement of others.' *J. Pers.*, **37**, 225-52.

SCHWARTZ, S. H., FELDMAN, K. A., BROWN, M. E. and HEINGARTNER, A. (1969) 'Some personality correlates of conduct in two situations of moral conflict.' *J. Pers.*, **37**, 41-57.

SILBERMAN, C. E. (1970) *Crisis in the Classroom.* New York: Random House.

SILBERMAN, M. L. (1971) (ed.) *The Experience of Schooling.* New York: Holt, Rinehart and Winston.

SIZER, N. F. and SIZER, T. R. (1970) Introduction. In *Moral Education: Five Lectures*. Cambridge, Mass.: Harvard University Press.

TURIEL, E. (1966) 'An experimental test of the sequentiality of developmental stages in the child's moral judgements.' *J. Person. soc. Psychol.*, **3**, 611-18.

WILSON, J. (1973) *A Teachers' Guide to Moral Education*. London: Chapman.

WILSON, J., WILLIAMS, N. and SUGARMAN, B. (1967) *Introduction to Moral Education*. Harmondsworth: Penguin Books.

WRIGHT, D. (1971) *The Psychology of Moral Behaviour*. Harmondsworth: Penguin Books.

The thinking and education of the adolescent

AUSUBEL, D. P. (1963) *The Psychology of Meaningful Verbal Learning*. New York: Grune and Stratton.

BRAINE, M. D. S. (1962) 'Piaget on reasoning: a methodological critique and alternative proposals.' In 'Thought in the Young Child,' *Monogr. Soc. Res. Child Dev.*, **27**.

CARVER, R. P. (1970) 'Analysis of "chunked" test items as measures of reading and listening comprehension.' *J. educ. Measurement*, **7**, 141-50.

CLARKE, W. D. (1974) 'A study of the development of adolescent judgment.' Ph.D. thesis, University of Birmingham.

DE SILVA, W. A. (1972) 'The formation of historical concepts through contextual cues.' In PEEL, E. A. 'The quality of thinking', *Educ. Rev.*, **24**, No. 3.

DIEDERICH, P. B. and PALMER, O. E. (1964) *Critical Thinking in Reading and Writing*. New York: Holt, Rinehart and Winston.

ELLIS, J. I. (1975) Unpublished research on secondary school pupils' understanding of human situations portrayed in literature.

MASON, J. S. (1974) 'Adolescent judgment as evidenced in response to poetry.' *Educ. Rev.*, **26**, No. 2.

PEEL, E. A. (1971) *The Nature of Adolescent Judgment*. London: Staples.

PEEL, E. A. (1972) 'Some aspects of higher level learning processes during adolescence.' In WALL, W. D. and VARMA, V. P. (eds.) *Advances in Educational Psychology 1*. London: University of London Press.

PEEL, E. A. (1975a) 'Analysis of comprehension and judgment.' *Educ. Rev.*, **27**, 2, 100-13.

PEEL, E. A. (1975b) 'Predilection for generalising and abstracting.' *Br. J. educ. Psychol.*, **45**, 177-88.

PITT, A. W. H. (1974) 'Adolescent thinking and levels of judgment in Biology.' M.Ed. thesis, University of Birmingham.

RHYS, W. T. (1972) 'Geography and the adolescent.' In PEEL, E. A. 'The quality of thinking,' *Educ. Rev.*, **24**, No. 3.

TAYLOR, W. L. (1957) 'Cloze readability scores as indices of individual differences on comprehension and aptitude.' *J. appl. Psychol.*, **41**, 12-26.

WELLS, J. (1972) 'Some aspects of adolescent thinking in science.' In PEEL, E. A. 'The quality of thinking.' *Educ. Rev.*, **24**, No. 3.

WERNER, H. and KAPLAN, E. (1952) 'The acquisition of word meanings: a developmental study.' *Monogr. Soc. Res. Child Dev.*, **15**, No. 1 (whole no. 51).

Language programmes for disadvantaged children

ALMY, M. (1966) *Studies of Young Children's Thinking*. New York: Teachers College Press.

BARTLETT, E. J. (1972) 'Selecting preschool language programs.' In CAZDEN, C. B. (ed.)

Language in Early Childhood Education. Washington, D.C.: National Association for the Education of Young Children.

BEARD, R. M. (1969) *An Outline of Piaget's Developmental Psychology.* London: Routledge and Kegan Paul.

BEE, H. L. *et al.* (1969) 'Social class differences in maternal teaching strategies and speech patterns.' *Dev. Psychol.*, 1, 6, 726–34.

BEREITER, C. E. (1972) 'An academic preschool for disadvantaged children: conclusions from evaluation studies.' In STANLEY, J. C. (ed.) *Preschool Programs for the Disadvantaged.* Baltimore: Johns Hopkins University Press.

BEREITER, C. E. and ENGELMANN, S. (1966) *Teaching Disadvantaged Children in the Preschool.* Englewood Cliffs, N.J.: Prentice-Hall.

BERNSTEIN, B. (1969) 'A critique of the concept of compensatory education.' Paper given at the work conference of the Teachers' College, Columbia University, New York. Published in BERNSTEIN, B. (1971) *Class, Codes and Control, Vol. I.* London: Routledge and Kegan Paul.

BERNSTEIN, B. (1971a) (ed.) *Class, Codes and Control. Vol. I: Theoretical Studies Towards a Sociology of Language.* London: Routledge and Kegan Paul.

BERNSTEIN, B. (1971b) 'Social class, Language and Socialization.' In ABRAMSON, A. S. *et al.* (eds.) *Current Trends in Linguistics, Vol. 12.* The Hague: Mouton Press. Reprinted in BERNSTEIN, B. (1971) *Class, Codes and Control, Vol. I.* London: Routledge and Kegan Paul.

BISSELL, J. S. (1973) 'Planned Variation in Head Start and Follow Through.' In STANLEY, J. C. (ed.) *Compensatory Education for Children, Ages 2 to 8.* Baltimore: Johns Hopkins University Press.

BLANK, M. (1973a) 'Implicit assumptions underlying preschool intervention programs.' In SPODEK, B. (ed.) *Early Childhood Education.* Englewood Cliffs, N.J.: Prentice-Hall.

BLANK, M. (1973b) *Teaching Learning in the Preschool: a Dialogue Approach.* Columbus, Ohio: Charles E. Merrill.

BLANK, M. and SOLOMON, F. (1968) 'A tutorial language program to develop abstract thinking in socially disadvantaged preschool children.' *Child Dev.*, 39, 379–89.

BLANK, M. and SOLOMON, F. (1969) 'How shall the disadvantaged child be taught?' *Child Dev.*, 40, 47–61.

BRANDIS, W. and HENDERSON, D. (1970) *Social Class, Language and Communication.* London: Routledge and Kegan Paul.

BRONFENBRENNER, U. (1974) 'Children, families and social policy: an American perspective.' In DEPARTMENT OF HEALTH AND SOCIAL SECURITY, *The Family in Society: Dimensions of Parenthood.* London: HMSO.

BRUNER, J. S. (1975) 'Poverty and childhood.' *Oxford Rev. of Education*, 1, 1, 31–50. Originally published in BRUNER, J. S. (ed.) (1971) *Relevance of Education*, New York: Norton.

CAZDEN, C. B. (1965) 'Environmental Assistance to the Child's Acquisition of Grammar.' Unpublished doctoral dissertation, Graduate School of Education, Harvard University.

CAZDEN, C. B. (1972) (ed.) *Language in Early Childhood Education.* Washington, D.C.: National Association for the Education of Young Children.

CHAZAN, M., COX, T., JACKSON, S. and LAING, A. F. (in press) *Studies of Infant School Children, Vol 2: Deprivation and Development.* Oxford: Blackwell (for Schools Council).

CHAZAN, M. and DOWNES, G. (1971) (eds.) *Compensatory Education and the New Media.* Occasional Publication No. 3, Schools Council Research Project in Compensatory Education. Department of Education, University College of Swansea.

CHOMSKY, N. (1965) *Aspects of the Theory of Syntax.* Cambridge, Mass.: M.I.T. Press.

COX, T. (1973) 'Review of Shiach, G. M., *Teach Them to Speak.*' *Br. J. educ. Psychol.*, **43**, 217-18.

DEPARTMENT OF EDUCATION AND SCIENCE (1975) *A Language for Life*. London: HMSO (The Bullock Report).

DEUTSCH, M. (1965) 'The role of social class in language development and cognition.' *Am. J. Orthopsychiat.*, **35**, 78-88. (Reprinted in PASSOW, A. H., GOLDBERG, M. and TANNEN-BAUM, A. J. (eds.) (1967) *Education of the Disadvantaged: A Book of Readings*. New York: Holt, Rinehart and Winston).

DEUTSCH, M. *et al.* (1967) *The Disadvantaged Child*, New York: Basic Books.

DONACHY, W. (1973) 'Promoting cognitive growth in culturally deprived preschool children.' Paper given at B.P.S. Education Section Annual Conference, Royal Holloway College, London.

DOWNES, G. (1975) 'An evaluation of a language programme.' Personal communication.

DOWNES, G. (to be published) *Language Development and the Disadvantaged Child*. Schools Council Project in Compensatory Education.

DUNN, L. M. and SMITH, L. O. (1964) *Peabody Language Development Kit*. Nashville, Tennessee: Institute for Mental Retardation and Intellectual Development, George Peabody College for Teachers.

ENGELMANN, S., OSBORN, J. and ENGELMANN, T. (1970) *Distar Language I and II*. Chicago: Science Research Associates.

FRANCIS, H. (1974) 'Social background, speech and learning to read.' *Br. J. educ. Psychol.*, **44**, 290-9.

GAHAGAN, D. M. and GAHAGAN, G. A. (1970) *Talk Reform*. London: Routledge and Kegan Paul.

GORDON, I. J. (1968) *Parental Involvement in Compensatory Education*. University of Illinois Press (for Eric Clearinghouse on Early Childhood Education).

GRAY, S. W. and KLAUS, R. A. (1970) 'The Early Training Project: a seventh year report.' *Child Dev.*, **41**, 4, 909-24.

GUILFORD, J. P. (1967) *The Nature of Human Intelligence*. New York: McGraw-Hill.

HALLIDAY, M. A. K. (1969) 'Relevant models of language.' *Educ. Rev.*, **22**, 26-37.

HALSEY, A. H. (1972) (ed.) *Educational Priority, Vol. I: E.P.A. Problems and Policies*. London: HMSO.

HAMMILL, D. D. and LARSEN, S. C. (1974) 'The effectiveness of psycholinguistic training.' *Exceptional Children*, **41**, 1, 5-15.

HARVEY, S. and LEE, T. R. (1974) 'An experimental study of educational compensation.' In *Educational Priority, Vol. 5: E.P.A.—A Scottish Study*. London: HMSO.

HERRIOT, P. (1970) *An Introduction to the Psychology of Language*. London: Methuen.

HESS, R. D. and SHIPMAN, V. C. (1965) 'Early experience and the socialisation of cognitive modes in children.' *Child Dev.*, **36**, 869-86.

KAMII, C. K. (1971) 'Evaluation of learning in preschool education: socio-emotional, perceptual-motor and cognitive development.' In BLOOM, B. S., HASTINGS, J. T. and MADAUS, G. F. (eds.) *Handbook on Formative and Summative Evaluation of Student Learning*. New York: McGraw-Hill.

KAMII, C. (1973) 'A sketch of the Piaget-derived preschool curriculum developed by the Ypsilanti Early Education Program.' In SPODEK, B. (ed.) *Early Childhood Education*. Englewood Cliffs, N.J.: Prentice-Hall.

KAMII, C. and RADIN, N. (1970) 'A framework for a preschool curriculum based on some Piagetian concepts.' In ATHEY, I. J. and RUBADEAU, D. O. (eds.) *Educational Implications of Piaget's Theory*. New York: Wiley.

KARNES, M. B. (1973) 'Evaluation and implications of research with young handicapped and low-income children.' In STANLEY, J. C. (ed.) Compensatory Education for Children Ages 2 to 8. Baltimore: Johns Hopkins University Press.

KARNES, M. B. et al. (1968) Activities for Developing Psycholinguistic Skills with Preschool Culturally Disadvantaged Children. Washington, D.C.: Council for Exceptional Children.

KIRK, S. A., MCCARTHY, J. J. and KIRK, W. D. (1968) The Illinois Test of Psycholinguistic Abilities (rev. edn). Urbana: University of Illinois Press.

LABOV, W. (1970) 'The logic of non-standard English.' In WILLIAMS, F. (ed.) Language and Poverty. Chicago: Markham.

LAING, A. F. (1968) 'Compensatory education for young children.' In Compensatory Education: An Introduction. Occasional Publication No. 1, Schools Council Research Project in Compensatory Education. Department of Education, University College of Swansea.

LITTLE, A. and SMITH, G. (1971) Strategies of Compensation: a Review of Educational Projects for the Disadvantaged in the United States. Paris: Centre for Educational Research and Innovation, Organisation for Economic Co-operation Development.

LURIA, A. R. (1961) The Role of Speech in the Regulation of Normal and Abnormal Behaviour (ed. TIZARD, J.) New York: Pergamon Press.

MCAFFREY, A. et al. (1970) Communicative Competence and the Disadvantaged Child: A Study of the Relationship between Language Models and the Development of Communication Skills in Disadvantaged Preschoolers. Final report to the US Office of Economic Opportunity: Harvard Graduate School of Education.

MCCARTHY, D. (1954) 'Language development in children.' In CARMICHAEL, L. (ed.) Manual of Child Psychology (2nd edn). New York: Wiley.

MCNEILL, D. (1970) The Acquisition of Language: The Study of Developmental Psycholinguistics. New York: Harper and Row.

NURCOMBE, B., DE LACEY, P., MOFFITT, P. and TAYLOR, L. (1973) 'The question of aboriginal intelligence: the first three years of the Bourke preschool experiment.' Med. J., Aust., 2, 625-30.

OSGOOD, C. E. (1957) 'Motivational dynamics of language behaviour.' In JONES, M. R. (ed.) Nebraska Symposium on Motivation. Lincoln: University of Nebraska Press.

PARRY, M. and ARCHER, H. (1974) Pre-school Education. London: Macmillan (Schools Council Research Studies).

PIAGET, J. (1952) The Origins of Intelligence in Children. New York: International Universities Press (original French edition, 1936).

PIAGET, J. (1954) 'Language and thought from the genetic point of view.' Acta Psychol., 10, 88-98.

PIAGET, J. (1959) The Language and Thought of the Child (3rd revised edn). London: Routledge and Kegan Paul (original French edition, 1923).

PHILLIPS, C. J., WILSON, H. and HERBERT, G. W. (1972) Child Development Study (Birmingham 1968-71), Part I. School of Education, University of Birmingham.

PHILLIPS, J. L. (1969) The Origins of Intellect: Piaget's Theory. San Francisco: W. H. Freeman.

PRINGLE, M. L. K., BUTLER, N. R. and DAVIE, R. (1966) 11,000 Seven-year-olds. London: Longman.

QUIGLEY, H. (1971) 'Nursery teachers' reactions to the Peabody Language Development Kit.' Br. J. educ. Psychol., 41, 2, 155-62.

SCHOOLS COUNCIL (1969) Scope: an introductory English course for immigrant pupils. London: Books for Schools.

SCHOOLS COUNCIL (1972) Concept 7-9 (Teaching English to West Indian Children Project): Units 1 to 4. Leeds: Arnold.

SEVERSON, R. A. and GUEST, K. E. (1970) 'Toward the assessment of the language of disadvantaged children.' In WILLIAMS, F. (ed.) *Language and Poverty*. Chicago: Markham.

SHIACH, G. M. (1972) *Teach Them to Speak*. London: Ward Lock Educational.

SINCLAIR-DE-ZWART, H. (1969) 'Developmental psycholinguistics.' In ELKIND, D. and FLAVELL, J. (eds.) *Studies in Cognitive Development*. London: Oxford University Press.

SKINNER, B. F. (1957) *Verbal Behaviour*. New York: Appleton-Century-Crofts.

SONQUIST, H. and KAMII, C. (1967) 'Applying some Piagetian concepts in the classroom for the disadvantaged.' *Young Children*, 22, 231-45.

STENDLER-LAVATELLI, C. B. (1968) 'Environmental intervention in infancy and childhood.' In DEUTSCH, M., KATZ, I. and JENSEN, A. R. (eds.) *Social Class, Race and Psychological Development*. New York: Holt, Rinehart and Winston.

TORRANCE, E. P. (1962) *Guiding Creative Talent*. Englewood Cliffs, N.J.: Prentice-Hall.

TOUGH, J. (1971) 'Some differences in the use of language between two groups of three-year-old children.' Paper given to B.P.S. (Education Section) Annual Conference.

TOUGH, J. (1973a) 'The language of young children: the implications for the education of the young disadvantaged child.' In CHAZAN, M. (ed.) *Education in the Early Years*. University College of Swansea Faculty of Education and Aberfan Disaster Fund.

TOUGH, J. (1973b) *Focus on Meaning: talking to some purpose with young children*. London: Allen and Unwin.

TOUGH, J. (1973c) 'Communication Skills in Early Childhood Project.' *Dialogue*, 14, 12-13.

VERNON, P. E. (1969) *Intelligence and Cultural Environment*. London: Methuen.

VYGOTSKY, L. V. (1962) *Thought and Language*. Cambridge, Mass.: M.I.T. Press.

WEIKART, D. P. (1967) 'Results of preschool intervention programs.' Ypsilanti, Michigan (mimeo).

WEIKART, D. P. (1972) 'Relationship of curriculum, teaching and learning in preschool education.' In STANLEY, J. C. (ed.) *Preschool Programs for the Disadvantaged*. Baltimore: Johns Hopkins University Press.

WILLIAMS, H. L. (1973) 'Compensatory education in the nursery school.' In CHAZAN, M. (ed.) *Compensatory Education*. London: Butterworths.

WILLIAMS, P. (1973) 'The Schools Council Research and Development Project in Compensatory Education.' In CHAZAN, M. (ed.) *Compensatory Education*. London: Butterworths.

WOLOTSKY, H. (1967) 'The Early Childhood Center.' In KLOPF, G. J. and HOHMAN, W. A. (eds.) *Perspectives on Learning* (Papers from the Bank Street Fiftieth Anniversary Invitational Symposium). New York: Bank Street College of Education.

Index

abstraction, 11, 18, 100, 133, 135, 139, 140, 143, 146, 172, 173, 175-6, 181, 185-6, 189, 193
acceleration (of development), 32, 38, 100, 123-4, 131, 143, 159, 160-2, 198
  see also programmes, stimulation, training
accommodation, 25, 31, 33, 44, 46, 47, 160
adaptation, xi, 12, 31, 43, 46, 110
adolescence, xiii, 6, 38, 46, 58, 72, 110, 133, 146-7, 149, 151, 154, 172-81 passim
affect
  and cognition, 43-4, 46-7, 50-3, 124, 178
  language of, 48
  moral, 97
  Piaget on, 44-6, 53-4
affective
  development, 45-8, 51-2, 155
  structures, 46-8
aggression, 49, 102, 169
ALC, see closure
altruism, 103
analogues, physical, 8, 9, 10
analysis
  functional, 125-8
  genetic, 46
  problems of, 93-4
  process, 25, 28
  task, 126, 127, 128
anxiety, 161
approval, 105
aptitude, 21, 58
arithmetic, 144-8
  see also mathematics, operations
assimilation, 6, 20, 25, 31, 44, 46, 47, 48, 51, 106, 133, 134, 150
asynchronism, 17, 18
attention, 88, 91-2, 94, 106, 107, 129
  visual, 87
attitudes
  moral, 99, 155, 158, 159, 164, 168
  to schooling, 37, 132

authority, 32, 98, 99, 104, 105, 156, 158, 159, 164, 167, 168
autism, 48, 124, 130
autoregulation, 7, 133

behaviourism, 8, 13, 26, 31, 85
behaviour modification, 25, 128-31, 159, 170, 190, 191
Bernstein, B., 32, 186, 187, 190, 195
biology, xi, 9, 31, 142, 179-80
Bloom, B. S., 13, 27, 167
body image, 126
brain, 8, 34, 37
  processes, 31
  structures, 23
British Intelligence Scale (BIS), 63, 64, 67, 72
Bruner, J., xiii, xiv, 3, 32, 71, 75, 76, 82, 159, 162, 185
Bullock Report on reading, 187, 188

categorisation, 115-17, 118, 135
  see also classification
causality, 4, 6, 74, 130, 134, 142
centration, 103, 135
cheating, 106-7, 158
child rearing, 35-6, 50
  see also home, mother, parents
Chomsky, N., 8, 27, 28, 186
'chunking' technique, 175
class, concept of, 29, 134, 135, 136, 138, 173
classification, xiii, 113, 119, 135, 136, 138, 153, 172, 185
  see also categorisation
clinical method, Piaget's, xii, 10, 48, 52, 57
closure, 11, 139, 142, 145, 146, 147-50
'cloze' technique, 175
cognition, xii, 13, 31, 132-43
  and affect, 43-4
  development of, xi, 15, 91, 133-9, 172-81, 182

cognition *cont.*
  and language, 7, 27-8, 84, 126, 133, 142, 172-6, 182, 196, 198-9
  measurement of, 57-61
  and perception, 74-83
  see also operations, scheme, structure
cognitive
  complexity, 103
  conflict, 7, 13, 50, 79, 81, 82-3
  growth, theories of, 15, 19, 22, 30
  organisation, 7
communication, 85, 88-9, 90-5, 187, 190, 192, 196
  and morality, 103
  mother-child, 34, 90-1, 92, 93, 94
  non-verbal, 90, 92, 93, 95
  pre-verbal, 89-90, 94
  recording, 93
compensation, 129
compensatory education, 128, 187-8, 195, 197
  see also programmes
comprehension, verbal, 8, 91, 174-5, 178, 185, 199
computer
  programs, 20-1, 62, 111
  technology, 9, 68, 94
conceptualisation, 13, 44, 50, 85, 87, 127
  moral, 106, 169-71
concrete operations, *see* operations
conditioning, 25, 27
conformity, 105, 106, 163, 164-5, 169
conscience, 102, 105, 106, 159
consciousness, 45, 48
consequences, of action, 98, 99, 100, 101, 102, 104
conservation, xiii, 6, 17, 21, 28, 29, 32, 57, 135, 144, 153, 156, 159, 160, 190
  of area, 57
  of length, 57
  and morality, 156-7
  of number, 57, 144
  of quantity, 17, 19, 25, 136
  tests of, 59
  of volume, 15, 57
  of weight, 16, 17
conservatism, 107
consistency, concept of, 145-8
constancies, perceptual, 75, 76, 127, 130
cooperation, social, 98, 99, 168
coordination
  body, 79, 89-90
  cognitive, 3, 13, 20, 53, 74, 83, 91, 133, 136, 137, 140, 141-2
  eye-hand, 76, 85, 86, 89, 127

'critical ages', 7
curiosity, 53, 88, 91
curriculum, school, xiii, 13, 123, 131, 144, 156, 166-8, 173, 181, 190, 195, 198, 199
  'hidden', 164, 168
  informal, 189

décalage, 60, 79, 80, 105-6, 160
  horizontal, 11, 17, 57, 136
  vertical, 11
decentration, 45, 46, 52
  and moral judgment, 103
decision making, moral, 98, 158-9, 161, 162-4, 170
'deficit', language, 185-7
delinquency, 158
deprivation, 32, 34, 35-7, 38, 39, 123-4, 168, 182, 183, 185-200
  sensory, 35
  see also environment
disadvantage, *see* deprivation
discipline, 99, 102, 161-2, 164, 169
  induction, 102, 108
  sensitisation, 102
discovery, cognitive, 189-90
discrimination, 127
  auditory, 126
  visual, 23, 28, 126, 127, 129, 195

Educational Priority Areas (EPAs), 194-5
egocentrism, xii, 45, 75, 76, 77, 78, 79, 81, 82, 98, 103, 157, 169
emotion, *see* affect
environment
  adaptation to, 8, 43
  concept of, 126, 130
  exploration of, 44
  and intelligence, 31-42, 45, 123
  interaction with, xi, 16, 25, 29, 44, 51, 83, 84, 88, 172
  and language, 183, 185-6, 190, 195, 196, 198
  and moral development, 97, 160, 161, 169-171
epistemology, xi, xii, 4, 5, 6, 12, 16, 31, 74
  genetic, xiii, 5
equifinality, 19
equilibration, 7, 19, 23, 24, 25, 27, 29, 45, 46, 51, 84, 160
equilibrium, xi, 12, 31, 43, 44, 45, 46, 47, 51, 52, 102, 160
equivalence, 8, 11, 71, 135, 139, 146
ethology, 9

evaluation, 167, 169
  see also tests
expectancy, 8
expectation, 37–8, 104, 106, 127–8, 131
experience
  and effect, 45
  and cognition, 5, 7, 12, 15, 24, 25, 32–3, 34, 39, 75–6, 78, 82, 87, 95, 130, 132, 133, 137, 139, 141, 172, 180–1
  and language, 185, 187
  and memory, 118, 172
experimental psychology, xii, xiii, 9, 21–3, 33, 86, 126

facial expression, 89, 90, 93
factor analysis, 22, 32, 106
family, 49, 104, 183, 187
  see also home, mother, parents
feedback, 86, 91, 92, 152, 167
figure-ground phenomenon, 77
formal operations, *see* operations
frame of reference, 4, 28, 29, 76, 78, 79, 81, 82–3, 85, 118, 136
Freud, S., 10, 48, 50, 51, 54, 99
Frostig, M., 126–7

generalisation, 13, 17–18, 26, 46, 47, 124, 127, 128, 131, 133, 146–7, 148, 153–4, 172, 173, 175–6, 178, 180
  hierarchies, 135
genetics, *see* heredity, individual differences, innate endowment
Gestalt psychology, 8, 53
goal-directed activity, 75, 87, 91
grouping, as aid to memory, 116–17, 118
guilt, 49–50, 169

handicap
  language, 129
  mental, 15
  social, 184–5
  see also retardation, subnormality
Hebb, D. O., 31, 33–4
heredity, 31, 32, 33–4, 36, 38, 39–41
  see also individual differences, innate endowment
home, influence of, 34, 36, 38, 39, 40, 132, 162, 183, 184, 185, 186–7, 191, 197, 200
  see also environment, family, mother, parents

identity, 11, 75, 78, 79, 80, 82, 83
imagery, 7, 8, 137
imagination, 134, 179, 180–1

imitation, 92, 103, 134, 191
implication, 138–9, 140
individual differences, 16, 20, 21–3, 30, 31–42, 57, 58, 61, 69, 104, 156, 188, 191
inference, 4, 8, 11, 12, 19, 28, 75, 76, 77, 78, 79, 82, 153, 174, 189
inferential links, 13
information, 9, 75, 79, 80, 131
  processing, 9, 12, 18, 20, 29, 76, 117, 118, 126, 129, 130, 192
  theory, 52
  see also abstraction
Inhelder, B., xiii, 12, 13, 20, 32, 44, 45, 51, 58, 84, 113, 126, 129, 130, 136, 137, 139, 142, 144, 145, 151
innate endowment, 5, 6, 11, 27, 28, 29, 31, 39–40, 76, 77, 87, 89, 90, 91, 186
intellectual readiness, 11, 190
  see also stage(s) of development
intelligence, xii, 7, 31–42, 58, 113, 155, 192
  assessment of, 22, 60, 64, 130
  and cognition, 7, 133, 181
  correlational studies, 32, 39–40
  determination of, 31, 33–42
  and emotion, 43–54
  'g', 32, 41, 59
  and moral judgment, 100, 103, 108, 158
  nature of, 31, 33
  see also IQ
intention, intentionality, 86, 88, 98, 100–4
  and memory, 112
  unconscious, 102
interest, *see* curiosity
interiorisation, internalisation, xi, 81, 84, 85, 102, 107, 133, 146, 157, 158, 159, 163, 165, 170
interpersonal relations, 37, 103, 107, 155, 156
  see also social interaction
intersubjectivity, 82, 89, 90, 91, 93, 95, 96
interview, diagnostic, xiii, 8, 9
inverse, concept of, 11, 141, 142, 145–6, 147, 148, 150, 151, 152
IQ, 32, 33, 34, 35, 36, 37, 39, 40, 61, 197
  see also intelligence

justice, immanent, 49, 99, 100

Kibbutz, 168
knowledge
  acquisition of, 3–4, 57, 74, 84–5, 95, 135
  intuitive, 140–1
  nature of, 5, 6, 7, 9, 87, 133–4
  organisation of, 21
  see also cognition

Kohlberg, L., 59, 72, 97, 103, 104-8, 155-61, 164, 166, 168, 169-71

language, xii, 7, 8, 12, 21, 33, 127, 133, 134, 142, 172-6, 182-200 *passim*
  acquisition of, 27-8, 32, 37, 39, 45, 94, 127, 134, 182, 183, 186-7, 198
  and affect, 48
  codes, 186-7, 190, 195
  and cognition, 7, 27-8, 84, 126, 133, 142, 172-6, 182, 196, 198-9
  handicap, 129
  and logic, 12, 133, 173, 182, 187, 190, 198
  and social class, 183-5, 186, 187
  see also comprehension, reading, speech
laterality, 125
learning, 11, 23, 24, 27, 35, 39, 113
  moral, 100
  observational, 26-7
  reception, 13
  social, 25, 26, 103-4, 161, 170
  theories of, 23, 25, 27
  see also conditioning, problem solving, specific disability
linguistics, 9, 27
  see also Chomsky, psycholinguistics
listening, 89
logic, xi, xiii, 5, 6, 8, 12, 44, 74, 108, 132, 140, 156, 159
  and language, 12, 133, 173, 182, 187, 190, 198
logical
  processes, 28, 75-6, 83
  rules, 74, 146, 147
  thinking, 6, 17, 33, 46, 105, 132, 134-5, 138-9, 182, 187, 190, 197, 198
  see also operations, rules, structure(s)

manipulation, 9, 52, 84, 94, 199
manual search, 79, 80-1
mathematical models, 10, 61-73
mathematics, xiii, xiv, 4, 5, 6, 12, 75, 136, 137, 144-54 *passim*, 173, 198
  see also arithmetic
maturation, 12, 31, 44, 190
  and developmental stage, 15, 23-4, 27, 34, 131
maturity
  cognitive, 177, 178-80
  functional, 19
  moral, 101, 103, 105, 157, 158, 159, 161
  social, 129
measurement, 57-73 *passim*, 136-7
  Rasch's model, 61-73

memory, 7, 8, 21, 24, 88, 102, 109-19 *passim*
  and affect, 50-1
  codes, 26, 29
  development of, 112-15, 117-19, 133
  and intelligence, 113
  long-term, 8
  and retardation, 109-10
  semantic, 21, 175
  short-term, 12, 109
  see also recall
méthode clinique, *see* clinical method
momentum, concept of, 140-1
moral
  development, 4, 45-6, 47, 72, 97-108, 155-171
  judgment, 59, 97, 99, 101-3, 105-8, 157, 158, 159, 161, 168
  maturity, 101, 103, 105, 157, 158, 159, 161
  principles, 102, 105, 158, 159, 168
  realism, 98-9, 101
  training, 100-1, 155
morality
  and discipline, 102
  Kohlberg's levels of, 104-5, 157-8
  and social class, 103, 108, 167
  see also decision making
mother, 47, 49, 51, 88-9
  and intellectual development, 34, 35-6, 37, 53
  and language acquisition, 90, 94, 183-4, 190-1
  and moral development, 157, 161
mother-child
  communication, 34, 90-1, 92, 94, 183-4
  interaction, 88-9, 91-4, 95, 187, 190-1, 197
motivation, 15, 32, 46, 186, 197
motor activity, 84, 90, 125
  organisation of, 79, 125
movement
  and language, 127
  and perception, 74-5, 76, 77, 78-81, 82, 91-2
  tunnel effect, 79-80

narcissism, 46
National Foundation for Educational Research, 64, 193, 195
nativism, 23, 27, 28
negation, 151-2
neurological
  characteristics, 39
  development, 29, 31, 87, 125
  impairment, 119, 125

neurophysiological
   development, 7, 125
   organisation, 23-4
number, xiii, 4, 5, 28, 33, 57, 72, 76, 113, 131,
   136, 144, 148

object permanence, 77-8, 82, 85-6, 87-8
objectives, 21, 25, 128, 130, 131
   educational, 25, 124, 126, 164, 166, 200
observation, xii, 6, 57, 84-9, 93-4, 128, 139
   and measurement, 57
operations, 7, 17, 18, 29, 31, 51, 58, 59, 71-2,
   74, 84, 125, 129, 143, 144, 157
   arithmetical, 145-54
   concrete, 16, 17, 19, 45, 131, 135-6, 139,
     141, 144, 149, 150, 152-3
   formal, 46, 72, 133, 138-43, 146, 149, 150,
     153
   temporal, 137
   see also logical thinking, scheme, stage(s) of
     development, structure(s)
organic defect, 125
orientation, 113

parents
   ambivalence toward, 49
   and intelligence, 32, 38, 39, 41
   and language, 183, 185, 191, 197
   and moral development, 45, 98, 99, 102,
     159, 161-2, 171
peers, 32
   and moral development, 46, 97, 99, 101,
     104, 107, 157, 161
perception, xii, 5, 7, 8, 9, 17, 25, 27, 28, 29,
   53, 126
   and cognition, 74-83, 85, 123, 129, 130,
     134, 136, 137, 138, 172
   cues, 8, 11, 76, 79, 86
   development of, 31, 33, 35, 85-92, 192
   social, 81-2
   visual, 11, 23, 28, 76, 77-81, 85-8, 91-2
   see also constancies, discrimination
performance, 19, 21, 22, 26, 29, 58, 125
   categorisation of, 137-8
   determinants of, 18-19, 25
   measurement of, 60, 71-2
personality, 23, 159
philosophy, xiii, 5, 6, 7, 91, 108
physiotherapy, 125
Piaget, Jean
   and affect, 43-54, 169
   appreciation of, 12-14
   biographical sketch of, xi-xiv

   and cognitive development, 15-16, 17, 18,
     20, 23, 24, 25, 29, 31, 32, 57, 58, 123, 126,
     130, 131, 132, 133-8, 139, 142, 144-8,
     151-3
   and memory, 109, 113
   and moral development, 97-9, 100, 101,
     102, 103-4, 107, 156-7, 158, 159-60, 169
   and perception, 74-7, 123, 126, 130
   publications of, v, xi-xiv, 3, 12, 47, 97,
     142-3, 198 (and references)
   and symbolic functioning, 84-5, 133, 182,
     189, 198-9
   see also clinical method, epistemology
play, 48, 49, 190
   therapy, 52
practice, 33, 37
prediction, 7, 22, 26, 33, 118, 134
preoperations, *see* stage(s) of development
'prise de conscience', 11, 13
privilege, 164
problem solving, 8, 25, 29, 35, 57, 109, 111,
   128, 134, 147, 186
process, xii, 16, 20, 21, 23, 24-7, 28, 75, 162-3,
   164-5
   v. content, 22, 25, 26, 27, 162-3
programmes
   cognitive, 35-6, 123-31, 138, 189-90, 195,
     199
   Head Start, 36-7
   language, 127, 182-3, 187-200
   moral, 166
   science, 138
   see also acceleration, training
proportionality, 137, 142, 145
psychoanalysis, xi, 45, 47, 49, 50, 51, 54
   see also Freud, S.
psycholinguistics, 18, 27, 175
   psycholinguistic training, 188, 191-2
psychometrics, xii, 21-2, 31-42, 58, 59, 73,
   126
   see also measurement, tests
punishment, 45, 50, 98, 99, 102, 104, 158, 159,
   161, 164, 168-9

Rasch, G., 61-73 *passim*
rationalisation, 115, 146
reading, 126, 127
realism
   intellectual, 99
   moral, 98-9, 101
reality
   and cognition, 139, 140, 145-7, 149, 152-4
   conceptualisation of, 75, 83, 87, 88, 104,
     134

reason, reasoning, *see* cognition, operations
recall, 112, 115-17, 174-5
  delayed, 113
  'improved', 114-15, 118
  see also memory
reciprocity, 13, 20, 47, 74, 98, 99, 102, 103, 104, 151-2, 156-7
reinforcement, 13, 26, 101, 159, 191
  see also punishment
rejection, 161
reminiscence, 115
representation, xii, 12, 84, 134
repression, 50
responsibility, 98
retardation, 32, 35, 59, 109-10, 117, 123, 124, 125, 131, 182, 192
reversal, concept of, 74-5, 135, 146, 147, 156
role taking, 89, 104, 107, 160-1, 190
rules, 7, 18, 19, 25, 79, 138
  logical, 74, 146, 147
  and moral development, 46, 97-8, 104-5, 166-7, 168, 170
  social, 94, 97-8, 105, 155, 163

scheme, schema, 13, 20, 24, 31, 74, 156, 157, 190
  affective, 46-7, 48, 49, 50, 51
school, schooling, 32, 34, 36, 177-81
  attitudes to, 37
  and intellectual development, 38, 41, 173, 177-81
  and language acquisition, 187, 193, 195, 198
  and moral development, 155-6, 157, 159-160, 162-71
  see also teacher, teaching
science, xiii, 4, 7, 12, 132-43 *passim*, 174, 179-180
  education, 132, 137, 138, 139, 142, 143, 162, 168, 181, 198
self
  awareness of, 45, 82, 134, 135
  concept of, 44, 162-3, 165, 168
  as frame of reference, 78, 83, 157
sensorimotor, *see* stage(s) of development
seriation, xiii, 9, 16, 21, 135, 136, 137, 138, 190
shaping, *see* behaviour modification
Smedslund, J., xiv, 3, 17
smiling, 90
  see also facial expression
social
  activity, 88, 95
  adjustment, 37
  class, 32, 34, 103, 108, 183-5, 187
  competence, 128, 184-5

interaction, xii, 31, 46, 85, 88-9, 92, 99, 101, 135, 157, 159, 164, 186
  learning, 25, 26, 103-4, 155, 161, 170
  perception, 81-2, 88-9, 92
  rules, 94, 97-8, 105, 155, 163
socialisation, 39, 45, 91, 105, 159-60
society, 12, 41, 157, 187
space, xiii, 4, 6, 10, 74, 75, 82, 83, 126, 134, 137
spatial
  ability, 33, 58, 127, 129-30
  conceptualisation, 11, 77, 78, 85, 126, 136
  judgment, 29, 80-1, 126
specific disability, 124, 129, 131
speech, 90, 93, 125, 186, 188
  see also language
stage(s) of development, 7, 9, 11, 12, 15-21, 31, 43, 57, 58, 80-1, 97-8, 99, 102, 106, 125, 128, 131, 136, 144-9, 160-2, 170, 190
  individual differences in, 21-3, 57, 104, 125
  measuring, 60, 71-3
  moral, *see* Kohlberg, moral, morality
  preoperational, 18, 32, 46, 47, 58, 101, 103, 152, 157
  sensorimotor, 12, 20, 32, 45, 47, 58, 74, 77, 83, 84, 94, 130, 190
  transition between, 15, 23-9, 57, 81, 83, 101, 131, 138
  see also maturation, operations
stimulation, 53, 82, 90
  and intelligence, 31-4, 36, 38-9
  linguistic, 182
  see also programmes
structuralism, 6, 7
structure(s), 6, 7, 8, 20, 31, 46, 50, 74, 82, 84, 133, 136, 190
  formation of, 19, 32-3, 58, 133
  logical, 9, 16, 17, 18, 20, 24, 43-4
subnormality, 124, 130, 131
sucking, 52, 87
symbolic
  activity, 46, 47, 84
  capacity, 45
  functioning, development of, 84-96, 133, 173-4, 190
  play, 46, 48, 134
  see also language
synchronism, 16, 17, 18
syntax, 27, 185

teacher(s)
  and cognitive development, 32, 38, 151, 180, 181
  and evaluation, 167, 169

teacher(s) *cont.*
  expectations, 37-8, 167
  and language acquisition, 188, 189, 190,
    191, 192-3, 194, 196, 197, 199-200
  and moral development, 159, 164, 166,
    167-8, 169
  moral reasoning in, 107-8
  ratings, 106, 183, 185
teaching
  and cognitive development, 130-1, 132,
    133, 139, 141, 143, 181
  and language acquisition, 182, 191, 193
  and moral development, 166
tests, xii, 15, 31, 33, 35, 37, 58-73, 128, 173-5,
    176, 183, 185, 186, 193
  construction of, 22, 59, 64, 174
  criterion-referenced, 59, 60
  norm-referenced, 59, 60, 64
  Piagetian, 59
  see also measurement, psychometrics
thinking, *see* cognition, logical thinking
time, xiii, 4, 6, 74, 75, 83, 85, 134, 136, 137
tracking, visual, 78, 79, 80, 87, 91-2
training, 12, 32, 34, 131, 141, 143, 192
  memory, 110
  moral, 100-1, 155, 166
  procedures, 12, 37

psycholinguistic, 188, 191-2
specific, 127-8, 189
see also acceleration, programmes
transfer, 13, 33, 141, 143
transformation(s), 5, 6, 7-8, 9, 84, 87, 106,
    133, 139, 146, 147, 149, 152
transitivity, xiii, 16, 21, 28, 29, 136
tunnel effect, 79-80
twins, 35, 36, 39-41

unconscious, 47, 48, 49, 50-1
UNESCO, xi
universals
  cognitive, 27-8
  cultural, 89, 170
  linguistic, 27
  logical, 105

vocabulary, 58, 173, 174, 185, 188, 197
volume, 6, 17, 57, 137, 139, 141, 142
voluntarism, 107
Vygotsky, L. S., 3, 95

weight, 6, 16, 17, 134, 136, 137, 139
will, the, 45, 46, 54, 106, 107
Wohlwill, J. F., xiv, 3, 16, 18, 19, 25, 75